Peacemaking in the twenty-first century

MANCHESTER
1824
Manchester University Press

Peacemaking in the twenty-first century

Edited by
JOHN HUME, T. G. FRASER
and LEONIE MURRAY

Manchester University Press
Manchester and New York

distributed exclusively in the USA by Palgrave Macmillan

Published by Manchester University Press
Oxford Road, Manchester M13 9NR, UK
and Room 400, 175 Fifth Avenue, New York, NY 10010, USA
www.manchesteruniversitypress.co.uk

Distributed exclusively in the USA by
Palgrave Macmillan, 175 Fifth Avenue, New York,
NY 10010, USA

Distributed exclusively in Canada by
UBC Press, University of British Columbia, 2029 West Mall,
Vancouver, BC, Canada V6T 1Z2

British Library Cataloguing-in-Publication Data
A catalogue record for this book is available from the British Library

Library of Congress Cataloging-in-Publication Data applied for

ISBN 978 0 7190 8793 6 *hardback*

First published 2013

The publisher has no responsibility for the persistence or accuracy of URLs for external or any third-party internet websites referred to in this book, and does not guarantee that any content on such websites is, or will remain, accurate or appropriate.

Typeset in Sabon by
Koinonia, Manchester
Printed and bound in Great Britain by
CPI Antony Rowe Ltd, Chippenham, Wiltshire

Contents

Any views expressed are those of the authors of the chapters and do not necessarily represent those of the editors, The Ireland Funds or the University of Ulster.

List of contributors[*]

Taoiseach Bertie Ahern, TD, Taoiseach, 1997–2008; President of the European Council, 1 January–30 June 2004.

Foreign Minister Dermot Ahern, TD, Minister for Foreign Affairs, 2004–2008; TD for County Louth, 1987–2011.

Secretary-General Kofi Annan, Secretary-General of the United Nations, 1997–2006; Nobel Prize in Peace, 2001.

Professor Paul Arthur, Emeritus Professor of Politics and Honorary Professor in Peace Studies (INCORE), University of Ulster; author of *Special Relationships: Britain, Ireland and the Northern Ireland Problem* (Belfast: The Blackstaff Press Limited, 2000).

Professor Kader Asmal, Member of the National Assembly, Parliament of South Africa, 1994–2007; Minister of Water Affairs and Forestry, 1994–1999; Minister of Education, 1999–2004; Professor of Law and Dean of the Faculty of Arts, Trinity College Dublin; Chairman, Irish Anti-Apartheid Movement, 1963–1990.

Senator Hillary Rodham Clinton, Senator, New York, 2001–2009; previously First Lady, and subsequently, from 2009 to 2013, Secretary of State.

President William J. Clinton, 42nd President of the United States of America, 1993–2001.

President Pat Cox, President of the European Parliament, 2002–2004; Member of the European Parliament, 1989–2004; International Charlemagne Prize, 2004.

Dr Garret FitzGerald, Taoiseach, July 1981–February 1982; December 1982–June 1987.

Professor T.G. Fraser, Emeritus Professor of History and Honorary Professor of Conflict Research (INCORE), University of Ulster; formerly Provost, Magee campus, University of Ulster; author of *Ireland in Conflict 1922–1998* (London and New York: Routledge, 2000); *The Arab-Israeli Conflict* (Basingstoke: Palgrave Macmillan, 3rd edn, 2007).

Dr Maurice Hayes, public servant; Town Clerk, Downpatrick; Chairman, Community Relations Council, 1969–1973; Permanent Secretary, Department of Health and Social Services; Northern Ireland Ombudsman; member, Independent Commission on Policing, 1998–1999; member, Seanad; Chairman, The Ireland Funds.

Professor John Hume, Tip O'Neill Professor of Peace Studies; formerly Leader of the Social Democratic and Labour Party, 1979–2001, and member of the European Parliament, 1979–2004, and Westminster Parliament, 1983–2005, and the Northern Ireland Assembly, 1998–2000; joint holder of the Nobel Prize in Peace (1998)[**]; awarded the Martin Luther King and Mahatma Gandhi peace prizes in 1999 and 2001.

Senator John F. Kerry, Senator for Massachusetts since 1985; Democratic candidate for President, 2004; Chairman of the Senate Committee on Foreign Relations, 2009; Secretary of State from 2013.

President Mary McAleese, President of Ireland, 1997–2011; previously Pro Vice-Chancellor, Queen's University Belfast.

Dr Leonie Murray, Lecturer in International Politics, University of Ulster; author of *Clinton, Peacekeeping and Humanitarian Intervention. Rise and Fall of a Policy* (London and New York: Routledge, 2008).

Rosemary D. O'Neill, eldest child of Tip and Millie O'Neill; retired from the US Foreign Service, she worked for the Department of State for some thirty-seven years, latterly as advisor to Richard Haass, point person on Northern Ireland, and as outreach coordinator for Afghan and Muslim women.

President Romano Prodi, President of the European Commission, 1999–2005; Prime Minister of Italy, 1996–1998, and 2006–2008.

Ambassador Mitchell B. Reiss, President George W. Bush's Special Envoy for the Northern Ireland Peace Process, 2003–2007; Foreign Affairs Award for Public Service; White House Fellow, 1988–1989; President, Washington College, 2010.

---

[*] The titles are those held at the date of the lecture.
[**] With David Trimble.

Preface

This book consists of lectures by distinguished public figures given under the auspices of the Tip O'Neill Chair in Peace Studies at the University of Ulster's Magee campus. The Chair acknowledges the contribution made to the pursuit of peace in Ireland by the late Speaker Thomas P. ('Tip') O'Neill (1912–1994), whose family had emigrated from County Donegal to Boston. On the invitation of the Chair's holder, Nobel Laureate John Hume, the lecturers were asked to address the theme of 'Peace'. Introduced by Professor Hume, the lectures were delivered before an invited audience drawn from the university and the community. This volume brings these contributions to a wider audience and in a permanent form. The Tip O'Neill Chair was inaugurated by President Bill Clinton during his historic first visit to Northern Ireland in 1995, when an honorary doctorate of the University of Ulster was conferred on him. It is, therefore, particularly appropriate that the lecture series should begin with his address on 'Peacemaking'.

These lectures were delivered at a significant time in the Northern Ireland peace process, which culminated in the restoration of devolved government on 8 May 2007. It was a process in which many of the lecturers had been intimately involved, and the book necessarily reflects their unique insights; crucially, however, this volume and its contributors also address broader aspects of peacemaking and international relations as reflected in the work of the European Union, the United Nations and at the individual state level. The lessons of the European Union for peacekeeping are particularly instructive, not least in the light of its subsequent financial crises. Moreover, while the peace process in Northern Ireland has been closely studied by those in other contested societies, no one should think of it simply as a template which can be applied elsewhere. Its lessons are there, nevertheless.

The lecture series was made possible as the result of a generous grant from The Ireland Funds. Kieran McLoughlin of The Ireland Funds was an unfailing source of encouragement and support. On Professor

Fraser's retirement from the university, his successor as Provost of the Magee campus, the late Professor Jim Allen, chaired the Tip O'Neill Project Board with his customary dedication. We regret that he did not live to see this publication. We also note with great sadness the passing of two of our contributors, Professor Kader Asmal and Dr Garret FitzGerald.

The lectures have been reproduced substantially as delivered, each with an introduction jointly written by Professor Fraser and Dr Murray. Dr Murray's chapter sets the individual contributions within the academic discourse on peacemaking. The editors are grateful to Rosemary D. O'Neill for the profile of her father, which sets his work in connection with Northern Ireland in the context of his political career, and to Emeritus Professor Paul Arthur for writing the Conclusion, which draws on his own extensive experience of the Northern Ireland peace process. Michael Longley kindly granted permission for Dr Hayes to quote 'The Civil Servant' and an extract from 'Ceasefire' from *Collected Poems* by Michael Longley, published by Jonathan Cape, reprinted by permission of The Random House Group Limited and US rights permission by Wake Forest University Press.

We gladly acknowledge the support of the University of Ulster, but especially of Mrs Janet Farren, secretary to the Tip O'Neill Chair, whose unfailing enthusiasm and professionalism sustained the project throughout. Dr Stephen Ryan gave helpful advice. We appreciate the help of the staff of Manchester University Press. Above all, we are grateful to the individual lecturers who so willingly shared their experience of a subject vital to the course of the twenty-first century.

John Hume, T. G. Fraser, Leonie Murray

Introduction
My philosophy of peace

Nobel Laureate John Hume

It was a great honour for me to be appointed Tip O'Neill Professor of Peace Studies at the University of Ulster's Magee campus, and to be given the opportunity of inviting so many distinguished speakers to share their thoughts and experiences of peacemaking. Tip O'Neill was a valued friend, who did not hesitate to use his considerable influence in Washington to advance the cause of peace in Ireland. He was the first Speaker of the House of Representatives to come to Northern Ireland. I was able to welcome him to my house in Derry and show him the area around Buncrana where his ancestors had lived before, like so many other Irish people, they migrated to the United States. Tip O'Neill joined with three other prominent politicians of Irish origin, Senator Edward Kennedy, whom I had known since 1972, Governor Hugh Carey and Senator Daniel Moynihan, to work for a peaceful solution to the problems here. Known as the 'four horsemen', they formed the Friends of Ireland. The Tip O'Neill Chair, which acknowledges the work that he did, was inaugurated by President Bill Clinton during his historic visit to Derry in 1995, and Senator Kennedy gave the Tip O'Neill Memorial Lecture on 'Northern Ireland: the view from America' in the Guildhall in January 1998.

I have always valued education and emphasised its importance. My parents were highly intelligent people, who lacked formal education and the opportunities it brings. My father left school when he was twelve, and never worked again after Derry's shipyard closed, and my mother, who was an outworker in the shirt industry, could only sign her name. But they taught me to be positive, to question and to transcend the attitudes of the past. I passed the Eleven-Plus Examination which enabled me to get a scholarship to Derry's St Columb's College, and then to attend Maynooth College. When my father encouraged me to 'stick to the books', he knew what he was saying. Education gave me the opportunity to give something back to my community.

I have often said that at the root of all conflict is difference, and that difference is seen as a threat. None of us asked to be born into a particular community, whether religious, racial or national. If peace is to be achieved and secured then the mindset which sees difference as a threat has to change. There are two mindsets in the conflict here, Nationalist and Unionist. Each has to face up to the challenge of respect for difference, and how this can be accommodated. I have been greatly influenced by my experience in Europe, where the European Union is a unique example of conflict resolution. In my Nobel Lecture in Oslo in 1998 I repeated the story of how in 1979, when I was first elected to the European Parliament, I walked across the bridge over the Rhine from Strasbourg to the German city of Kehl, and meditated on what had changed since 1945 when Europe was in ruins, with 25 million dead, for the second time that century. If anyone had said then that we would all be together in a new Europe, and that we would all be working in our common interests, they would have been sent to a psychiatrist. But that is what has happened.[1]

What the European Union teaches us is that we have to create institutions that respect difference. All member countries are represented in its institutions, the Council of Ministers, the European Commission and the European Parliament. As the members work together in their common interests, the ancient barriers of distrust and hatred have eroded and a new Europe has emerged. These are the very principles which are at the heart of the Agreement which we negotiated here. When I visited the grave of Abraham Lincoln, I read the Latin words *E Pluribus Unum*, or 'out of many, one'. Those who make up America are drawn from many lands where famine, injustice and conflict existed, but a determination to avoid such things in their new country led them to build a unity based on respect for diversity. The principles behind the European Union and the United States of America are the same.

As we carry forward this Tip O'Neill lecture series, we are not just honouring the legacy of a great friend of peace in Ireland, we are exploring through a variety of experiences how peace may be reached in our new century. We are living through a period of revolutionary change – technologically, in telecommunications and in transport – which is bringing people closer together. This revolution makes the pursuit of peace more achievable, but, as I have so often said, if we are to do so, then it must be through dialogue and by spilling our sweat and not our blood.

Notes

1 John Hume, Nobel Lecture, Oslo, 10 December 1998, © The Nobel Foundation, www.nobelprize.org/nobel_prizes/peace/laureates/1998/hume-lecture.html (last accessed 13 February 2013).

1

Peacemaking – challenges for the new century

Dr Leonie Murray

Introduction

The pursuance of peace as a philosophy and of peacemaking as an activity, contrary to the suppositions of those who would call them 'modern' preoccupations, has a long and richly textured history.[1] Since the earliest times during which human beings organised themselves into social groupings there has been violent conflict, to which the 9,100 year old vestiges of fortress walls around the ancient city of Jericho attest, and there is no shortage of great minds to tell us of the innately aggressive and bellicose nature of 'man': St Augustine, Hobbes, Rousseau and Freud, to name but a very few. The adage that 'history is written by the victors' highlights the salient fact that until relatively recently in human historiography, history has been about, or in some way revolved around, war and violent conflict. It is hardly surprising that a cursory glance at this 'history', then, would produce the conclusion that it is one of discord and bloodshed. For if history is written by victors then it follows that it is written by those concerned with victory; by those whose primary focus is contest not conciliation.

However, the human 'instinctive imperative' towards peace and peacemaking can be traced back to prehistory and beyond to our primate ancestors, which have an instinct for peaceful coexistence and engage in peacemaking activities in the face of conflict and tension.[2] Equally because, and in spite, of the frequency of conflict, both biogenetic and cultural imperatives ensured that the maximising of peace emerged as a social good.[3] From ancient times, people in social groups, large and small, have promoted peace and been actively involved in arbitration of violent disputes. Consequently, that humans also possess just as natural an inclination towards peace can be as strongly affirmed.

Whilst it is undoubtedly true that our past as a species is replete with conflict and although it may have seemed so at times, the world has not been at war without end for millennia; there have been extended periods of peace and harmonious coexistence. Therefore, it is possible to suggest that ours is, in fact, a tale of two realities: one of war and the other, less well explored, of peace. The purpose of this chapter is to walk a little while along that road less-travelled with the aim of clarifying for the reader such efforts as have been made to date in the area of peacemaking, placing our volume within the context of that ongoing endeavour. It will also outline the terms of greatest significance in this volume – peace and peacemaking – and introduce the reader to some of the key themes of importance in what is at once both an intellectual and practical project. *Peacemaking in the twenty-first century* looks to the complex nature of contemporary conflicts and the global nature of the forces exerted on them; to root causes, sub and supra state structures and multi-level challenges. The global nature of the twenty-first-century peace challenge requires a cosmopolitan-multicultural, universal-globalist response that focuses on accepting diversity and transcends conflict and division through progress on common goals and recognition of common humanity.

This chapter will address the normative challenge of twenty-first-century peacemaking, define the terms used herein and explore notions of negative and positive peace in historical context before moving on to discuss three key themes in this century's peacemaking project: the root causes of conflict, its complex and global nature and the requirements of a universal-globalist response.

The normative challenge

It is possible to describe the pursuance of peace as a perpetual human project: a 'peace project' that encompasses all human activity designed to achieve peace in all of its forms, be it political, religious, civil or academic. The one thing that links the diverse, multi- and inter- disciplinary nature of those involved in the 'peace project' (statespersons, IGO and NGO representatives, practitioners, civil activists, scholars) and something that has attracted criticism, certainly in the academic sphere, is an agreement on the normative basis of the project: that peace is the ideal state for humanity to inhabit. As Ramsbotham, Woodhouse and Miall confirm, for its scholars, it is a 'proactive peacemaking project' that is 'normatively associated with the promotion of peace'.[4]

For others peace is 'worth the risks' in the getting, as President Bill Clinton acknowledged in his dialogue; a point elevated by Hillary Clinton even further to the 'most essential and noble goal'. Indeed, Taoiseach Bertie Ahern saw peace and its realisation as the 'triumph of humanity and cooperation over division and despair'. Still, peace partners from most quarters would view the peace project in the twenty-first century from the perspective taken by Dr Maurice Hayes who precisely encapsulated the goal of the venture in the contemporary world when he affirmed that 'no problem which results in a continuance of human suffering can be simply left to fester'.

Such is the contemporary mission: problems that result in human suffering give rise to a deficit of peace and since peace is the ideal, the role of the twenty-first-century peace project is to find solutions. A judgement has been made and unashamedly so, and it is this judgement that divides it from a purely academic pursuit and draws in statespersons, international civil servants and activists and NGO practitioners from around the world; it is what brought every one of our contributors to the task of peacemaking, from which combined experience this volume draws its lessons for peace.

The lexicon

What, then, exactly does this volume mean by peace and, indeed, by the peacemaking of its title? Peace as a concept is extremely difficult to capture in the abstract and as a result it is often defined as the absence of conflict, violent or otherwise. It is not within the parameters of this chapter to accurately bring such a multi-layered and nebulous idea to a satisfactory definition; however, what is important is our acceptance of what Johan Galtung (1964) crystallised as the distinction between 'negative' and 'positive' peace.[5] Negative peace describes the absence of violent conflict, but not necessarily all conflict. Neither does it say anything about the presence of balance, justice, equality, etc. As Rodgers and Ramsbotham (1999) state, the 'absence of war could obscure deep injustices which made a mockery of notions of peace'; this is the 'oppressive peace' model first established, in recorded history, in Pharaonic Egypt and which became the pattern, perhaps exemplified in the Pax Romana, so expertly described by Roman historian Tacitus that variants of his well-known idiom can be found in most writings on the subject.[6] In such a context: 'they made a wasteland and called it peace'.[7]

A condition of positive peace, by contrast, contains those elements of a harmonious society that negative peace cannot ensure and whose absence give rise to the underlying causes of violent conflict. Negative peace may be characterised as the absence of direct violence, but might still witness indirect violence or structural violence, such as uneven development, poverty, gendered social violence and inequality, economic, social and political injustice and environmental degradation. For positive peace to exist, therefore, a holistic approach to the overall equity and justice of society, domestic and international, must be undertaken, over-and-above safeguarding from direct violence. In this sense, although negative peace has been achieved in many conflict situations around the world, it can be argued that few, if any, societies have yet managed to achieve true peace in the positive sense.

It follows, then, that contemporary peacemaking may be concerned with any and all of these positive and negative factors, which brings us on to the term peacemaking itself. In specificist peace and conflict resolution literature peacemaking tends to refer to a tailored response to a particular stage of conflict intervention; top-down, elite-centred settlement of armed conflict.[8] In broader discursive circles (and often involving the same range of academics and practitioners, as well as policymakers) it is regularly used to describe the gamut of activities associated with mitigation, management, resolution, settlement and transformation or transcendence of conflict and creating and promoting both negative and positive peace and reconciliation in and across divided societies. In fact, in this present volume peacemaking can be seen to refer to all of these aspects.

In the sense that all contributors to this volume have acted as elite peacemakers of some form or other, the activities in which they engaged can be described as peacemaking in the specificist sense. Each has, however, also been involved in peacemaking in the broader sense and their discussions incorporate and reflect a diversity of peacemaking activities and, therefore, the broader discursive definition also applies. In short, peacemaking herein refers to the whole range of activities directed at making peace, which includes, but is not limited to, elite settlement of armed conflict.

A potted history of peace: negative and positive peace explored

A burgeoning interest among peace project confederates in putting together the pieces of humanity's historical record in the areas of peace and peacemaking, as an antidote to centuries of history focused almost exclusively on war, has produced some refreshing scholarship and can be claimed as a feature of the twenty-first-century peace project whilst the following exploration of negative and positive peace in history firmly embeds the writings of this volume within the broader context of peacemaking in the twenty-first century.[9]

Although what we would now describe as negative peace certainly pre-existed modern politics by centuries, its achievement has been the main focus of rulers, politicians and those primarily concerned with advancing peace as a project since Napoleon's late eighteenth-century European outing. In the ancient and classical worlds there were periods of extended negative peace; an ideal sought by rulers in ancient Mesopotamia and Sumeria.[10] In Ancient Egypt, one of the Pharaoh's most central functions was the preservation of peace on earth, for which purpose a Philanthropia or 'state of peace' was sought and habitually imposed; that negative or 'oppressive peace' through which he most often ruled and which set the standard for many future negative peace's.

Members of Ancient Greece's Amphictyonic or Delphic League made pledges to each other to abstain from mutual attack and in some ways progressively surpassed the League of Nations more than three thousand years later, in that offenders, be they members or not, faced collective attack if they contravened the League's rubric.[11] The League centred around the famous Oracle of Delphi, to which rulers came from near and far to seek the means of ending conflicts, one such instance of which, it is said, resulted in the foundation of the Olympic Games. The ruling tenets of the Games contained clear peacemaking elements as every four years combatants were required to lay down their weapons in order to participate in the sporting events.[12] Negative peace leagues also existed in Classical Greece: the Peloponnesian, Hellenic and Delian Leagues were usually dominated by a stronger state (Sparta) and designed to produce military unity rather than peace, per se. However, members pledged not to fight one another and to use diplomacy rather than the threat of force in their relations.

Perhaps an interesting insight into the *Pax Romana*, or (negative) 'Peace of Rome' may be found in the linguistic origins of the Latin 'pax', which evolved from the initial sense: a pact in which the defeated surrendered to the will of the victor, to a 'social condition devoid of war'.[13] What this sublimation meant in practice was Romanisation for those who capitulated and enslavement for those who did not; nonetheless, the Peace of Rome was aspired to as a beacon of order and civilisation, perhaps, by nearly as many as those who laboured under its barbarism and cruelty. Whilst the Greeks and Romans were caught up in a seemingly endless round of war and peace, so, too, were the peoples of the Ancient 'East' caught in their own cycles. In the ancient Chinese Dynastic tradition, peace and prosperity were avidly sought by rulers and during the Zhou Dynasty, for example, prolonged periods of warfare and discord meant that the ruler had offended the god of heaven and so, despite otherwise 'divine' status, could be rightfully replaced in the cause of guaranteeing (negative) peace.[14]

Both Judeo-Christian and Islamic histories and traditions contain strong combative elements.[15] Nevertheless, peacemaking as a duty is central to all three religions and the avoidance of war was often an overwhelming enough prospect, though there are significant positive peace elements in all three traditions also. In Judaism, peace (negative) was recognised as a guiding practice and in time acquired important social and political connotations and after expulsion from the 'Holy Land', Jews who inhabited Christian or Islamic societies tended to be strong peace advocates and could be found to occupy peacemaking roles throughout their kingdoms. In terms of negative peace in Islam, the Qur'an contains quite specific instructions regarding war, peace and peacemaking. Whilst war is permitted when necessary, there are a whole host of qualifications. If peace is offered or peacemaking attempted, it *must* be accepted, and if enemies will not fight peace must also be made since in such a case 'Allah has not given ... a way against them'.[16] Indeed, the Prophet Mohammed himself was a famed peacemaker.[17]

The early Christian Church was fundamentally pacifist in nature; a fact that brought it into direct confrontation with the Roman Empire, as its members refused to serve in the Roman Legions. The Christian Church of the Middle Ages endeavoured, as far as was possible in such times of upheaval as this formative period of European statehood, to limit war: instituting the *Treuga Dei* or 'Truce of God', which banned combat on Sundays and other 'holy days' (holidays) and the *Pax Dei* or 'Peace of God', which prohibited fighting on holy ground, gave immunity to ecclesiastics such as priests, monks and nuns and proclaimed 'sanctuary' inside the walls of holy orders etc. – such attempts also sought to extend protection to peasants who had not the means for their own defence.[18]

Over the centuries, pure peace traditions also emerged from Christianity, such as the Waldesians in the twelfth century and the Anabaptists in the sixteenth century as well as the Society of Friends or Quakers (which was founded by George Fox in the mid-seventeenth century and remains a potent force in conflict resolution), Mennonites and Brethren, which came to be described as 'peace religions' since the pursuance of peace and active personal resistance to violence in society and government is a key feature. Indeed, it is difficult to over-emphasise the input, particularly from Quakers, that has been ongoing in all subsequent periods of development.

Renaissance Humanism gave rise to a focus on human versus divine worth that stimulated an emphasis, albeit among a small minority outlook, on the desirability of (negative) peace in what was a conflict-ridden period of European history. In what was likely a reaction to the seeming endless bloodshed of the Hundred Years War, writing in the early sixteenth century, Dutch philosopher and priest Desiderius Erasmus denounced war: 'If there is in the affairs of mortal men any one thing which it is ... incumbent on every man by every lawful means to avoid, to deprecate, to oppose, that one thing is doubtless war' (Erasmus, 1507). In a later work, writing as peace personified, he called down judgement on the rulers and powerful of the day for waging war and causing suffering, discord and strife to be visited upon the ordinary people (Erasmus, 1521). We can date the modern advancement of negative peace as the most desirable state of human existence from this period of intellectual flowering.

Centuries of warfare (power struggles that after the Reformation took on the additional colouring of religious campaigns) resulted in the creation of the modern state system in 1648 with the Treaty of Westphalia, which put an end to the religious conflicts of the previous generations by decreeing that the ruler of a state would decide the religion therein, free from external interference and in doing so, established the principles of sovereignty and non-intervention that still dominate our contemporary international system, in an effort to foster stability and a negative peace by regulating state behaviour.

The Enlightenment saw the emergence of several important philosophical strands which were boons to both war and peace. Discourses on natural rights and liberties arose from the conditions of social dislocation, uneven development and increased literacy and secularisation that were by-products of the Industrial Revolution, and these in turn gave rise to nationalist and socialist doctrines, both of which provided justifications for violent struggle, as well as the basis for non-violence.[19] Discourses on the roles of democracy and capitalism and peace also emerged.[20] Such philosophical development of this period as Immanuel Kant's *Perpetual Peace*, in addition to earlier classical and Renaissance works, created the context from which contemporary western peace philosophies grew.[21]

Reactions to the Napoleonic Wars helped launch the secular peace movements of the nineteenth century, which developed apace with technological advancements of that century (which in turn spurred arms races) and in response to particular localised conflicts such as the Mexican and Indian Wars for Americans and the Crimean War for Europeans and were, thus, focused primarily on preventing war. The Concert of Europe, which was established in the wake of Bonaparte's campaigns on the continent (and also, in part, in reaction to the revolutionary events that preceded him in France) was intended to safeguard the established state system through balance-of-power governance; but importantly, it was also designed to preserve the fragile (negative) peace that had been secured through Napoleonic defeat, by way of dialogue and the pursuance of common goals.

The nineteenth century also saw the growth of international civil groups concerned with the eradication of war; various peace associations or foundations were founded in this century and symposia held, such as the Hague Peace Conferences, which met between 1899 and 1909. Additionally, the First Geneva Convention was adopted in 1864, which although not designed to achieve peace, was important in its recognition that war had an abominable human cost and if it could not be stopped altogether, must at least be regulated in international law, and vitally, laid the foundation for the extension of later protocols to non-combatants after the Second World War.

An interval in concerns regarding peace was experienced as large portions of the globe 'discovered' nationalism and organised itself thusly into states. The inevitable consequence of this flourishing of nationalist sentiment and statism was its overflow into the orgy of violent national confrontation of the First World War; the horrors of which, conversely, caused a great outpouring of pro-peace sentiment (negative) and firmly implanted the appreciation that the absence of war was the most desirable condition for the contemporary world. Importantly, however, this time the mood appeared also to have pervaded the halls of power. War, as an acceptable extension of state policy, for the first time in modern international history had become delegitimised. This interval saw mass efforts for peace break out across the globe. There was a noteworthy international civil push towards disarmament; significant enough to cause governments to embark on a series of disarmament conferences. Internationally, there was an overall rise in pluralism, and cosmopolitan liberal internationalism rose to ascendance in the global political system, culminating in the foundation of the League of Nations; the international community's most radical effort to-date to exorcise the spectre of war once and for all, with its newly institutionalised principles of collective security and open dialogue. (Of course, this cosmopolitan world-view could trace its roots back to classical times and more recently to the eighteenth century musings of the likes of Kant.)

Great minds looked to new ways of avoiding war, such as Mitrany and functionalism, which focused on the idea of creating functionally specific cross or supra state institutions that would unite people on the basis of shared needs and common interests rather than state allegiance, and eventually fed into European integration following the Second World War.[22] World War I also gave rise to the new study of International Relations that was born of this understanding – lately furnished by revulsion at the carnage of the previous four years – that vigorous, serious work on affairs between states was vital in order to ensure such horrors never again occurred. The first chairs in International Relations, such as at Aberystwyth in Wales, were endowed in the name of peace, meant as a memorial to the many students who gave their lives in the First World

War'. Consequently, at its birth the study of International Relations had (negative) peace as its purpose and in this way can be seen also as the birth of Peace and Conflict Studies. Having witnessed, first hand, the horrifying damage that total war had on yielding human flesh and vulnerable human psyche, physicians and behaviourists were among the first to engage in the new project to prevent war, bringing an interesting perspective to the new sphere of academic study emerging from political science and history. Indeed, interest began to emerge from many other quarters also: the natural sciences, anthropology, mathematics and the social and health sciences in a multi- and inter- disciplinary manner that came to characterise peace and conflict as a field of study.

Unbeknown to these peace pioneers, however, the orgy of nationalistic violence had not seen its ultimate manifestation; that was yet to come in its most extreme expression of the Fascism of Hitler's Germany that engulfed Europe in 1939 and one-by-one drew the countries of the world into total war for the second time in twenty years. The aggressive expansionism that it engendered (in concert with imperialist Japan) and the moral repugnancy that this display inspired, for most, simply *required* confrontation, and so because it must be combatted, war experienced a revived credibility in the furtherance of 'right cause'; a fact that carried through to the post-Second World War wars of anti-colonialism in the vein of Jefferson's 'tree of liberty' and engendered renewed discussions surrounding Just War theory, all of which the perceived realities of the Cold War maintained, to a certain degree.[23]

Whilst the study of International Relations had been born of a cosmopolitan desire to end war, the failure of the League of Nations to prevent the outbreak of war in 1939 disillusioned many statesmen and theorists regarding what was now considered a discredited and unrealistic, utopian venture.[24] The academic field, and by reflection, the international system itself, came to be dominated by power-centric Realism, the focus of which was on the politics of insecurity, self-interest and zero-sum gains and for which violent confrontation between states was an unavoidable, and not always negative, consequence of the anarchical nature of the international system. For some scholars, then, International Relations as a discipline was no longer suited to the rigorous prevention of war. Driven, primarily, by the fear of nuclear extermination (at least initially), a handful of academics took up the challenge.[25] Working initially from a state-centric and negative peace perspective, the discipline that emerged in the post-Second World War period became the contemporary manifestation of the historical record of humanity's quest for peace. Partly as a result of those doctors and psychologists who had taken up the banner of peace in the aftermath of World War I, and partly because

of the preliminary focus on the nuclear threat, early influences from the
natural and health sciences played a unique role in the construction of
the discipline's taxonomy, and one that meshed well with the normative and analytical goals of this 'new' field: the establishment, not only
of a philosophy of peace or a moral rationale for its appeal, which had
been attempted by many before them, but of a 'science' of peace that
would generate well-founded and practical methods of preventing war.
Adopting the language and sometimes methodological approaches of
the scientific community, a frequent analogy saw war as a disease and
their task: to treat the illness; to discover its root causes; to prevent its
contraction in the first instance.

Despite the rise of *realpolitik*, after two world wars, war had largely
come to be seen not only as 'illegitimate' as a policy means, but also
iniquitous, and through the establishment of the United Nations (UN)
system, deemed *illegal* in international law.[26] The extent to which war
was now considered entirely illegitimate can be additionally demonstrated by the fact that in the immediate aftermath of the Second World
War, most 'war departments' changed their names and became departments tasked with their nation's 'defence'; one of the only permissible
applications of military power left under the new international system.
Also illustrative of the general revulsion for total war was the revival of
concepts of limited war popular in the nineteenth century, which was
exhibited in the proxy wars of the Cold War period; which were also
partly initiated by what in the nuclear era had become the overriding
concern of many statespersons: the avoidance at all costs, of nuclear
war. In this way nuclear weapons also had an impact on perceptions of
war and peace; as the first generation with the capacity to destroy all of
creation it could go either way.[27] Both concerns over nuclear arsenals
and such 'limited' conflicts as, in particular, Vietnam for the US and
Afghanistan for the Soviet Union, fuelled vast anti-war (negative peace)
movements across the globe.

The examination of war and peace, as a manifestation of the twenty-
first-century peace project, has gone through several stages of development since its first emergence-proper from the ashes of pre-First World
War cosmopolitanism, with many of the key thinkers nominally associated with each phase, in fact, moving with, and even driving, the devel-
opmental forces that have produced them.[28] In this first wave, the input
of scientists concerned about the nuclear threat was exemplified in the
publication of the *Bulletin of the Atomic Scientists of Chicago* in 1945
(in 1947, shortened to simply the *Bulletin of the Atomic Scientists*).
Centres for the study of conflict and/or peace sprang up at the Universities of Michigan and Groningen. At Stanford University the Centre for

Advanced Studies in the Behavioural Sciences was the incubator for the *Journal of Conflict Resolution*, which issued its first edition in 1957; significant names associated with which were Herbert Kelman, Kenneth and Elise Boulding, Anatol Rapoport and Lewis Richardson (whose work was published posthumously). Driven by the overriding concern of the previous century (the avoidance of war) and the dread of nuclear obliteration these peace project associates were concerned originally with the prevention of war (advancing negative peace).

At the Norwegian Institute of Social Research, Johan Galtung established the precursor to what became the Peace Research Institute in Oslo (PRIO) in 1959, from which the *Journal of Peace Research* (1964) arose. The Conflict Resolution Society was founded in London in 1963, welcoming John Burton as its first honorary secretary and producing its first publication in 1966. In Sweden the Stockholm International Peace Research Institute (SIPRI) commemorated 150 years of peace in 1966 and a variety of other peace institutions and centres for research were founded in this period in Canada, Japan and elsewhere. It is also at this juncture that the contemporary peace project began to move past its primary focus on preventing war or advancing negative peace. In what they termed their 'friendly quarrels', Boulding and Galtung represented what became a minimalist/pragmatist vs maximalist/structuralist split in these early days over what the discipline's true focus should be, often characterised by peace researcher's' position on a particular side of the Atlantic: preventing war (producing negative peace) or generating positive peace.[29]

Boulding's work concentrated on evolving a knowledge base that would prevent conflict from occurring through the production of warning signals; whereas Galtung developed work on multiple layers of peace and violence, both positive and negative, indirect/structural and direct, that as a consequence required investment in a broader spectrum of issues relating to equality and combatting conflict through transformation of structures as well as including views from non-western sources. A third 'founder', John Burton, meanwhile utilised systems and games theories to extend this broadening approach with his problem-solving and Basic Needs proposals.[30] Also significant was the influence of social change and counter culture in the West at this time, which led to the development of new ways of solving local social and labour disputes and the emergence of Alternative Dispute Settlement (ADR) in community relations, which also began to filter into the work being conducted on peace and conflict issues. Gradually, linkages between peace and development, inequality, injustice and environmental degradation began to become clear, and as a result the peace project began to shift towards tackling such underlying causes of conflict in the pursuit of both negative and positive modes of peace.

As evidenced both in and by the structure of the United Nations, despite the preponderance of Realism in the international system, the post-war period witnessed a growth of pluralist doctrines, concurrent with the *realpolitik* of the day. This growth is substantiated by the development of traditional peacekeeping which grew out of the stalemate on the Security Council caused by Cold War confrontation as a way of enabling the UN to live up to its role as global peacemaker, as well as concepts of human rights, international social and economic justice and environmental preservation and the concomitant structures that were established over the course of the twentieth century. Such matters simmered away, during this period, on the back-burner of concern at the highest echelons of power, but increasing in significance for activists and ordinary citizens the world over. So, too, the scope of activity among academics, practitioners and activists expanded to include 'three great projects': 'avoiding nuclear war, removing glaring inequalities and injustices in the global system, and achieving ecological balance and control'.[31] This second wave saw an expansion in the nature of approaches designed to promote peace. Most significant was the increasingly practical application of research and the feedback loop that this created for understanding. There was an increasing acceptance of the interconnections between domestic and international levels in conflict analysis and a real absorption of recently professionalised ADR strategies into the work that was being done at that time. Problem-solving ideas were progressed in workshops; significantly by the London Group (which included Burton) and the Harvard School, most importantly by Herbert Kelman.[32] Essential work was carried out on principled or 'interest-based' negotiation by the likes of Roger Fisher and William Ury; and Adam Curle, among others, moved mediation approaches beyond 'Track I', or power-based mediation, towards 'Track II', or good offices mediation, and beyond.[33]

The end of the Cold War presented the peace project with a series of difficult challenges and fresh opportunities. The collapse of the bipolar system was accompanied by an intensification in ethnic and intra-state conflict. Both the complexities of these 'new wars' and their number gave rise to increased demands for innovative and multi-layered 'solutions'.[34] The expiration of the restrictive concerns that revolved around endless confrontation also allowed a rise to prominence of those 'secondary' matters that had been all the while growing in the global consciousness whilst politicians had haggled over the status of Intercontinental Ballistic Missiles: the increasing gap between global spheres of rich and poor, human rights abuses, gender inequalities, the environment, etc. Those issues that peace scholars and activists had been pressing for answers were now given leave to enjoy attention at the highest levels. The prominence of global problems *not* Cold War-related, the potential for global solutions and the optimism surrounding that potential was high. Additionally, many in positions of authority and influence at this time endorsed a basic cosmopolitan perspective and underlined the power of global governance, internationalism, humanitarianism, rights, democracy and economic interdependence, including many of the contributors to this volume.[35] A combination of these forces meant that perhaps more so than mainstream International Relations, in this particular geopolitical atmosphere Peace and Conflict Studies provided a better framework context for dealing with the issues and so too enjoyed an increased authority.

Perceived successes in places like Cambodia, Angola and El Salvador, triumph of right over oppression in South Africa and progress in intractably divided societies such as Israel/Palestine and Northern Ireland seemed to suggest incredible possibilities and gave the 'peace project' immense encouragement. However, problems associated with peace operations in places like Somalia and the former Yugoslavia and the abject failure to respond in any effective way in the face of the Rwandan genocide, followed by a reversal in the fortunes of the Middle East peace process, disillusioned international statespersons and sent many academics back to the drawing board, armed with the lessons of both the achievements and disappointments of this period.[36]

The al Qaeda attacks of 11 September 2001 and the period of US policy that followed also had a serious impact upon the 'peace project' as the globe reoriented itself towards the 'Islamist threat'. If the field had fit the post-Cold War bill, researchers and peace activists now found themselves on the outside in the search for a response; momentarily wrong-footed by the US 'War on Terror' and liberal statebuilding of the decade. Liberal internationalism, concepts of humanitarian intervention and, indeed, liberal peacebuilding were discredited in some circles because of their association with these policies; however, this in some ways reflected an already existent split in the field, regarding military force and peace. Since they had 'encroached' on peace project 'territory' so to speak, such issues as the use of force and how the US projects its power globally became questions not just for traditional International Relations but for the peace project also.

Greater interest and scrutiny during this period resulted in a greater sophistication and professionalisation in the peace discipline and, unsurprisingly given the context, significant work was conducted on the intractability and complexity of intra-state conflict. New approaches, building on work carried out in the immediate post-Cold War period by the likes of Boulding and Adam Curle, charted a move away from the idea of peace as something *brought* to a conflict by external parties and enacted 'from above' (with inevitable questions concerning interest and motivation, highlighted at that time by the US liberal statebuilding agenda) towards indigenous sources of peace; peace 'from below', or what scholar-practitioner John Paul Lederach (1995) terms 'indigenous empowerment', resulting in the development of conflict resolution techniques such as 'Track III' or indigenous mediation, and on to consideration of conflict resolution as a discourse: the result of interaction between external and internal sources of peace.[37] Complementary studies on ethnicity, gender, culture and civil society (likewise the successors of earlier work) emerged during this period too, with noteworthy contributions and cross-permeations with the NGO community. Critical and post-structural debates provided a useful critique of conflict resolution and liberal peacebuilding as reinforcing the exploitative liberal-capitalist structure of the global political system and failing to recognise the validity of indigenous and non-northern values.[38] One emergent concept that negotiates its way around this accusation of a lack of vision in contemporary conflict resolution is that of hybridity: the 'fluid and intersecting identities shared by all', the uncovering of which creates a middle path between difference, fundamental to which is the acceptance of difference itself as a 'method of peace'.[39]

The lessons of the previous years have fed into the present in which work on culture (what Beck calls the 'otherness'), globalism/global civil society, multiculturalism and social pluralism will be the important markers for the future of both the discipline and the human project itself; in this way combining traditional peacemaking issues with the post-Cold War complex social-ethnic conflict issues and post-September 11 clash of culture claims.[40] In this contemporary conceptualisation the effort to draw more firmly on positive modes of peace from the past and, particularly, from non-northern cultures features heavily and is of vital importance in moving the field forward past its apparent liberal European and North American roots. In recent scholarship, history has been re-plumbed for sources of a human emphasis on positive peace. Homer's great Hellenic literary colossi – *The Iliad* and *The Odyssey* – though appearing on the surface to glorify war, have been reinterpreted as tales with an inherent anti-war core, which although celebrating warriors of this Heroic Age of man, singled out those who, through wisdom or skill, manage to avoid conflict or bring it to a swifter conclusion and provided contemporary readers with hope for a return to the

Golden Age in which 'man' lived in peace and harmony with each other, the earth and the cosmos.[41]

The cradle of many western philosophies, Classical Greece, has been revisited in the search for philosophical antecedents to positive peace; finding that for Pythagoras, peace meant harmony, whilst for Herodotus, it was the natural pattern of existence, and war, the aberration. So, too, in the art of Sophistry, from which emerged the great discourses of Socrates, Plato and Aristotle, can be found a celebration of reason, debate and critical dialogue as methods of dispute settlement rather than the resort to armed conflict. All of which is reflective perhaps of the etymological roots of the Greek word for peace, *eireinei*, as comprising harmony and justice as well as the usual absence of turmoil.

Critical eyes are looking for new insight from eastern philosophies such as Buddhism and Hinduism (already partly explored), and also Taoism, Confucianism and Mohism, which emerged from the Hundred Schools of Peace of the Chinese Warring States period.[42] Taoism's main text, the *Tao Te Ching* states that military force is not the *tao*, or the *way* that humans should follow and life demands balance; a philosophy that was taken to extremes by philosopher Zhuangzi, who wrote in the fourth century BCE that 'when opposing weapons are crossed, he who deplores the situation conquers', advocating inaction and withdrawal from and non-involvement in violent governments and societies in a manner redolent of the so-called 'peace religions' of latter-day Anglo-Centric Christianity.[43] Confucius held that the accomplishment of internal peace was the definitive human goal and that peace comes from social harmony and balance. In his most famous tract, *The Analects*, he wrote of *jen* (or empathy) and of the golden rule of human relations: 'treat your subordinates as you would like to be treated by your superiors'.[44] In Mohism violence was denounced and was to be replaced by good deeds and thrift as a path to universal love, peace and harmony: the highest goal. Mohists also advocated dialogue as a means of mitigating conflict. Again, indigenous cultural interpretations of peace are often embedded in linguistic traditions. In Mandarin, peace is a composition term *he-ping*: *he* denoting balance and *ping* signifying harmony and unity from diversity.

Islamic and Judeo-Christian traditions are also being re-examined given their core emphasis on the achievement of positive peace and of peacemaking as a duty of their adherents. The Arabic word *'salaam'* and Hebrew *'shalom'*, both used in greetings, as cognates have essentially the same meaning; both the absence of violence, but also personal happiness, fulfilment and harmony – our contemporary understanding of positive peace. As a result of the prominence of the global Islamist challenge in twenty-first-century discourse, significant attention is being directed towards reviewing the central peace tenets of Islam, in which one of Allah's titles is 'giver of peace'. The word 'Islam' in Arabic, means 'submit', and 'Muslim' means 'one who submits', and individual peace in the Muslim faith is achieved through submission to the will of Allah. Even 'Jihad' or 'struggle', a provocative term in today's environment, can be viewed as a struggle with oneself in accepting and submitting to the will of Allah, which is not to say that Jihad was/is never used as a rallying cry to holy war, but merely that this popular perception is not necessarily its most commonly understood significance within Islamic culture.[45] A period of conquest in the decades after Mohammed's death culminated in the establishment of the *Pax Islamica*, which was established and upheld, in the main, with an official policy of tolerance and remarkably low levels of violence, and certain offshoots also grew up within Islam concerned with a specific focus on the achievement of inner peace and purification, such as Sufism, but the 'essential message' of mainstream Islam is one of 'peaceful unity based on tolerance and benevolence'.[46]

These 'non-western' traditions which stress good deeds, tolerance of diversity, justice and balance find resonance in Judeo-Christian values. In Judaism the god of the Torah *chose* Abraham and his descendants and made a 'covenant of peace' with them and despite the fire and brimstone professions of most of the prophets, there were also those, such as Isaiah, who preached peace; all predicted the coming of the Messiah, in and through whom, '*shalom*' would be realised.[47] Whilst Christians emphasise the teachings of Jesus Christ as the son of God and Saviour, Jews meanwhile, focus on good deeds, peace and non-violence.[48] In the end, the more effort is expended in studying peace in different world cultures and religious traditions, the more obvious it becomes that the well-known adage from the New Testament, 'blessed are the peacemakers', far from 'damning' the twenty-first-century peace project by singular association with northern values, is in fact echoed in cultures and traditions the world over.[49]

A holistic approach

Given how recently we have begun to re-explore positive aspects of peace and multicultural and historical sources of inspiration, in addition to a deeper approach to the attainment of peace, against the centuries-long focus on war and, only latterly, its avoidance, it is quite remarkable that so many statespersons have adopted concerns regarding positive peace and the range of issues associated with a maximalist approach to peacemaking; a fact that is reflected in the silent assumptions and articulated concerns of our contributors, all of whom recognise the importance of the broadest range of issues and methods in advancing peace in the twenty-first century. One of the key characteristics of today's peace project is the recognition of the need to take a 'holistic' approach to peacemaking. In the twenty-first century engaging with peace requires that we go deeper than merely considering what prompted a violent outburst, in order to: firstly, identify the underlying causes of conflicts, which requires, secondly, recognition of their global nature and, finally, the multi-level, integrated, universal-globalist approach that is needed to mitigate, manage, resolve, settle and transform or transcend conflict and create and promote both negative and positive peace and reconciliation in and across divided societies.

Root causes of conflict

Disentangling the root causes of conflict is one of the most fundamental tasks in contemporary twenty-first-century peacemaking. Simply attempting to predict triggers for violent conflict and guarantee the absence of direct violence in society clouds deeper realities and structures that contain the seeds and perpetuate cycles of future violence in and across societies and states. What this acknowledgment means is that it is necessary to look below the surfaces and above traditional limits to identify sub and supra social structures of inequality and injustice; issues such as political, economic, gender and cultural discrimination, inequality of access to opportunity, education and empowerment and resource competition. Such root causes are recognised across the contributions to this volume. Both President Clinton and Hillary Clinton refer meaningfully to problems such as hunger, lack of clean water, poverty and disease in facilitating conflict and in contrast, to promoting diversity, debt relief, fair trade and economic opportunity as well as 'education and citizen service among people' in progressing peace; whilst Kader Asmal underscores the negative impact of 'inequality and uneven development' and the 'widening gap between rich and poor' against the constructive potential of 'education, employment and particularly civil society'. The role of education is also picked up by John Kerry and Mary McAleese, who further reiterate the importance of equality, justice, human rights and 'civic society' in peacemaking.

In twenty-first-century peacemaking, recognition of such root causes is vital, but must go further in tackling them and, as Romano Prodi further notes, must be underpinned by 'structures' that do just that; something, he emphasises, that the European Union had been learning to put into practice. Moreover, former United Nations Secretary-General, Kofi Annan, warns us that as past experience taught him, where the 'underlying causes of conflict had not been resolved' failure for peace-making efforts was almost guaranteed. Clearly, therefore, emphasis on core sources of violent conflict has risen from the grass-roots level to be adopted at the highest strata of global governance.

The global nature of the contemporary peace project

Acknowledgement of the causal sources of conflict is vital, but a second central factor must also be explored before twenty-first-century peace-makers can move on with the job of tackling such conflicts and that is recognition of the unmistakably complex, multi-level and global nature of conflict in the contemporary world. Such complex social-ethnic conflicts, although more often than not in today's world intra-state in nature, have equally sub, inter and supra state aspects and origins and are often impacted upon, or even caused by, larger global problems; for instance: unequal global politico-economic structures, environmental degradation or ideological struggle, as represented most prominently today by the global Islamist campaign.[50]

Bertie Ahern, Kofi Annan, Maurice Hayes and Mary McAleese all take care to highlight the complexity of contemporary conflict; indeed, Annan and McAleese are almost identical in their emphasis that there is 'no one size fits all' conflict type or resolution model. Kadar Asmal describes globalisation as a 'source of despair' for many, bringing with it 'tremendous political and economic instability and rupture'. He adds that the phenomenon locks states into 'entrenched patterns of inequality and uneven development', triggering a sequence that can only end in violent conflict; whilst Bill Clinton raises the importance of 'trying to provide economic opportunity to poor communities' at home and 'around the world' and of tackling 'poverty and ignorance and disease and global warming' all in the cause of peace. Global environmental problems are broadly recognised as having a causal role in conflict, with what Garret FitzGerald calls 'ecological action', or environmental sustainability, as Pat Cox would have it, forming part of the overall picture.

One of the most recent challenges to the peace project in the twenty-first century has been the threat of global Islamism and the international community's response to that threat. As John Kerry puts it, 'discon-nects' in today's global society have influenced the development of what represents one of the most 'critical challenges of our time', but one that must be countered with words as well as deeds, or as Romano Prodi puts it 'both force and brainpower'. President Clinton takes this idea a little further by suggesting that leading the world in the fight against poverty, disease, environmental challenges, etc. will do as much, if not more, to stem the tide of fanaticism in the Islamic world, as military force. Our contributors each engaged with this issue in its relation to the progression of both domestic and international peace in the contemporary world. Most, such as Hayes and Asmal, note the impact of the terrorist attacks of the 11 September 2001 on both the global context and the pursuance of peace, more specifically; although not all link the two as intrinsically as Hillary Clinton does when she tells us that in today's world, peace 'always a noble goal, is now a strategic imperative'.

A universal-globalist response

Once we appreciate that the nature of twenty-first-century peacemaking must deal with root causes and the complex, multi-level and global nature of conflict, then we must recognise that so too must the response be multi-faceted and interconnected; a universal-globalist approach to conflict resolution. Ramsbotham, Woodhouse and Miall (2011) make an excellent case for what they term 'cosmopolitan conflict resolution' as the appropriate response.[51] The importance of a broad spectrum approach from local, national and regional to international and of the role of supra-national institutions and an international pluralist agenda is one of the most widely recognised features within this volume; as Kader Asmal comments, peace must be secured at both domestic and global levels. Most of our contributors talk about contemporary politico-economic structures as in some way contributing to conflict and, consequently, in need of some manner of adjustment: be it radical, or in the form of free trade, development aid, the encouragement of sustainable development, etc.

Speaking from a considerable, amassed experience, a multi-level approach to peacemaking is endorsed by virtually all. The importance of locally empowered indigenous peacemakers (Track III mediation) makes a significant appearance in discussions.[52] Hillary Clinton stresses how peace must be 'built in neighbourhoods', whilst Dermot Ahern tells us that peace must begin 'on the ground in local communities' and Kader Asmal highlights the inadequacy of 'elite representation'. Indeed, even Annan, whose primary focus is on elite intervention, stresses that peacemaking must be 'deeply rooted in local communities and identities'. Outsiders, he says, 'however well-intentioned, do not always know best' (although he continues in his belief 'that outsiders can help' and goes on to detail how this help can be applied to greatest success).[53] Focusing on domestic and international levels President Mary McAleese talks about the role of 'unofficial' (Track II) and 'official' (Track I) organisations and groups in mediation and finding ways to 'reach out to one another' in the Northern Irish context, and many contributors emphasise the influence of powerful external peace partners, such as the United States and the EU, in progressing peace within the province ('crucial dynamics' as McAleese called them) as an exemplar of the role of 'good offices' (Track II) as well as elite or 'muscular' (Track I) mediation in conflict resolution.[54]

Bill Clinton recalls the time he 'stayed up all night before the Good Friday Agreement calling everybody' he could get on the phone, as representative of the important role that elite peacemakers have to play in contemporary peace efforts; put even more firmly by Hillary Clinton when she says that 'American involvement [in Northern Ireland] was essential' and to be viewed as a 'lesson' for other conflict situations. The magnitude of the United States and European Union as forces for peace is, in fact, a theme returned to again and again by contributors. Both Bill and Hillary Clinton, John Kerry and Mitchell Reiss are confident of the positive role that America can and should play in promoting peace around the globe, whilst Bertie Ahern, Pat Cox, Garret FitzGerald, Maurice Hayes and Romano Prodi all emphasise the lessons that can be learned from the European Union as both a model for cooperation and conflict resolution in divided societies (a 'powerful force for transformation and creative reconciliation' as Cox puts it) and, as FitzGerald comments, 'an extraordinarily positive force' for peace in the world; which point he advances through discussion of Europe's humanitarian and peace missions, a subject further explored by Ahern. Most agree that international organisations have a key role to play in the contemporary peace project, as Bertie Ahern underlines, saying that a 'synergy' between supra-national institutions is vital since solutions to contemporary peace problems 'can only be achieved through collective action by the international community as a whole'; or rather an effective 'international framework' as Hillary Clinton would have it.

Hillary Clinton further states that 'peace and reconciliation begins, not by eliminating differences, but by creating the ground of mutual respect'; one way of doing that is by identifying common goals, interests and needs; a lesson that Prodi points out was learned by experience in the EU, where members 'realised that common and converging interests are powerful tools for building peace'.[55] Encouraging conflicting parties to work together on, as Dermot Ahern notes, 'issues that all sides care about' is, therefore, another theme to which our contributors return, again and again. The terms 'political partnership' (Dermot Ahern), 'partnership politics' (Bertie Ahern) or the 'politics of partnership and peace' (Mary McAleese) are used to describe when parties come together to work on what Hayes calls 'common problems' that are, Cox remarks, 'in the common interest', thereby breaking down 'the barriers of the past ... [in order to] ... build a common destiny'. President Clinton maintains that the way to build peace in the face of diversity is to 'construct a system of shared benefits ... [and] ... shared responsibilities', whereas John Kerry talks of 'harnessing people's energies for the common good'.

Globalism, or international pluralism, solidarism or, indeed, cosmopolitanism, depending on how one views the question, is strongly represented within the volume. Bill Clinton, Mitchell Reiss and John Kerry all describe the benefits and opportunities created by our globalised world. For Kerry, in our twenty-first-century existence, making 'a better future' requires that people 'connect to the rest of the world'; whilst Clinton quotes Martin Luther King Jr. in an effort to describe the interconnectedness that has the power to transcend national or identity politics and craft a more just global society, which once created, makes it 'virtually impossible to dominate, kill or jail all of your adversaries'. Asmal speaks at length about the importance of what he calls 'cosmopolitan multiculturalism' trumping nationalism and narrow or oppressive concepts of sovereignty (which Reiss describes as now 'contingent' on good governance), and of the importance of 'global citizenship ... international solidarity' or activism and 'global governance' and 'harnessing global forces to a politics of hope' in transcending conflict. This idea is taken up by McAleese, when she speaks of the significance of 'global civil society' and of 'today's new global reality in which more and more politicians, civil society leaders, students and professionals are engaging in dialogue across these [conflict] situations, discussing each other's experiences and deepening their knowledge of conflicts, how to manage them, how to avoid them and how to get out of them'.

The importance of this globalism, or cosmopolitan-multiculturalism (what Cox defines as a 'dialogue of cultures'), as a theme of significance in twenty-first-century peacemaking is stressed in this volume. Bill Clinton draws from the Christian Bible, the 'Koran' and the Talmud in seeking to demonstrate multicultural endorsement for the task of peacemaking. Dermot Ahern describes peace as existing when 'identity, culture and tradition are no longer identified with discord and division, but are seen through the prism of tolerance, generosity and mutual respect'; tolerance as a theme being echoed by both Kerry and Reiss. For Maurice Hayes, one of the key issues for peacemakers is to move societies towards a situation in which 'differences can be accommodated and diversity positively cherished'; or as Prodi explains, a context in which 'no religious, ethnic, cultural or other component ... [is] ... able to dictate to others, but all ... have equal dignity'. However, Kader Asmal, in particular, devotes significant space to the 'cosmopolitan multicultural ethic', maintaining that 'human dignity is to be found in genuine multicultural societies'. In his view tolerance of diversity is fundamental to peaceful societies and a peaceful world.

Conclusion

Although in no sense exhaustive, this introductory chapter has shed some light on the history of humanity's longest project – securing peace and harmony – and in doing so has placed those writings that now follow within the context of ongoing endeavours in the areas of peace and peacemaking, which terms it also took pains to define. Finally, this introduction has presented three of the key themes of importance in twenty-first-century peacemaking; looking to the complex nature of contemporary conflicts and the global nature of the forces exerted on them, to root causes, sub and supra state structures and multi-level challenges. It has highlighted the global character of the twenty-first century peace challenge and the necessity that any response must be cosmopolitan-multicultural, universal-globalist and focused on accepting diversity and transcending conflict and division through progress on common goals and recognition of common humanity. As Ramsbotham, Woodhouse and Miall (2011) conclude: '[i]n the end ... it is an awareness of shared humanity that underpins the global enterprise ... And the task of the next generation of workers in the field is to push forward the widening of the circle of recognition ... that subordinate identities, whether of family, clan, ethnic group, nation, state, class, gender, culture or religion, do not cancel out the deepest identity of all – humanity',[56] or as President Clinton simply reminds us: 'our common humanity matters more'.

Notes

1 See, for example: Michael Howard, *The Invention of Peace* (New Haven, CT: Yale University Press, 2000); Anthony Adolf, *Peace. A World History* (Cambridge: Polity, 2009).

2 Adolf, *Peace. A World History*, p. 14; Leslie Sponsel, *A Natural History of Peace* (Nashville, TN: Vanderbilt University Press, 1996); Frans de Waal, *Peacemaking Among Primates* (Cambridge, MA: Harvard University Press, 1990).

3 Adolf, *Peace. A World History*, p. 14.

4 Oliver Ramsbotham, Tom Woodhouse, Tom and Hugh Miall, *Contemporary Conflict Resolution*, 3rd edn (Cambridge: Polity, 2011), p. 36.

5 Galtung is regarded along with Kenneth and Elise Bouldings, John Burton, Herman Kelman, Lewis Richardson, etc. as a primary founder of peace and conflict studies.

6 Paul Rodgers and Oliver Ramsbotham, 'Then and now: peace research – past and future', *Political Studies*, 47:4 (1999), 744; Adolf, *Peace. A World History*, p. 29.

7 Publius Tacitus, *De vita et moribus Iulii Agricolae* (c. 98 CE).

8 Ramsbotham, Woodhouse and Miall, *Contemporary Conflict Resolution*, p. 32.

9 Such as Adolf, *Peace. A World History*.

10 Adolf, *Peace. A World History*, pp. 21–8.

11 A significant problem for the League of Nations in the 1930s was what to do about aggressive states that were not members, since its collective security provisions contained no guidance for dealing with offenders that were external to the collectivity; a fact that was partly responsible for the organisation's ultimate failure and collapse amid the outbreak of the Second World War.

12 See, for example: United Nations General Assembly GA/10872 Sixty-fourth General Assembly Plenary, 21st Meeting (PM). 'General Assembly calls upon member states to uphold Olympic truce during Vancouver Winter Games, cooperate in effort to use sport as a tool for peace' (19 October 2009).

13 Adolf, *Peace. A World History*, p. 49.

14 Adolf, *Peace. A World History*, p. 66.

15 Certainly, the Yahweh of the Old Testament could be quite a ruthless and unforgiving god when crossed, and seemed to frequently foment war, and modern Israel maintains strong militaristic conventions. In the Middle Ages, European Christians launched a series of crusades in the name of their belief and warriors of Islam have declared holy war on several occasions in different contexts over the years. The Roman Catholic Church unleashed the bloody Inquisition in a panicked response to the Reformation and for the next hundred years or so Europe almost consumed itself in wars of religion.

16 Qur'an, 2.11.

17 See S. Jafar and A. A.Said, 'Islam and peacemaking', in S. Allen Nan, Z. C. Mampilly and Andrea Bartoli (eds), *Peacemaking from Practice to Theory. Volume 2* (Westport, CT: Praeger, 2011).

18 The Canons of the First Lateran Council: I (1123).

19 Such as Georg Wilhelm Frederik Hegel, Johann Gottfried Herder, John Locke, Edmund Burke vs Thomas Paine, Karl Marx, etc.

20 Exemplified by the likes of Adam Smith and Immanuel Kant.

21 Immanuel Kant, *Perpetual Peace* (1795).

22 D. Mitrany, *The Progress of International Government* (New Haven, CT: Yale University Press, 1933). See also D. Mitrany, *A Working Peace System* (Chicago: Quadrangle Books, 1966); D. Mitrany, *The Functional Theory of Politics* (New York: St Martin's Press, 1976).

23 'The tree of liberty must be refreshed from time to time with the blood

of patriots and tyrants', Thomas Jefferson, 13 November 1787, letter to William S. Smith. Just War theory takes its modern roots from Hugo Grotius, *Ways of War and Peace* (1625).

24 Alan Sharp, *Consequences of Peace. The Versailles Settlement: Aftermath and Legacy 1919–2010* (London: Haus, 2010).

25 Ramsbotham et al. suggest five categories: precursors, founders, consolidators, reconstructors, cosmopolitans. Ramsbotham, Woodhouse and Miall, *Contemporary Conflict Resolution*, pp. 44, 424.

26 Except under very specific and internationally sanctioned contexts. *Charter of the United Nations* (1945).

27 On one hand the principle of Mutually Assured Destruction should guarantee the avoidance of war since no side would strike in the knowledge that they were ensuring their own destruction. On the other hand, tensions were so high during certain periods of the Cold War, it seemed that even such knowledge was no surety against the initiation of nuclear war; a particularly pertinent fact after the development of miniaturisation and tactical nuclear weapons that could be used in conventional combat settings. United States Conference of Catholic Bishops, *Pastoral Letter on War and Peace, 'The Challenge of Peace: God's Promise and Our Response'* (1983).

28 Ramsbotham, Woodhouse and Miall, *Contemporary Conflict Resolution*, p. 45.

29 Americans associated with the former and Europeans, the latter: K. Boulding, 'Twelve friendly quarrels with Johan Galtung', *Journal of Peace Research*, 14:1 (1977), 75–86.

30 For example: J. Burton, *Conflict and Communication. The Use of Controlled Communication in International Relations* (London: Macmillan, 1969).

31 Ramsbotham, Woodhouse and Miall, *Contemporary Conflict Resolution*, p. 49.

32 See, for example: H. Kelman, 'The problem-solving workshop in Conflict Resolution' in, R. Merritt (ed.), *Communication in International Politics* (Urbana, IL: Illinois University Press, 1972).

33 Roger Fisher and William Ury, *Getting to Yes. Negotiating Agreement Without Giving In* (London: Penguin). 1981); Adam Curle, *In the Middle: Non-Official Mediation in Violent Situations* (Oxford: Berg, 1986).

34 M. Kaldor, *New and Old Wars: Organized Violence in a Global Era* (Stanford: Stanford University Press, 1999).

35 Ramsbotham, Woodhouse and Miall, *Contemporary Conflict Resolution*, p. 3

36 Leonie Murray, *Clinton, Peacekeeping and Humanitarian Interventionism. Rise and Fall of a Policy* (London: Routledge, 2008); T. G. Fraser, *The Arab-Israeli Conflict*, 3rd edn (Basingstoke: Palgrave Macmillan, 2007); Ramsbotham, Woodhouse and Miall, *Contemporary Conflict Resolution*, p. 6.

37 J. P. Lederach, *Preparing for Peace: Conflict Transformation across Cultures* (New York: Syracuse Press, 1995).

38 Prominent in this third wave are: Kevin Avruch, Elise Boulding, Hans-Georg

Gadamer, Jurgen Habermas, Mark Hoffman, John Paul Lederach, Roger MacGinty, Michael Pugh, Oliver Ramsbotham, Oliver Richmond, Paul Rodgers, Stephen Ryan, Tom Woodhouse, etc. In addition, Galtung founded the TRASCEND initiative during this period.

39 Oliver Richmond, *Peace in International Relations* (London: Routledge, 2008), p. 147.
40 Ulrich Beck, *The Cosmopolitan Vision* (Cambridge: Polity, 2006); Ramsbotham, Woodhouse and Miall, *Contemporary Conflict Resolution*, pp. 425–6.
41 Adolf, *Peace. A World History*, pp. 36–7.
42 Roughly from the end of the fifth century BCE to the beginning of third century BCE.
43 Lao Tzu, *Tao Te Ching* (sixth century BCE), translation by S. Mitchell (1995), http://academic.brooklyn.cuny.edu/core9/phalsall/texts/taote-v3.html.
44 Confucius, *The Analects* (c. 500 BCE).
45 J. Kelsey and J. Johnson (eds), *Just War and Jihad: Historical and Theoretical Perspectives on War and Peace* (Westport, CT: Greenwood, 1991), p. iii.
46 M. Sicker, *The Islamic World in Ascendancy: From the Arab Conquests to the Siege of Vienna* (Westport, CT: Praeger, 2000), p. 10; Adolf, *Peace. A World History*, p. 102.
47 See for example: the Book of Isaiah or Job 22:21.
48 See for example: the Gospel of Matthew, Mark 12:31 and John 14:27.
49 Matthew 5:9.
50 For more on complex social and ethnic conflicts see: Tom Woodhouse and Oliver Ramsbotham, *Humanitarian Intervention in Contemporary Conflicts. A Reconceptualisation* (Cambridge: Polity, 1996). Ramsbotham, Woodhouse and Miall, *Contemporary Conflict Resolution*, pp. 55, 62.
51 Ramsbotham, Woodhouse and Miall, *Contemporary Conflict Resolution*, p. 426.
52 Negotiation, mediation Tracks I, II and III, peace enforcement, peacekeeping, elite peacemaking, peacebuilding, conflict transformation, reconciliation, etc. are all aspects of peacemaking covered by contributors.
53 For Track III indigenous peacemaking, see, for example: J. P. Lederach, *Building Peace: Sustainable Reconciliation in Divided Societies* (Washington DC: US Institute of Peace Press, 1997).
54 For Track I see for example: Oran Young, *The Intermediaries. Third Parties in International Crises* (Princeton, NJ: Princeton University Press, 1967); and moving into Track II: Curle, *In the Middle*.
55 For more on interest-based negotiation see, for example: Fischer and Ury, *Getting to Yes*.
56 Ramsbotham, Woodhouse and Miall, *Contemporary Conflict Resolution*, p. 426.

Bibliography

Adolf, Anthony, *Peace. A World History* (Cambridge: Polity, 2009).

Allen Nan, S., Mampilly, Z. C. and Bartoli, Andrea, *Peacemaking from Practice to Theory. Volume 2* (Westport, CT: Praeger, 2011).

Beck, Ulrich, *The Cosmopolitan Vision* (Cambridge: Polity, 2006).

Boulding, K., 'Twelve friendly quarrels with Johan Galtung', *Journal of Peace Research*, 14:1 (1977), 75–86.

Burton, J., *Conflict and Communication. The Use of Controlled Communication in International Relations* (London: Macmillan, 1969).

The Canons of the First Lateran Council: I (1123).

Confucius, *The Analects* (c. 500 BCE).

Curle, Adam, *In the Middle: Non-Official Mediation in Violent Situations* (Oxford: Berg, 1986).

de Waal, Frans, *Peacemaking Among Primates* (Cambridge, MA: Harvard University Press, 1990).

Erasmus, Desiderius, *Antipolemus; or, the Plea of Reason, Religion, and Humanity, Against War* (1507).

Erasmus, Desiderius, *The Complaint of Peace* (1521).

Fischer, R. and Ury, W., *Getting to Yes: Negotiating Agreement Without Giving In* (London: Penguin, 2006).

Fraser, T. G., *The Arab-Israeli Conflict*, 3rd edn (Basingstoke: Palgrave Macmillan, 2007).

Galtung, J., 'An editorial', *Journal of Peace Research*, 1:1 (1964), 1–4.

Galtung, J., 'Violence, peace and peace research', *Journal of Peace Research*, 6:3 (1969), 167–92.

Grotius, Hugo, *Ways of War and Peace* (1625).

Howard, Michael, *The Invention of Peace* (New Haven, CT: Yale University Press, 2000).

Kaldor, M., *New and Old Wars: Organized Violence in a Global Era* (Stanford: Stanford University Press, 1999).

Kelman, H., 'The problem-solving workshop in Conflict Resolution', in Merritt, R. (ed.), *Communication in International Politics* (Urbana, IL: Illinois University Press, 1972).

Kelsey, J. and Johnson, J. (eds), *Just War and Jihad: Historical and Theoretical Perspectives on War and Peace* (Westport, CT: Greenwood, 1991).

Lao Tzu, *Tao Te Ching* (sixth century BCE), translation by S. Mitchell (1995), http://academic.brooklyn.cuny.edu/core9/phalsall/texts/taote-v3.html (last accessed 25 February 2013).

Lederach, J. P., *Preparing for Peace: Conflict Transformation across Cultures* (New York: Syracuse Press, 1995).

Lederach, J. P., *Building Peace: Sustainable Reconciliation in Divided Societies* (Washington DC: US Institute of Peace Press, 1997).

Mitrany, D., *The Progress of International Government* (New Haven, CT: Yale University Press, 1933).

Mitrany, D., *A Working Peace System* (Chicago: Quadrangle Books, 1966).

Mitrany, D., *The Functional Theory of Politics* (New York: St Martin's Press, 1976).

Murray, Leonie, *Clinton, Peacekeeping and Humanitarian Interventionism. Rise and Fall of a Policy* (London: Routledge, 2008).

Rodgers, Paul and Ramsbotham, Oliver, 'Then and now: peace research – past and future', *Political Studies*, 47:4 (1999), 704–54.

Ramsbotham, Oliver, Woodhouse, Tom and Miall, Hugh, *Contemporary Conflict Resolution*, 3rd edn (Cambridge: Polity, 2011).

Richmond, Oliver, *Peace in International Relations* (London: Routledge, 2008).

Sharp, Alan, *Consequences of Peace. The Versailles Settlement: Aftermath and Legacy 1919–2010* (London: Haus, 2010).

Sicker, M., *The Islamic World in Ascendancy: From the Arab Conquests to the Siege of Vienna* (Westport, CT: Praeger, 2000).

Sponsel, Leslie, *A Natural History of Peace* (Nashville, TN: Vanderbilt University Press, 1996).

Tacitus, Publius, *De vita et moribus Iulii Agricolae* (c. 98 CE).

Woodhouse, Tom and Ramsbotham, Oliver, *Humanitarian Intervention in Contemporary Conflicts. A Reconceptualisation* (Cambridge: Polity, 1996).

Young, Oran, *The Intermediaries. Third Parties in International Crises* (Princeton, NJ: Princeton University Press, 1967).

2

Thomas P. 'Tip' O'Neill Jr.: the honour of public service

Rosemary D. O'Neill

A 'New Deal' Democrat

Thomas P. 'Tip' O'Neill Jr. was Speaker of the Massachusetts General Court (1949–1952) and Speaker of the US House of Representatives (1977–1986). A quintessential urban ethnic politician who rose to national prominence, he was often called 'the last of the New Deal liberals'. From the era of political party dominance to the period of media domination of public life, Tip O'Neill was a shrewd practitioner of the political arts.

Background

Like so many Americans before and after, Tip O'Neill's life was the story of an impoverished immigrant family succeeding in a land of opportunity. His grandfather Patrick O'Neill fled famine ravaged Ireland in 1851 to work for the New England brick company in North Cambridge, Massachusetts. His father, Thomas Sr., also a bricklayer, was elected to the Cambridge City Council and later, through civil service examination, became Cambridge Commissioner of Sewers, where he supervised the work of 1,000 city employees.

Tom Sr. imbued in his son the importance of: loyalty; integrity – the imperative to lead a clean and honest life; responsibility to his fellow man; never to forget where he came from; and, public service as an honourable and noble calling. Like his heroes before him, New York Governor Al Smith and President Franklin Delano Roosevelt, Tip O'Neill's keen sense of fair play propelled him, especially during the Depression, to reject the reality of a nation where many were ill-fed, ill-clothed and ill-housed while a favoured few prospered.

This imperative for social justice, instilled in him by his father, was strongly reinforced by the working-class community of Irish Americans in which he lived, and by his Roman Catholic faith. It was inculcated in him by the Church and his parochial grade school and high school education at St John the Evangelist parish in North Cambridge. The Jesuits at his alma mater, Boston College, where he received a classical liberal arts education, further honed the importance of fairness.

'All politics is local'

To paraphrase his eldest son, Tom III, Tip was an Irish American without a dark side. A shrewd observer of human behaviour, his enthusiasm for life and keen sense of humour won him many friends. He parlayed this popularity to run for a seat in the Cambridge City Council. Following his defeat in this initial campaign, Tip's Dad pointed out that while seeking the vote in parts of the city where people did not know him, Tip had paid little attention to his own neighbourhood. His father advised him that all politics is local; first he had to mobilise support in the neighbourhood where people knew him.

In 1936, at the age of twenty-four, he won his first election as a member of the Republican dominated Massachusetts legislature, representing the working-class immigrant neighbourhoods in North Cambridge. Tip relished the crucible that was Boston politics: mobilising support among his constituents for New Deal policies; servicing the people in his area; the thrust and parry of political debate and negotiations; the collegiality of his fellow legislators. An ardent partisan for Democratic principles, he nevertheless understood that politics was the art of compromise and that good governance required you to work with others who might not share your ideas or beliefs.

The young legislator mastered the arcane rules of parliamentary procedure. His speciality was not any single area of expertise but rather his deep understanding of the mechanics of the political process. Myra MacPherson of the *Washington Post* once wrote, 'his success was his genius as a political strategist who could broker a consensus from disparate corners, partly because he was so likeable'.

Speaker of the Massachusetts General Court

In the late 1940s, Congressman John McCormack encouraged Tip to travel around the state to recruit popular young men home from the war to run as Democrats for the state legislature. For the first time in the history of Massachusetts, the Democrats won the lower house by the narrowest of margins, and Tip O'Neill was elected Speaker – the first Democrat, the first Irish American and the first Catholic in Massachusetts ever to do so. With Paul Dever, also of Cambridge, elected Governor, the Democrats were able to push through liberal proposals under the rubric of 'the little New Deal'.

On to the US Congress

In 1951, Congressman John F. Kennedy gave Tip advance notice that it was his intention to run for the Senate. Tip, whose highest ambition had been to be elected Governor, saw the opening of this Congressional seat as a stepping stone to that goal. In a bitter ethnic campaign, Tip narrowly won the Democratic primary race by enlisting the support of independent as well as Democratic voters. Winning the primary in this Congressional district was tantamount to being elected as no Republican could displace the Democrats in the general election.

In Washington, Tip soon became a protégé of Majority Leader John McCormack of Boston. As such, Speaker Sam Rayburn invited him to join the powerful Rules Committee, overseeing those procedures that would govern each piece of legislation going to the floor of the House. Using every parliamentary tool at their disposal, the few liberals on the Rules Committee battled the Chairman, Judge Howard Smith of Virginia, to allow civil rights proposals to advance to the floor of the House. The epic struggle lasted years, but finally advanced when Lyndon Baines Johnson mobilised the Congress following the assassination of JFK.

Tip's position on the Rules Committee allowed him to help expedite LBJ's Great Society legislation. Thus he had an important hand in seeing that Medicare, Medicaid, Vista and early childhood programmes were adopted. Millions of federal dollars found their way to the cities as block grants. Throughout his tenure as a member of Congress, Tip pushed social legislation which would protect the weakest in society: Pell grants for college students, free school lunches, medical research, particularly on cancer, and on and on.

Vietnam

In 1966 Tip O'Neill broke with the President over Vietnam. Military and intelligence officials, who had concerns about the conduct of the war, told him that the US was not taking the steps necessary to win the war, and that we should end our participation. Tip was the first of the mainstream Democratic members of Congress to oppose the conflict. For years after, he fought for legislation to limit funding and thus end American involvement in Vietnam. The working-class people of Tip's Congressional district supported LBJ; many of their sons were fighting in the war and their families were stunned at Tip's opposition. He spoke at scores of communion breakfasts, elder facilities and other venues to explain his change. Eventually he convinced the voters of his position. He survived this difficult time in part because of his reputation for excellent constituent service.

The House Leadership and Watergate

In 1972 when Carl Albert of Oklahoma became Speaker and Hale Boggs of Louisiana became Majority Leader, they choose Tip to be Majority Whip, a job which sought to ensure that Democratic members would vote the party line. Two years later, Hale Boggs disappeared in a plane as he flew over Alaska. Tip succeeded him as Majority Leader, and it was as such that he faced his next great political challenge. The Watergate burglary and, more importantly, the cover-up galvanised Tip. He quietly mobilised the members of the House to prepare for impeachment. He ensured that Peter Rodino, Chairman of the Judiciary Committee, would undertake the investigation. Twenty-one months after winning a landslide election, Richard Nixon resigned as President.

Speaker of the House

On Carl Albert's retirement from Congress in 1976, Tip was elected Speaker. One of the first major pieces of legislation was an ethics bill that strengthened House rules on outside income for Members of Congress and made more transparent the donors of campaign contributions. Tip also strengthened the position of Speaker. Adoption of a ground-breaking energy bill early in his service as Speaker pointed to his tenure as a strong leader. In his many meetings with international leaders, Tip emphasised that power in Washington was based at the two ends of Pennsylvania Avenue: the White House and the Capitol.

Ireland and Northern Ireland

At the beginning of the Troubles in Northern Ireland, most Irish Americans, separated from the Emerald Isle by more than a hundred years, two world wars and a depression, had little understanding of the disturbances there. Starting in the early 1970s, John Hume journeyed to Washington several times a year to educate a generation of political leaders, including Tip O'Neill, about the need for a peaceful resolution in the North. He briefed the Speaker and others about the Civil Rights Movement in Northern Ireland and how it received its inspiration from the Civil Rights Movement in the United States. In sharing his compelling vision of a Northern Ireland at peace with itself, John Hume found an enthusiastic partner in Tip O'Neill.

Through the Congressional Friends of Ireland, annual St Patrick day luncheons on the Hill, speaking engagements around the country and interventions with President Reagan, Speaker O'Neill ensured that John Hume's message of non-violent political discourse was the tactic of choice in resolving the Troubles. On a trip to Northern Ireland in the early 1980s, Tip clearly saw the extent of unemployment in Northern Ireland. One of the Speaker's last acts before his retirement was to provide for US government participation in the International Fund for Ireland, through which thousands of jobs were created.

'The loyal opposition'

The nadir of his speakership came during the first year of the Reagan administration. The defection to Reagan of Southern Democrats enabled the Republicans to spend massive amounts on defence while they simultaneously gutted domestic spending and made deep cuts in taxes. Even as he gained national attention for his opposition to these policies, Tip allowed the bills to come to the floor of the House. He was convinced that the public would soon realise the folly of 'trickle-down economics'. Two years into Reagan's tenure, Tip's prediction proved true. The country faced a serious recession with unemployment reaching 10 per cent. The Democrats won some twenty-five seats, retaining a strong hold on the House of Representatives.

Despite policy disagreements, Tip and Reagan famously made a point to get along 'after six p.m.'. Tip truly believed that politics was an honourable profession; he believed in 'the loyal opposition'; and while competing furiously, and sometimes bitterly, his politics were seldom personal. His son, Tom, once noted that Tip's brand of politics was one 'that defends the working people, but does not depend on class resentment', and that 'he took a very Catholic view toward Republicans ... hate the sin, but not the sinner'. His politics 'loved justice and hated no one'.

There were victories during the Reagan years: most importantly, Tip, emphasising the need for fairness, ensured that Social Security was not only protected, but strengthened.

The legacy

When at the time of his retirement he was asked how he wanted to be remembered, he replied that he 'came to Washington with a set of ideas, and stayed with them all the way'. Indeed, he was constant and loyal to one wife, old friends and old values. He seldom discussed religion, but was a devout Catholic. He had a deep and abiding sense of purpose. Father Monan of Boston College observed that Tip's faith was 'never a badge or an ornament to make others uncomfortable, but always a star he checked to set his own course'.

He was proudest of the fact that, during his life time, Democrats had passed legislation to build the middle class. By the time of his retirement in 1986, poverty in America had been reduced to 10 per cent. In describing Tip's bedrock beliefs, Senator Ted Kennedy said, 'He was never afraid to speak out for the average man and woman – the worker trying to keep a job, the child going hungry in the night, the senior citizen trying to live in dignity in retirement'. Politics for Tip was not only a noble profession, it was a joyous profession, and this joy extended to all he met.[1]

Notes

1 See Tip O'Neill with William Novak, *Man of the House: The Life and Political Memoirs of Speaker Tip O'Neill* (New York: Random House, 1998).

3

Peacemaking

President William J. Clinton

Introduction

On the 6 July 2003, former President of the United States of America, William J. (Bill) Clinton offered assembled listeners his insight to guide them and others making a similar ascent out of conflict, at a time when the much-lauded Northern Irish peace process was, it seemed, poised on the precipice of collapse.[1] Electoral movement away from the more moderate parties, the Social Democratic Labour Party (SDLP) and Ulster Unionist Party (UUP), towards the more polarised Sinn Fein (SF) and Democratic Unionist Party (DUP) since 2001, had increased friction in devolved government; particularly, over such issues as decommissioning, parades, policing and justice. In the course of 2002, already tense working relationships were stretched to breaking point and in October, then Secretary of State for Northern Ireland, John Reid, suspended devolved government at Stormont under controversial circumstances. Although London and Dublin came together in April 2003 to announce a joint proposal for forward movement, elections scheduled for May were postponed amid gloomy political prospects in the province.

Neither was the path to peace in Northern Ireland alone in yielding obstacles upon which its travellers might stumble. The Road Map for Peace announced by the 'Quartet' in April 2003, and designed to pursue an elusive Israeli-Palestinian peace settlement, had already strayed into the wilderness; the wars in Afghanistan and Iraq were, for many, on a proscribed course.[2] North Korea had withdrawn from the Non-Proliferation Treaty and for many, globally, the threat from terrorist attack felt alarmingly high. It was against such a background that President Clinton framed his thoughts on making and building peace at this time, telling listeners that 'the rewards of peace are worth the risks'.

Of course, President Clinton spoke from his own illustrious experience: initially, his studies in international relations at Georgetown and Oxford, as well as law at Yale and in the US political system as Governor of Arkansas and Chair of the National Governor's Association. Of greatest consequence, however, were his two terms as President of the most powerful country in the world, during which time it was his fortune to confront, arguably, the most fractious US legislature since the Second World War and from which he learned many valuable lessons about how domestic politics works; can work; does not work.

Add to this expertise the unique and grave international experience that he garnered as the first real post-Cold War President of the remaining global superpower. The opportunities presented during this time of momentous change in world politics meant that his was a Presidency characterised by internationalism and multilateralism; the attendant volatility of global politics and multiplicity of conflict meant that the search for peace, stability and justice in places like South Africa, Somalia, Bosnia, Haiti and the former Soviet Union also demanded his attention.

During Clinton's Presidency a now estimated 500,000–1,000,000 people perished in the Rwandan genocide, but the peacebuilding efforts that occurred in the aftermath of those hundred bloody days, combined with the ongoing struggle for peace in Israel–Palestine, which he worked so tirelessly to move forward from the 1993 Oslo Accords, gave him particular food for thought when it came to the practice of waging peace.[3]

The quest for peace in Northern Ireland absorbed a great deal of Clinton's time in office. For an American President to visit a tiny province in the far corner of Europe three times in four years and sit up all night cajoling politicians to come to a peace deal, whilst a myriad of other high-priority domestic and international crises demanded his attention, was truly remarkable, and the impact of the timely encouragements, economic incentives and powers of persuasion upon the final crafting of the Good Friday Agreement cannot be overstated and will never be forgotten.

It was within this context that, as the inaugural speaker of the Tip O' Neill Lectures in Peace, Clinton chose as his theme three of the most important lessons learned by Tip O'Neill over his long and distinguished political career and applied them to Northern Ireland and other areas attempting the path towards conflict resolution at that time, within the global context of ever-increasing interdependence. Firstly, he said, when things are difficult that is when you must work the hardest and accept help from your friends; secondly, people like to be asked, and thirdly, and most importantly, all politics is local.

How, then, could O'Neill's lessons be applied to help make peace work in Northern Ireland and elsewhere, in culturally and/or religiously diverse post-conflict societies in a progressively globalised world? The answer, Clinton told his audience, was to create a system of 'shared benefits, shared responsibility and shared values' by promoting the ideal in society that '[e]verybody counts, everybody deserves a chance, everybody has a responsible role to play'. Here, the key, he emphasised, was to encourage the growth of a civil society that would help nurture a new social and political environment, from which true peace might mature. Nonetheless, he said, as his host, the newly inaugurated Professor of Peace Studies, John Hume, knew better than most, such developments must also be attended by economic advancement.

Whilst recognising the problems inherent in globalisation and the contemporary system, the benefits of the increasing interconnectedness that accompanies that phenomenon were also highlighted. The interdependent nature of the world, he argued, increased the chances of defeating injustice and oppression and promoting peace, because international solidarity and a global civil society in an economically interreliant world meant that 'you cannot kill, jail or occupy all of your adversaries' and so in the end 'you have to make a deal'. Politics has to be engaged in.

He ended by comparing the problems that must be overcome in Northern Ireland to other zones of conflict and asked his audience whether they were 'tougher' than those faced in trouble-spots the world over; by reminding listeners, again, that all politics, domestic or global, was local in our new age of international connectivity and that by recognising our common humanity we might avoid the mistakes and the bloodshed of the past. Finally, and because it was what Tip O'Neill would have done for peace, he asked for it.

Lecture

Thank you very much and good afternoon, Vice-Chancellor, University Officials, Leaders of The Ireland Funds, Mr Mayor, John, Pat, Mark Durkan, thank you for coming.

I thank the representatives of the American government who are here with our Consulate, for coming. I note at the outset that I was very pleased that President Bush named Richard Haass as his envoy to the Irish peace process. I have a very high regard for him and I think that it shows the concern of the United States for peace in Ireland is as bi-partisan and continuing.

John, I thank you for the introduction. You probably should be here, you began your career as a teacher, you never stopped being a teacher. I must say I have had a hard time calling you Professor today, however. Your predecessor in this position, Roelf Meyer, is a friend of mine:

we worked together in South Africa to build a civil society there and continue to do so, and I am delighted to be invited here today.

The most important lesson of your life is that the rewards of peace are worth the risks and I hope I can make that case again here today at a difficult time in the Irish peace process. In 1995 I was honoured to be the first American President to visit Northern Ireland and as you noted I had the privilege then to help announce the establishment of this Tip O'Neill Chair.

Tip O'Neill was a giant of a man with a big heart and a large role in American politics. He helped to make America a more decent, more just, more fair place and he fought for peace in Ireland. I imagine somewhere he's looking down on us, laughing, to see that his partner for peace has the august title of Professor, and that a President who consistently got his best vote in the state of Massachusetts is here to give a speech for him.

I should also say that I am grateful for the establishment by some of my friends of the Clinton International Peace Centre in Enniskillen and for that centre's commitment to global peace and reconciliation and for the interesting and important work they are doing there and I thank Martin Maguire, the director of the centre, for being here today.

John mentioned one of the most lasting memories of my Presidency: the night I stayed up all night before the Good Friday Accord, calling everybody I could get to the phone, John, Gerry Adams who is here today, thank you sir, David Trimble, Bertie Ahern, Tony Blair, George Mitchell. I could never figure out whether I was giving instructions or getting them. It's inevitable in the dynamics of such a thing that every time I called anybody or all of them, every one of them said, 'Oh you have to call someone else, they have a problem'. And so I did: I didn't sleep that night – and the next morning we all know what happened.

I would like to organise my talk today around three of Tip O'Neill's rules of politics. Beginning with how I felt on that historic morning and how I am sure all the exhausted parties felt. Once, Tip O'Neill asked one of his colleagues from Massachusetts, Joe Moakley, who passed away recently, who was another great Irish politician and a very close friend of mine, to cast a particularly tough vote for the party's leadership. Moakley said, 'Jeez Tip, that's a hard one'. Tip responded with rule one of politics, 'Joe, I don't need you on the easy ones'. Well the Good Friday Accord was a hard one and, as we are still learning, making it work is a hard one. Which brings me to Speaker O'Neill's second rule. The day before his first election his neighbour across the street, Mrs O'Brien, said, 'Tip I am going to vote for you tomorrow even though you didn't ask me to'. And Tip said, 'Mrs O'Brien I shovel your walk in the winter, I mow your grass in the summer, I didn't think I had to ask for your vote'. She replied, 'Let me tell you something, Tip, people like to be asked'. That's rule number two. Because he had taken the votes of his neighbour for granted, Tip O'Neill lost that election. But it was the only one he ever lost. For the rest of his life, on every election day, over fifty years, Tip O'Neill would leave his house to go to vote, but first would turn to his wife and say, 'Millie, I'd like to ask for your vote'. Her reply was always the same, 'I will give you every consideration'.

Tip's third rule of politics became his signature, his guiding philosophy, the title of his book. John mentioned that it is now a law in American elections – all politics is local. It is difficult for us today to know exactly what that means in our globalised world. But I am convinced that it still matters just as much as ever. We just have to figure out how.

How can all politics be local in an Ireland where I've been told more people use mobile phones more than any other country in Europe? In the United Kingdom now connected to the European continent by tunnel. In an EU with a new constitution and soon to have twenty-five members. In a world where far more email is sent everyday than postal mail, where satellites deliver news around the world in the blink of an eye, where a sneeze in Hong Kong can lead to a SARS quarantine in Toronto. In a world where open borders and emigration make us more diverse within our borders but also vulnerable to terrorists from without it. Still we hold on to our locality, don't we? To our family, to our faiths, to our culture, to our history, to our heritage.

It makes our interdependent world inherently unstable when we cannot figure out how to merge our locality, its history and its meaning with our responsibilities and possibilities in the global world of the twenty-first century. The great challenge for people everywhere is to move from interdependence to an integrated global community where local meanings are kept but reconciled with global possibilities. In order to do this we have to create everywhere a system of shared benefits, shared responsibilities and shared values. How can you create shared values in diverse societies?

Shortly after September 11 my wife and I went down to Lower Manhattan to visit an elementary school which was meeting in a makeshift place because their school had been destroyed by the ashes blowing through the windows when the Trade Center buildings collapsed and I looked out on several hundred bright young people who came from this one school in Lower Manhattan, eighty different national, racial, religious and ethnic groups, eighty. That is the trick, but I am convinced there are some simple values we can all share. Everybody counts, everybody deserves a chance. Everybody has a responsible role to play. We all do better when we work together and most importantly our differences are significant. They make life a lot more interesting but our common humanity matters more. For all the conflicts today around the globe with all their differences I think they can be distilled into one, everywhere from Northern Ireland to the Middle East, from the tribal conflicts in Africa to the Balkans, the great conflict of this new century is between the forces of integration and harmony, democracy, diversity, peace, trade, information technology, shared advances in health and sciences, a raid against the forces of disintegration, chaos, terror, weapons of mass destruction, environmental destruction, poverty, disease, ignorance, racial, religious, ethnic and tribal hatred.

These conflicts didn't just happen, they are rooted in painful truths about the modern world in our collective psychology. At a time when trade and globalisation have lifted more people out of poverty in the last twenty years than ever before, a billion of the world's people still live on less than two dollars a day. Half the world's people, three billion, one billion live on less than one dollar a day. A billion people go to bed hungry every night, one billion and a half people never get a clean glass of water.

At a time when we have sequenced the human genome and made huge advances in the diagnosis and treatment of disease which I am convinced will lead the children of the young people here today to be born with life expectancy of somewhere in the range of ninety years, more than 10 million children still die every year of completely preventable childhood diseases and one in four of all the world's deaths this year will come from AIDS, TB, malaria and infections related to diarrhoea.

Most of them will be little children who die just because they never got a clean glass of water in their entire lives. At a time when education brings economic success in rich countries and poor ones with every year of schooling adding 10 to 15 per cent a year to the income of young people in poor countries, a billion of the world's people still cannot read a single word and somewhere between 120 million and 130 million children never set foot in a schoolhouse.

Given all these problems it is interesting to contemplate how they will be aggravated when the population of the world is expected to increase by 50 per cent in the next fifty years, with all the greatest increases in the poorest countries. At a time when more and more people live in societies thriving because of their diversity, racial, religious, ethnic and tribal conflict along those same lines continues to fuel fanaticism, fundamentalism and hatred and cause most of the deaths by violence around the world today. It almost seems as if the twenty-first century has sparked two great parallel trends of lives with half the people of the world living in a positive way growing together, growing more prosperous, growing more wealthy, growing more diverse, the other half of the people continuing to be poor without much hope and very vulnerable to the claims of extremists. The response of people caught in the middle to these parallel lives will determine what kind of world we have in the twenty-first century and that response depends more than anything else on whether they have the hope and vision necessary to imagine a different future.

Bono loves to tell that old joke over and over again about two guys who see a large mansion, the first one says, 'Someday I'm going to live in that place', the second says, 'Someday I'm going to get the guy who lives in that place'. The first person has hope and vision to imagine a different future and the second doesn't.

John Hume has known from the beginning that lasting peace here would have to be tied to economic opportunity for the people of Northern Ireland to build more people who can imagine a different future. We are, I hope and pray, about to get back around to that vision in the Middle East. In 1993 when we had the historic signing of the Middle East peace agreement on the White House lawn, which I'm sure most of you will remember, where Yitzhak Rabin and Yasser Arafat shook hands for the first time before over a billion people watching on television, a very important meeting took place the next day when I got 600 Jewish American and Arab American business people to come together for the first meeting they had ever had together in the White House and I challenged them to set up funds to invest in the Palestinian areas so that the children there would imagine a different future. They all committed to do so – almost none of them did.

Why? Because the rejectionist groups who did not buy the peace were clever and they knew it would only take one or two or three bombs a year to terrify investors. One or two or three bombs a year to force the Israelis to close the borders and keep the Palestinians pinned up inside Gaza unable to work.

Those one or two or three bombs a year before the horrible intifada of the last two and a half years which we hope is coming to an end, just those were enough to ensure that after seven years of peace and a continuing high birth rate among the Palestinians that the Palestinian people were both younger and poorer at the end of the process than they were at its beginning. So that's why it's important for the United States to look at our role, not only to lead the world against terrorist threats but also to lead the world's efforts against poverty and ignorance and disease and global warming. And why whenever possible we should work in cooperation with others so that more people will have the vision and the hope necessary to believe the future can be different from the past.

That's why when I was President I worked not only to strengthen and expand our military alliances and to include Russia and China, but also to help take down Russian nuclear weapons, destroy them, secure the materials that were left, to help other people deal with biological and chemical stocks and to help build more educational and other opportunities, why we did the millennium debt relief initiative for the poorest countries of the world so that they could educate more of their children, why we opened up trade to Africa, so that we could buy products from them.

Not very long ago I was in Africa where I do a lot of work with my Foundation and I was in Ghana in West Africa to launch a programme for working capital for the poor with a great Peruvian economist, Hernando De Soto, some of you may know of his work.

And I was on my way to the airplane at the airport in Accra and as I was walking to the airplane, this woman was screaming at me, 'President Clinton don't go, don't go', and she's got some package in her hand, she's waving this package. So I turn around and she runs up to me and she said, 'I want you to know because of your Africa trade bill I'm one of 400 women who has a job here in a factory making shirts, so here's your shirt'. And I figured, I'm not in office anymore, so I took the shirt – and when I got home I put that shirt in a place in my house where I have to look at it every day. Literally every day in my house, I cannot avoid looking at this shirt and I did it for this reason.

That woman is not mad at me, she is not mad at America, she is not angry at Europe, she knows that you have more money than she does, but she believes that we want her to be a part of our future. She does not want her children to be killed in African tribal wars or to contract HIV and AIDS at an early age and die. She has something to live for and she can imagine a different future.

We came up with 300 million dollars, which is a paltry amount in our big budget, to offer through the international food organisation in Rome a nutritious meal to children in schools in poor countries, but they would have to come to school to get the meal. In Rome it's gone up by 7 million, and I'm convinced that the families of those kids were not mad at us.

If you live in an interdependent world where you cannot kill, jail or occupy all of your adversaries, in the end you have to make a deal – it's called politics. It doesn't matter whether it's in Northern Ireland or East Timor or Bosnia or Kosovo or the Middle East or Rwanda. If you live in an interdependent world it is virtually impossible to dominate, kill or jail all your adversaries. In the end you have to make a deal.

That's why Tip O'Neill's rules are important.

One thing I want to say before concluding my remarks is that there are things that all of us can do who don't have political power. When I left office there is no job description for former Presidents, you have to sort of make it up as you go along and only four or five of my predecessors ever made a real difference in the life of America after they left office. Only two of them have assumed better offices.

William Howard Taft became Chief Justice of the Supreme Court and most importantly John Quincy Adams who was defeated by Andrew Jackson in the 1830s went to Congress for sixteen years and became the leading advocate for ending slavery in our country. So that the sixteen years he spent after he left the White House were more important in the life of our country than the four years he spent as President. Herbert Hoover who left office in disgrace in the Depression devoted thirty years of his life to other worthy projects and lived a quite good life. Theodore Roosevelt started a new political movement and as we all know President Carter won the Nobel Prize for twenty years of efforts in human rights, peace and reconciliation.

I decided I would focus on the things that I cared most about where I thought I could still have an impact. On trying to do what I'm trying to do today, convince people to overcome their differences, on trying to provide economic opportunity to poor communities in my country and around the world, on promoting education and citizen service among young people.

We have a great project in South Africa working on that now and on fighting HIV and AIDS which has the potential literally to destroy large numbers of democratic countries around the world: 80 per cent of the people dying of AIDS are between the ages of twenty and fifty.

There are some places in Africa where we can't bring a farm crop in now because there is nobody able to harvest the crop. There are villages in China where grandparents and great grandparents are the only people left to raise children under ten.

It is going to be difficult for us to build an integrated world if we permit diseases to consume us. So I do a lot of work on this. We are working in sixteen countries in the Caribbean and three in Africa to try to get medicine to people. This is unbelievable, a global scandal that outside Brazil and the United States only 40,000 people are getting the anti-retroviral medicine, even though there are 40 million people infected with AIDS, and 6 million of them have their lives hanging in the balance at any given moment, they could be saved if they had access to the medicine. So we are working on that.

I mention that, only because there are Irish people from the north and from the Republic all over the world always doing this non-governmental organisational work. And the most important new development in this integrated world in the last thirty years is the rise of non-governmental organisations committed to public purposes. And lots and lots of your people are involved in this work but it's very, very important. Having said that, in the end politics will matter and often be decisive. And yet even if you construct a system that has shared benefits and shared responsibilities, first there must be shared values and that requires certain habits of heart which are not all that easy to develop.

I spent a lot of time in the Middle East and I always marvel that the Middle East was the home of the world's three great monotheistic religions, in order, Judaism, Christianity and Islam. They all said the same thing. The Christian Bible said, all the law is fulfilled in one word: even in this thou shalt love thy neighbour as thyself. The Koran says, requite evil with good and he who is your enemy will become your dearest friend. The Talmud says, the man is a hero who can make a friend out of a foe.

Easy to say, hard to do.

The significance of doing it now is much greater than ever before, because for the first time in human history, what Dr Martin Luther King referred to as the inescapable network of mutuality in which we are all caught is a web that embraces the entire world.

Which brings me back to the lessons of Tip O'Neill. Lesson number one, people like to be asked. So I ask you to stay the course and lead the world by your example. When the Middle East peace fell apart, when the future was uncertain in Bosnia, when Africa was still reeling from losing 10 per cent of the people in the entire country of Rwanda and 2 million died in the Congo, I could always point to the Good Friday Accord.

You need to think a long time before you give it up.

Lesson number two, we need you for the tough ones. If this were easy, somebody would have done it a long time ago. By definition the only things worth talking about are the difficult ones. Do you really think that it is more difficult than what they face in Rwanda? In 1994 in ninety to a hundred days 700,000 people died in Rwanda. A country of under 8 million. They lost about 10 per cent of the population. Almost all of the people were killed with machetes. No bombs, few guns.

You couldn't even chalk it up to colonial oppression and its legacy because Rwanda has been a more or less coherent country for 500 years. With the majority Hutu population they were always economically and politically subordinate to a minority Tutsi population. A couple of totally unscrupulous Hutu politicians convinced the Hutus that the Tutsis were going to kill them and they had better do the killing first.

And before anyone knew what had happened, in ninety days, poof! – that is no time at all, 700,000 people were dead.

You know what they are doing in Rwanda, the Tutsi President of Rwanda has organised reconciliation villages. He has told the Hutu soldiers to come home from their hideouts in the Congo and that if they were not involved in ordering slaughters, but only followed orders, if they were not leaders, they can come back to a village, live there, and all they have to do is say what they did. And work to regain the confidence of the people in their village through service.

I met two women sitting next to each other, also living next to each other. One of them was a Tutsi who had lost her husband, her brother and her brother-in-law in the slaughters. Her next-door neighbour was a Hutu woman whose husband was a leader of the slaughter, in jail awaiting war crimes trials. But they were neighbours – and they were beginning again.

Is it tougher than that?

I just came back from the Dead Sea in Jordan where I met with leaders of the current Israeli government and some of the Palestinians who have long been friends of mine. In this last intifada they lost 1,800 Palestinians and over 600 Israelis. They are talking as if they have a new beginning right ahead of them.

Is it tougher than that?

Finally, all politics is local. What does that mean for Northern Ireland? Look at the context. Over the next twenty years the economies of the UK and the Irish Republic will inevitably grow closer together. Over the next twenty years, formally or informally you will all be drawn more closely into the European Union politically and economically. It will still be something to be Irish. People like me will still want to know where our ancestors came from. No one will be asked to give up their faith or their freedom of political speech. But in a world that is coming together I think that the Good Friday Accord is about the best you could ever do. The principle of consent, majority rule, minority rights, shared political responsibilities, shared economic benefits, special relations with both the UK and the Irish Republic. The assumption that if everyone is treated fairly now when one religious or political group is in the majority, that thirty years from now if present birth rates continue and immigration doesn't render it totally irrelevant, the other will be in the majority – it will work out fine then too, when we are all integrated into much bigger units anyway. I don't think you could do much better than that. I think that's why the deal was made in the first place.

So, you have been asked.

I know it's hard.

You have done the best you can to preserve the locality of the meaning of your lives and your history, in terms of the possibilities of the modern world. The truth is that all throughout history, since people first rose up out of the African savannah 100 thousand years ago we have had to cling to our crowd because we felt threatened by those who were different from us and in the beginning there were very good reasons, food was limited, shelter was limited, fuel was limited.

Over time there have been other good reasons, but all of human history has basically been erased between our ability to see the common humanity of people who were different from us and our increasing ability to kill them with technological advances. In the twentieth century, humanity nearly got it wrong.

The millions of people who died in World War I and World War II, the millions more who were slaughtered in the totalitarian purges of the Soviet Union and China. 1945 comes along and we finally have for the first time in all of human history the acknowledgement of our common humanity in the universal Declaration of Human Rights and the UN charter. It had never happened before.

By then there had been 7,500 years of civilisation and 100,000 years of human existence had never happened. But there were words on paper because the Cold War divided us in profound ways. The Cold War ended in 1989. There has been a lot of trouble in the world since 1989, but if you compare the troubles of the world since 1989 with the slaughters of the whole twentieth century – they don't seem too bad. And if you look at the good things the United Nations has done, the growing of the European Union, the broadening of NATO, the ending of the slaughter in the Balkans, what you did here, the world sticking up for that tiny speck of land in Asia called East Timor, to save them from a religious slaughter.

I could give you example after example after example: we're not doing too badly here.

I know terror is a problem, I know people are worried about weapons of mass destruction: we should be.

Terror has never destroyed a society yet. And it will not now if we keep remembering that what our obligation is, is to give people the possibilities of the modern world without asking them to give up their fundamental identities.

I have studied every peace agreement made and everyone not made, everywhere in the world in the last fifty years. Nobody could have done a better job in reconciling the complicating and conflicting interests than you did in this agreement. So it's about as local as you can get and still sees the possibilities of the modern world.

I know implementing it is tough. All I can do is to ask you to remember all the other hard places in the world and how much better it is sitting here today talking to each other and not worrying about a bomb going off.

And so I am asking, just like Tip O'Neill would, I want your vote for peace.

Thank you and God bless you.

Postscript

After leaving office President Clinton continued to tackle poverty, disease and conflict, establishing the William J. Clinton Foundation to that end. In 2005, then UN Secretary-General of the UN, Kofi Annan, appointed him to lead the relief effort following the Asian Tsunami and in that same year, with former President George H. W. Bush he founded the Bush-Clinton Tsunami Fund (January) and Bush-Clinton Katrina Fund (October). He campaigned for his wife Hillary Rodham Clinton and subsequently Barack Obama in the 2008 presidential race, and in 2009 intervened in North Korea's detention of two US journalists and was appointed United Nations' Special Envoy to Haiti. In 2010, Clinton and former President George W. Bush created the Clinton-Bush Haiti Fund to help raise money for the stricken Caribbean nation. He continues to back the work of peace and progress in Northern Ireland, visiting once more in September 2012 in support of US Secretary of State Hillary Clinton's economic efforts in the province.

Notes

1 At the same time culminating in and arising from the Good Friday Agreement (1998) that had spelled the end to nearly 30 years of conflict in the province.
2 The 'Quartet' consisted of the US, Russia, the EU and the UN.
3 Leonie Murray, *Clinton, Peacekeeping and Assertive Multilaterialism: Rise and Fall of a Policy* (London: Routledge, 2008), p. 123.

4

The European Union:
a force for peace in the world

The Taoiseach Bertie Ahern, TD

Introduction

Taoiseach Bertie Ahern's lecture in March 2004, on 'The European Union: a force for peace in the world', came at a critical juncture in the institution's history; and in the Northern Ireland peace process. Importantly, he was speaking in his capacity as President of the European Council, a position held by Ireland, as it did by rotation amongst member states, from 1 January until 30 June that year. By then, he had intimate and extensive experience of government at all levels, both domestic and international. The son of a politically aware family from Drumcondra in north Dublin, he entered city politics in 1978 in the Fianna Fail interest, becoming Lord Mayor in 1986. In 1977, he was elected to the Dail from the constituency of Dublin-Finglas, and subsequently, as the result of redistribution, representing Dublin Central, a testing seat with a high level of social deprivation. In 1994, he was elected leader of Fianna Fail, the political party founded by Eamon de Valera in 1926. In June 1997, he led the party to victory, becoming Taoiseach, a success that was repeated in 2002 and 2007.

He could not have come into office at a more testing time, since the affairs of Northern Ireland were about to enter a critical phase with negotiations over its political future about to get under way, chaired by the American Senator George Mitchell. As Taoiseach, Bertie Ahern was central to these complex events, earning respect for his commitment to the discussions during the period of mourning for the death of his mother. His central role in helping to secure the Good Friday Agreement of 10 April 1998 firmly established his credentials to speak on the topic of peacemaking, as did his subsequent contribution to the St Andrews Agreement of 13 October 2006.

If the Northern Ireland peace process owed much to his persistence and skill as a negotiator, so, too, did the fortunes of the European Union during his period of responsibility. Three critical issues engaged his Presidency. The Union was in the process of being expanded in a way that the statespersons who assembled at Messina in June 1955 could scarcely have imagined. Europe was then divided politically, militarily and ideologically by the Iron Curtain into two opposing systems. The unexpected collapse of the Soviet system in Eastern Europe, and then of the USSR itself, transformed the continent. In addition, new states were coming into existence. When Bertie Ahern took up office, the European Union, which had already grown to a membership of fifteen states, was about to be joined by a further ten. Malta and Cyprus were former British possessions. Slovenia had just emerged from the wreckage of Yugoslavia. Poland, Hungary and the former partners, the Czech Republic and Slovakia, had been part of the Soviet system, while Estonia, Latvia and Lithuania had been integral parts of the Soviet Union. Their accession to the Union marked by any measure a historic transformation of the continent. On 1 May 2004, the Day of Welcomes in Dublin marked the accession of the new members. After a century when Europeans had endured two wars, and then been divided by the Cold War, most of their continent was united and at peace, confirming the European Union's unique contribution to peacebuilding. The Irish Presidency of the Council was also occupied by the ongoing negotiations over the Constitution for Europe, and the need to repair relations with the United States, since much opinion in Europe had opposed the war in Iraq. All of these preoccupations formed the context of Bertie Ahern's lecture.

Central to his theme was the pursuit of what he termed 'effective multilateralism' in the achievement of global security. One of Ireland's responsibilities during its Presidency of the Union was to carry forward the Security and Defence Policy, which had been adopted on 12 December 2003 under the title 'A secure Europe in a better world'. Reassured that a large-scale aggression against a member state was unlikely, the document identified the threats facing Europe as terrorism, the proliferation of Weapons of Mass Destruction, regional conflicts, state failure and organised crime. The key to the policy was, as Bertie Ahern said, effective multilateralism, international law and the United Nations Charter, as well as partnership with the United States.[1] The operation of the policy was about 'getting the various international organisations to work more effectively together'. It was not about the creation of a military superpower, he argued, nor was it incompatible with Ireland's tradition of neutrality. Its core purpose was the prevention of conflict, in tandem with the work of the United Nations. In that regard, Ahern reminded listeners of the work that the European Union and the United Nations had recently carried out in the Democratic Republic of the Congo, the military monitoring mission in Macedonia and the Police Mission in Bosnia-Herzegovina; indeed, since his lecture, the EU has undertaken military and civilian missions in a variety of locations, including the Balkans, Georgia, Afghanistan and parts of Africa, including Somalia.[2]

He focused clearly on the EU as 'perhaps one the best examples of multilateralism in practice'. Although he was principally concerned with the role of the European Union in the prevention of conflict, humanitarian relief and peacebuilding, he did not neglect the peace process in Northern Ireland, where he clearly set out what he believed Republicans and Unionists needed to commit to in order to secure 'an irreversible path to peace, stability and progress'. There could not, he said, be a process that was continually in crisis, emphasising 'that partnership politics on this island is the way forward'. In his conclusion, relating the Northern Ireland peace process to his broader theme of the European Union, he reminded his audience that 'the EU has shown that it is not only interested in peace outside its borders. It also has, and is, supporting peace closer to home'.[3]

Lecture

Bishop Edward Daly; Bishop Seamus Hegarty; John Hume; Dr Don Keegan, Lord Lieutenant; Professor Gerry McKenna, Vice-Chancellor; Professor Jim Allen, Pro-Vice-Chancellor; members of the City Council; distinguished speakers; distinguished guests.

It is a great honour to be here in Derry today. Derry is for all of us a beacon of hope and an example of the triumph of humanity and cooperation over division and despair. It is, I feel, the ideal location to address the challenges facing Ireland, Europe and the world.

I am particularly happy to be in the company of John Hume. He is, in so many ways, a living symbol of Derry. John has worked tirelessly for peace his whole life. As well as being a statesman whose tenacity and conviction are widely admired, he is a visionary.

He was a visionary on Ireland. But for his courage and wisdom we might never have achieved the progress of recent years.

And he was a visionary on Europe, recognising from day one its potential to contribute, not only to easing division in Ireland, but as a force for peace and good in the wider world.

Ladies and gentlemen, it is nowhere pre-ordained that international security and the lot of humanity will inevitably and continuously improve. It is up to each generation to engage with the wider world so as to help shape it for the better.

This generation of Irish men and Irish women – this generation of

Europeans – have an important role to play. We must all play our part.

The world has changed fundamentally in the past decade and a half. In the matter of international security and the prevention, management and resolution of conflict, the context has undergone profound change. Unprecedented challenges face the entire global community.

If these challenges are to be met, Europe must play its part and we must do this to the full, using all of the instruments available to us and guided by principles which have served the wider world well.

Europe is in the process of changing and organising itself so that it can play this important role.

It cannot play this indispensable role from the sidelines.

The Secretary General of the United Nations has repeatedly welcomed the enhancement of Europe's various capacities and the steadily growing role that Europe is playing.

The theme today, 'The European Union: a force for peace in the world', has never been more valid.

The Irish Presidency is taking place against the background of what may be seen in years to come as a defining period in the broader field of international relations. Divisions in the international community over the past year have highlighted the need to develop a more effective multilateral international system.

The challenges facing us cannot be resolved through unilateral action by any one country, or group of countries, no matter how large the resources or resolute the determination to go it alone.

A few years ago, Kofi Annan captured this point clearly when he noted that, 'Challenges to peace and security today are predominantly global ... They require complex and collective responses, which are possible only if the web of multilateral institutions is adequately developed and properly used'.[4]

So how does this relate to the EU?

Let us not forget what binds Europe together in the first place. As a community of shared values, the Union is uniquely placed to play a stronger role in support of peace and security, human rights and development. With the accession of ten new member states in just under two months' time, an enlarged EU will comprise over 450 million people producing a quarter of the world's gross national products.

There is no doubt that the European Union is a global player. Our size and wealth brings not only opportunities but also obligations.

As Presidency, Ireland is facilitating the dynamic to enhance the role of the EU as a force for peace.

This is the thinking behind the European Security Strategy, which was adopted by the European Council last December. The increasing focus on the role of the Union in international affairs led to the decision to draw up such a strategy. It signals a step towards the Union taking a more strategic approach in the external action area. This is both timely and necessary, not least in light of the enlargement of the Union. Enlargement is, in itself, a response to the new challenges the Union is facing – that of reinforcing political stability and economic security on our own continent.

The European Security Strategy is a comprehensive approach to security, going beyond purely military aspects. This is now it should be – security is everybody's business.

The Security Strategy identifies the global challenges and opportunities facing the Union and the need for a coherent and all-embracing response.

In the past, the Union has tended to react to developments. But the Security Strategy sets the context for a more proactive approach, stemming from an awareness of the need to define a common perception of security threats and of the role the EU can play in tackling them.

The Security Strategy is not about creating a military superpower. Nor is it a charter for military intervention or foreign adventures. Those who seek to present it in these terms are profoundly wrong.

It is Ireland's responsibility, as Presidency, to guide the Union's first steps towards implementing the strategy. As Presidency, we have been tasked by the European Council with conducting follow-up work in four areas – these are effective multilateralism, the fight against terrorism, strengthening relations with the Middle East region and the Arab world, and, not least, developing a comprehensive strategy for Bosnia-Herzegovina.

It is on one of these themes in particular that I would first wish to focus this morning. And that is – effective multilateralism. Both as Presidency, and nationally, this is an area to which we attach particular importance.

'Effective multilateralism' is a much-used phrase. But what does it actually mean in practice. Why is it so important?

In essence, it means getting the various international organisations to work more effectively together. It is a recognition that global security can only be achieved through collective action by the international community as a whole. In the Security Strategy, the EU makes it clear that the United Nations is the crucial organisation in this regard. The primary responsibility of the United Nations Security Council for international peace and security is clearly endorsed.

As Presidency, we wish to see the Union use its voice at the UN to better effect, and to contribute to the current process of UN reform.

The EU is perhaps one of the best examples of effective multilateralism in practice. It is natural that the EU would support this principle and work closely with the UN on crisis management issues. The United Nations itself sees growing benefit in fostering this cooperation to the benefit of both organisations. Kofi Annan has welcomed the Union's developing capabilities for civil and military crisis management. As Presidency, we want to build on this synergy between what the UN and the EU are doing. And there are practical steps that we can take. In September 2003, the UN and the EU agreed a political declaration on cooperation on crisis management. The Irish Presidency is implementing this important declaration.

Minister Cowen has met Kofi Annan and agreed that the two organisations will build on the cooperation between them for the very successful stabilisation mission in the Democratic Republic of the Congo last summer. This mission was undertaken by the EU at Kofi Annan's request.

The more effective contacts and coordination between the two organisations, which are now being put in place, will enable them to respond to other challenges that require a rapid response from the international community.

The strategy then is already paying dividends in terms of EU and UN cooperation. It is also paying dividends in the field of conflict prevention.

Prevention is at the heart of the Security Strategy. A culture of prevention infuses the document. It makes the clear statement that 'conflict prevention and threat prevention cannot start too early'.[5] The EU is, therefore, developing an increasingly strong and coherent policy on the prevention of violent conflicts. I do not have to remind an audience here in Northern Ireland this morning that we cannot achieve security if we do not tackle the root causes of conflict. And this, as the Northern Ireland experience illustrates so clearly, goes beyond the immediate threats to take account of the environment in which those threats are generated and sustained.

I think we should also remember, as John Hume has so correctly highlighted, the extent to which the European Union is itself probably the most successful example of conflict prevention in history. The EU came forward in a Europe recovering from the horror of two global wars. Out of the devastation of war we created a unique union dedicated to peace. As such, the EU is a remarkable experiment in collective action to address problems that are beyond the reach of any one country to solve.

Conflict prevention is already implicit in much of the work and priorities of the EU. But the Presidency is mainstreaming this area and giving it greater visibility. This includes a focus, not only on enhancing the

Union's capacity for early warning to prevent potential conflict, but also looking at how better to match such early warning capacity with early action.

When it comes to conflict prevention, the European Union is playing to its strengths. It has at its disposal a wide range of capacities, which sets it apart from any other organisation. As well as developing capabilities for military and civilian crisis management, the resources available to the Union also encompass development cooperation assistance and trade policy, as well as diplomatic and political measures.

Bringing greater coherence and effectiveness to our collective EU external action means harnessing these instruments. This enables the Union to develop a broadly based approach to the complex problems which face us as an international community.

As part of the Presidency's commitment to the conflict prevention area, we will also host a conference on this subject in Dublin which will focus on the role of civil society and non-governmental organisations.

The European Security and Defence Policy is fully consistent with Ireland's neutrality policy. Our policy has always expressed itself in support for conflict prevention and crisis management. The European Security and Defence Policy now allows us to play our true role in building peace in the world, hand in hand with our EU partners. It enables us to be far more active in areas which traditionally have been so central to our foreign policy.

Already the Union has undertaken several operations under the European Security and Defence Policy.

I have already referred to last summer's mission aimed at stabilising the situation in the Democratic Republic of the Congo. The EU and the UN worked in close harmony on this mission, which helped to alleviate a situation of great humanitarian distress. The military monitoring mission in the former Yugoslav Republic of Macedonia, which concluded last December, has also proved highly successful.

Both of these operations illustrate, in tangible terms, how far the EU has travelled in a short period of time in terms of our ability to meet our international responsibilities.

The Irish Presidency is also facilitating the ongoing EU Police Mission in Bosnia-Herzegovina. This mission is playing a central role in building the sustainable policing capacity that Bosnia requires if it is to continue along the road to recovery. I am pleased to say that an Irish police officer, Assistant Commissioner Carty, has been charged with overseeing some 470 police officers and sixty civilian personnel who are an important element of the EU's overall contribution to peace and stability in the region.

The Union's commitment to developing policing capacity in the Balkans is also reflected in the ongoing EU Police Mission in the former Yugoslav Republic of Macedonia.

Looking ahead, the EU is being called upon to provide a follow-on mission to the current multinational peace stabilisation force, SFOR, in Bosnia-Herzegovina. This will represent a key challenge for the Union. SFOR is a significantly larger and more complex operation than any undertaken to date under the European Security and Defence Policy. It can be envisaged that any EU follow-on force would continue to operate under a mandate from the UN Security Council.

As Presidency, Ireland is facilitating the arrangements for the EU follow-on to SFOR. This is fully consistent with the importance we attach to the international community continuing to play an active and constructive role in the Balkans region.

It is, perhaps, as much as any other factor, the experience of the Balkans that underlines the imperative of the EU continuing to strive towards the maintenance of peace and security in our own neighbour-hood and beyond.

The EU has already done much to establish its credentials as a force for peace in the wider world. As Presidency, we want to play our part in facilitating this role. The steps we take towards implementing the recommendations of the Security Strategy will lay a foundation for the positive and constructive role that the EU should play in advancing the cause of peace and stability.

At the heart of John Hume's vision, based on his understanding of the European experience and ideal, was his conviction that the differences that divide people can be transcended by working together to overcome their common problems.

As John succinctly puts it, we must spill our sweat and not our blood.

Our common membership of the European Union has provided a new teamwork within which Ireland and Britain have been able to address their relationships.

And never has there been a more opportune time to make progress. Ireland, North and South, can take real advantage of the tides in world affairs if we act promptly and constructively.

I firmly believe that if we build a lasting peace on this island, we can be both a force for positive change in the world and a beneficiary of the ever-quickening globalisation of the world economy.

We know that partnership politics on this island is the way forward.

We know that the people of Northern Ireland yearn for stable politics.

We know that they want their own elected politicians to get on with the job of making positive differences in areas like health, education, transport and tackling the problems of economic and social disadvantage in deprived loyalist and republican communities.

In summary, we know that the people of Northern Ireland want to move beyond the old politics of confrontation that have failed them and to embrace the new politics of partnership that will provide a positive future for their children.

It is, therefore, immensely frustrating that, as we collectively strive to find a way forward towards realising this vision of partnership politics, yet another manifestation of the destructive agenda of the past should convulse the political process.

We cannot have a process that is continually in crisis because there are those who will not relinquish the ways of the past.

Recent events have brought into very sharp relief what was, in any event, the reality for some time. We have reached a bedrock situation in the political process and it is this.

The continuation of paramilitary activity by the Republican movement negates any prospect of achieving inclusive partnership politics in Northern Ireland.

I believe that the Sinn Fein leadership understand this reality and are working towards achieving that objective of ending paramilitarism. The problem is that time is no longer a friend to the process.

It is now almost six years since the Good Friday Agreement was signed. In that time, we have had significant historic events. But we have only periodically been able to see the Agreement working at its best.

Remedying the deficits of trust and confidence that now exist require a fast-forwarding to completion. That is the task that all parties of influence must now focus on.

We all know what must be done.

Some parties seem to believe that a policy of exclusion is the answer. It is my belief that any such policy would not be workable.

Arrangements which exclude the largest party in one community would scarcely be the best expression of partnership government, would in practice not provide political stability and would not be conducive to achieving closure on paramilitarism.

I fully agree with Prime Minister Blair when he says that the people of Northern Ireland wants the Republican movement to commit to peace, the Unionists to commit to power-sharing and for everyone to get on with the job of delivering good governance and a better future for all.

For that to happen, the Republican movement needs to fully understand and accept the imperative of definitively ending – both in words and deeds – the culture of paramilitarism.

And Unionism needs to unequivocally embrace the principle and practice of inclusive partnership politics.

If these core issues, which are inextricably linked, can be resolved, I believe that Northern Ireland will be on an irreversible path to peace, stability and progress.

The governments too must meet our commitments.

Regardless of political context, we must press on with the implementation of the outstanding aspects of the Good Friday Agreement – not as concessions to one side or another but because they are the objective requirements of the new and fair society that the Agreement envisaged.

The EU has been of enormous help in underpinning the peace we have already achieved in Northern Ireland. The financial support provided by the PEACE I and PEACE II programmes has brought significant benefit. Some €1 billion has been committed through these programmes. In addition, the EU has committed over €200 million to the International Fund for Ireland which, as a result of the contributions received from its international donors, has done extraordinary work in promoting economic development and reconciliation.

We hope when the PEACE II programme ends later this year that it can be followed by a further programme. We will be working closely with the British to try to assure this. The work is not yet finished. But the EU has shown that it is not only interested in peace outside its borders. It also has, and is, supporting peace closer to home.

Thank you.

Notes

1 'A secure Europe in a better world. European Security Strategy', Brussels, 12 December 2003, www.consilium.europa.eu/uedocs/cmsUpload/78367. pdf (last accessed 11 March 2013).

2 'Overview of the missions and operations of the European Union August 2012', www.ue.eu.int/media/1730495/map_en_august.2012wl.pdf (last accessed 15 March 2013).

3 Bertie Ahern with Richard Aldous, *Bertie Ahern. The Autobiography* (London: Hutchinson, 2009), *passim*.

4 Kofi Annan, 'Implementation of the United Nations Millennium Declaration', Report of the Secretary-General, 2 September 2003, UN General Assembly A/58/323, p. 8, www.un.org/millenniumgoals/sgreport2003. pdf?OpenElement (last accessed 26 February 2013).

5 'A secure Europe in a better world. European Security Strategy'.

5

Europe and peace

President Romano Prodi

Introduction

Professor Romano Prodi's lecture on 'Europe and peace', delivered on 1 April 2004, came at a particularly important juncture in European affairs, not least since the Constitutional Treaty was being advanced under the leadership of the Irish Presidency. He began with a salutary reminder, to those who would doubt it, that the post-war reconstruction of Europe rested on the necessity to build peace and security in a continent which had been ravaged by ancient hatreds raised to a new level of ferocity by advances in science and technology. No one who glimpsed the devastated cities of Europe in the immediate post-war years, then scarcely recognisable as what they had been or were to become again, could think otherwise, but memories fade and new generations are born.

Physical losses were irreparable: the old city of Warsaw; mediaeval Nuremberg, the home of Hans Sachs; the Wren churches of London; the Roemerplatz in Frankfurt where the Holy Roman Emperors were crowned; streets in Dante's Florence; Saint Benedict's monastery of Monte Cassino.[1] The list could go on, but the human cost had, of course, been even infinitely more tragic. The events of 1914–1945 have been described as a second Thirty Years' War, and for the peoples of Eastern Europe their consequences were to continue for another generation. At least, men and women of vision could begin the task of rebuilding Western Europe on new foundations, and extend their hands eastward after the dramatic events of November 1989 unfolded.

He brought impeccable credentials to the topic. Graduate *cum laude* in Jurisprudence from the Catholic University of Milan in 1961, he then studied at the Universities of Milan and Bologna, as well as at the London School of Economics. From 1963, he followed an academic career at the University of Bologna, founded in 1088 and the oldest in Europe, and was Visiting Professor at Harvard and the Stanford Research Institute. From 1974 to 1978, he presided over the *Societa Editrice Il Mulino* in Bologna, one of Italy's leading academic publishing houses. Already experienced in public service, in 1995 he formed a centre-left coalition, *Ulivo* or the Olive Tree, becoming their candidate for President of the Council of Ministers. In May 1996, he was invited to form a government, which he led until October 1998. In 1999, he published *Un'idea dell'Europa* with *Il Mulino*, which was published in English as *Europe As I See It*, and also went through Spanish, Romanian, Serbian and Ukrainian editions. In the same year, he was chosen to be President of the European Commission at a time when the European Union was facing fresh challenges. It was, then, with a wealth of experience, both in the academic and political worlds, that he came to focus on 'Europe and peace'.

Comparing the situation in 1945 with the Europe of 1648, when the Peace of Westphalia brought an end to the Thirty Years' War, he noted that the latter had ushered in an era when the sovereign state was the principal actor on the international stage and that states would respect each other's internal affairs. This, he argued, meant security within each state, but instability in their external relations. The European Union, in contrast, brought together sovereign states that shared common interests but respected diversity. The Union was challenged by the break-up of Yugoslavia and the conflicts which followed. These and other considerations led to the provision in the 1992 Treaty on European Union, commonly known as the Maastricht Treaty, for the introduction of a possible future common foreign and security policy, and to the decision to work towards the admission of countries from Central and Eastern Europe. By April 2004, the Union was on the point, exactly four weeks later, of admitting ten new countries, expanding its membership to twenty-five states.

Equally significant for the future, and building on the Maastricht Treaty, was the European Security Strategy, unveiled on 12 December 2003, as 'A secure Europe in a better world'. The thrust of this document was the Union's role in countering: organised crime; state failure, as in Somalia and Afghanistan; regional conflicts, such as in the Great Lakes Region, and especially in the Middle East; weapons of mass destruction, where again the Middle East was identified; and terrorism. In addressing this key document, Prodi focused particularly on terrorism. That this should be the case was hardly surprising, since his lecture had been preceded on 11 March by the bomb outrages on trains in Madrid which killed almost 200 people. Conceding that there had to be a military response, he argued for the need to tackle the root causes of terrorism. His hope was for what he called a ring of friends from Russia to Morocco, which should include sovereign Israeli and Palestinian states. Without an Israeli-Palestinian settlement, the Middle East would continue to generate a terrorist threat, he warned.

Lecture

Greetings and thanks

It is a pleasure and a privilege to be here. I wish to thank Professor McKenna and the University of Ulster, together with Professor John Hume, for their kind invitation.

Tribute to John Hume

Let me pay a personal tribute to John Hume. His part in bringing peace to this land is an example and an inspiration to us all.

Together with David Trimble, his contribution to healing the sectarian divide has been immense. It has brought benefits all of you here appreciate. Better than any, you Irish know what peace means, and what a difference it makes.

The Irish people and the communities of Northern Ireland have always been close to our hearts. We will continue to support them so peace continues to prosper.

When he received the Prize in Oslo in 1998, John gave the credit to the Irish people in these words: 'we owe this peace to the ordinary people of Ireland, particularly those of the North who have lived and suffered the reality of our conflict'.[2]

He also said how much the European experience inspired him in his work for peace. I could not agree more with him, and today I want to explain the reasons why I believe this so strongly.

The European Union can be seen in many ways. But to me it is one thing above all others: *the fostering and flourishing of peace*.

We should never forget that the basic reason for the European integration process – and the European Union – is peace.

That was the overriding objective of our founding fathers: Jean Monnet said that building Europe meant building peace. You cannot be clearer than that.

At a time when Europe lay in ruins, devastated by war and devoured by the hatred it had generated, an onlooker would have found it difficult to believe in reconciliation between France and Germany.

Half a century later, we know it was much more than a dream. I agree with John when he says that 'the European Union is the best example in the history of the world of conflict resolution'.[3]

Our continent has been transformed. It was once a cauldron boiling over with conflicts. And today Europe is a powerhouse for peace, generating stability and prosperity beyond its borders.

The Union has brought us one of the longest periods of peace in our history. And it has set an example that gives hope to millions around the world.

Our success shows we have found a model that works. A model to draw on in managing relations between states in our neighbourhood and even beyond.

We can be proud of these achievements. We have learned the lessons of the past. We have realised the importance of respecting diversity. Above all, we have discovered ways of consolidating peace through structures that tackle the *root causes of conflict.*

We Europeans know a lot about conflict. As a continent, our past is dominated by war, with short interludes of uncertain peace.

Look at the political map of Europe over the last five centuries. It illustrates the perpetual unrest on a continent with few natural frontiers. They reflect little more than the arbitrary ebb and flow of power between empires and fiefdoms.

The lessons of the past

For hundreds of years, war was the only way for Europeans to ensure their security. It was a matter of attacking before being attacked and destroying your enemies' cities before they burned yours. *And we should never forget that those dark days could return.*

The great walls of this town are there to remind us of that age of conflict and insecurity, when people had to build colossal defences to survive. And often Europe's peoples paid the price in blood and grief for very little protection.

This is the world Thomas Hobbes described. The great English philosopher saw the natural condition of mankind as '*that condition which is called war … where every man is enemy to every man*'.

Leviathan, his great work published in 1651, explains how it takes a powerful state to deal with the constant threat of war.[4]

That was just two years after the Peace of Westphalia put an end to the Thirty Years' War. It closed a terrible chapter when Man was truly wolf to Man.

And when those three decades of religious conflict were finally over, people counted the losses.

For most of Europe, they were shocking. Germany – the main battlefield – had lost almost half its population. Cities lay in ruins, trade had collapsed, serfdom was reinstated. Pillage, famine, disease, widespread rape and social disruption turned the clock back a century.

And elsewhere the picture was equally bleak.

The end of the Thirty Years' War reminds us of 1945 – with many important differences.

The Treaty of Westphalia *did* bring a sort of peace to Europe. It did this by introducing the modern sovereign state as the protagonist of power politics.

This marked a new stage in European history. It laid the foundations for a new order of inter-state dynamics. And it ushered in a new form of instability.

A new era of European order and disorder began. A new, desperate search for stability in a new round of the zero-sum game I have described.

The Netherlands and Switzerland gained their independence, the German states were strengthened. And these new players agreed on the principle that states had no right to intervene in each other's internal affairs.

This meant that the people's security was guaranteed within each state. Let us not underestimate what this progress meant to people.

But peace and security within the state brought only a small improvement. Because Hobbes's vision of man's relations with his fellows continued to apply between states. And Europe's states kept on as wolves to each other, building unstable coalitions and fighting for territory.

In the absence of clear international law, the law of the jungle applied: across the continent, states did as they liked.

This was the backdrop against which the political ideas of the Age of Enlightenment must be seen.

Shaping a lasting peace

Immanuel Kant, who died exactly 200 years ago, saw clearly that there could be no lasting coalition between such states.

He realised that relations between states were indeed like the world Hobbes had described – a *'state of nature'* when war could break out at any moment.

So how could this unbearable situation be changed? This is the question Kant tried to answer in *Perpetual Peace*, a work he published in 1795, shortly after the French Revolution.

To make perpetual peace possible, Kant proposed a *'federation of "republican" states'*. He believed there was no place for war between states *that had a civil legal order and respect for moral law*.

Nowadays we might call that *sharing the same basic values*. And as we also believe today, Kant thought that if citizens have a direct interest in peace to safeguard their prosperity and well-being, they will always oppose war in a republic.

Kant was not thinking of some kind of world republic or superstate – any more than we are in the European Union.

He wanted to find a practical and realistic way for states to coexist peacefully, to truly enjoy security.

In this, Kant was very modern. He did not seek to do away with our nations and states any more than we want to see the end of individual nations.

The crucial point is that Kant wanted an alliance of states that agreed on certain *principles and rules*.

He believed perpetual peace could be achieved by a peaceful federation of states that agreed not to go to war with each other. And that federation would be strengthened by trade and underpinned by a system of international law.

Like Kant, we believe the rule of law should apply within states just as it should between states.

Kant may have been pleased to see what we have done in the European Union – a form of supra-national democracy in a Union of sovereign member states. In some ways, our Union enshrines the essence of Kant's federation of sovereign democracies.

We too have realised that common and converging interests are powerful tools for building peace. And we have founded our Union on shared values and a system of common rules.

So let us see how we have got where we are today in terms of peace and stability.

Reconciling enemies and bolstering stability

We founded our Union on reconciliation between the peoples and nations of our continent, on tolerance for others, on individual freedoms and minority rights.

United in our diversity, we based the Union on a willingness to see the other's point of view rather than imposing our own, on reciprocal undertakings, freely entered into and democratically accepted.

It is striking to note the great differences in our member states' constitutional origins. The checks and balances introduced over time have considerably altered the original structures. So whether they started as constitutional monarchies or republics, they all function today as highly developed democracies respecting the same values and principles.

Respect for diversity has allowed each individual state to retain its own characteristics. This has not impaired our collective respect for the values and principles we share. But it means our conflicts do not degenerate into violence. As John Hume says:

'All conflict is about difference, whether the difference is race, religion or nationality. The European visionaries decided that difference is not a threat, difference is natural. [...] The answer to difference is *to respect it*. Therein lies a most fundamental principle of peace – respect for diversity'.[5]

How the European Union did it

The principle of diversity is enshrined in our institutional framework. Our rules are there to safeguard the interests of our member states, both large and small.

At least two generations of our citizens have now grown up without seeing war in their countries. This is our greatest achievement, but we should not be complacent.

We tend to take for granted our stability, prosperity, democracy and respect for human rights and basic values. As if things could never be any different.

Among the reasons for success were the founding fathers' combination of low-key rhetoric and modest ambitions. They kept their sights on the achievable steps.

For fifty years we added brick to brick, building a structure of institutions, rules and principles.

The four freedoms of movement – goods, services, persons and capital – have led to our single market.

Many of our member states share a single currency. And they have done away with passport checks. This was possible because we have stepped up cooperation between our police and judicial authorities.

All this has made our internal borders much less important than in the past.

We have developed common policies to consolidate our stability and prosperity.

We are now in the process of taking big steps in the area of justice and home affairs. Protecting our citizens' security is vital, particularly at a time of terrorist threats. And we can safeguard our internal security more effectively by working together.

All this has shown us that the multilateral approach is the only one that can work. Because living on a continent with few natural borders means we cannot ignore our neighbours.

On the world scene too, we support multilateralism, because we know individual states cannot go it alone.

Since 1945, there have been enormous changes on the international scene. New institutions designed primarily to ensure peace and security and foster cooperation have given form and substance to the multilateral approach.

We have built up a system of overlapping layers to reinforce security. This has meant supporting other regional and international structures to bolster our security – such as NATO, the United Nations, the Council of Europe, the OSCE and, most recently, the International Criminal Court.

It has meant setting up an international system to manage and underpin our prosperity – through such organisations as the World Trade Organisation and agreements like the Kyoto Protocol to the United Nations Framework Convention on Climate Change.

1989: time for a proper policy for peace

There are some dates that stand out in history because they mark great periods of change. We must take care to learn the right lessons from them. Remember Mikhail Gorbachev telling Erich Honecker that '*he who comes too late will be punished by life*'.[6] 1989 was a watershed in European history.

Conventionally, for historians the nineteenth century started back in 1789. And I believe the twenty-first century started in 1989.

Some have seen 1989 as marking the triumph of liberal democracy and economic liberalism. And they claim this amounts to the end of history.

For my part, I believe 1989 marks the time history started again. It is the end of the Cold War – *not* the end of history.

Closing the Cold War, it ended a period that was neither war nor peace, but more like a truce.

But 1989 also brought a return to armed conflict with the break-up of the former Yugoslavia.

Our institutions were, of course, already established. We had started to think about external policy. As a Union we had never before had a war on our doorstep. And we all know we were caught totally unprepared.

But in 1993 we took two strategic decisions. We signed the Maastricht Treaty that introduced a common foreign and security policy. And we opened our doors to the countries of Central and Eastern Europe.

In other words, we took strategic decisions to bolster our security in the light of the post-Yugoslavia experience. And these involved both 'hard' and 'soft' power.

Security in a complex and dangerous world

An intelligent multilateral approach involves both 'hard' security and 'soft' security.

We all know what 'hard' security means: the credible threat – or the use – of force. And it is perfectly legitimate where it complies with the rules of international law.

We built our Union for peace. We would have liked to do away with all weapons. But we know the world is still a dangerous place.

The 11th of March this year has brought home the importance of joint action to protect our people and ensure security. The scale of the atrocity and its implications have altered the political landscape.

The way people responded was impressive. It has strengthened my faith in the Europeans.

They demonstrated in silence in their millions across Spain – and across Europe – against the bombs in Madrid's stations.

Only days later, the Spanish people voted massively to show they believed in democracy and were not daunted by terrorism. The turnout at the elections was 10 per cent higher than in 2000.

Their message was clear. They fought back against the logic of violence and fear.

This should be Europe's response, too. We must fight terrorists, we must protect our citizens and we must defend our way of life. We must safeguard our values of democracy, openness and tolerance. We must ensure our minorities and our legal immigrants continue to enjoy the benefits of our open societies.

In December last year, the Union outlined a European Security and Defence Strategy for the first time. The problem of terrorism and its root causes figure prominently in the strategy. This timely initiative on the part of the High Representative for the Common Foreign and Security Policy now needs implementing urgently, as last week's Spring European Council stated.

The Council also decided to establish a European counter-terrorism coordinator, whose task will be to improve the exchange of information. It also endorsed a set of measures including:

- sharing of intelligence,
- controlling terrorists' sources of financing,
- action along the lines of the solidarity clause in the draft Constitution.

Of course, internal security goes hand in hand with security on the external front. Since the Maastricht Treaty, we have started to organise our foreign and security policy. We need to develop this further.

And since the Anglo-French defence initiative at St Malo, things have indeed moved. A European security and defence policy has started to take shape.

The aim is to strengthen the European pillar of NATO. NATO continues to bear the main responsibility for our security. But we need to ensure we can take action militarily where our American partners are not concerned.

Events gathered pace in 2003. In January, the Union undertook its first mission under the European Security and Defence Policy. This involved taking over the monitoring and mentoring of police activities in Bosnia and Herzegovina from the UN-led International Police Task Force. And the Union is preparing to undertake a follow-on mission to SFOR, the NATO stabilisation force in Bosnia and Herzegovina.

In March, we launched an EU stabilisation mission called *Concordia* in the former Yugoslav Republic of Macedonia that drew on NATO assets. Following the successful completion of the operation, we set up *Proxima* – the EU Police Mission in the former Yugoslav Republic of Macedonia in December.

Outside Europe, the Union has already conducted a military operation called *Artemis* in the Democratic Republic of the Congo.

These examples show that, where this is needed, the Union is capable of a modulated response that takes account of each individual situation and can include aspects of hard security.

However, I am convinced that wars are not won by weapons alone.

This is all the truer where you are fighting not a state, but a terrorist organisation. In a war against terrorism, the concepts of the past do not work. The balance of terror of the Cold War does not work with terrorists. Deterrence has no effect on suicide bombers. Targeted killings just boost the terrorists' recruits.

We have to get realistic about solving the problem of terrorism. It is a dangerous illusion to think it can be defeated without tackling the root causes. Force alone is not enough to defeat terrorism. Both force and brainpower must be used. Alongside the military option and repression, political avenues need to be explored with equal determination. And for both options the multilateral approach needs following: unilateral approaches are no longer enough.

Hard facts about soft security

Let me tell you the hard facts about soft power. Soft power is not about wearing kid gloves. There is no easy way to peace. It is easy to see how states fail. *Building* nations is the real tough job. And that is only done when you no longer need occupying troops.

It cannot be achieved overnight. And it may not hit the headlines. But it gets the job done in the long term. Preventing is better than pre-empting.

Good examples are fostering our democratic principles through development assistance to bolster peace and security internationally. And I am proud to say the European Union's role is second to none here.

The Union is by far the world's foremost donor of overseas development assistance.

We are also an active promoter of sustainable development. Because development is a key factor in building peace.

The Union is addressing certain major root causes of conflicts – such as poverty, demographic pressure and competition for scarce natural resources, like water and land.

The Cotonou Agreement between the Union and seventy-seven African, Caribbean and Pacific countries stresses poverty eradication and smooth integration into the world economy, good governance, democracy and the rule of law.

And how does soft power work? To explain, let us take a step backwards in time and look at what happened.

As we said, the European Union's role in fostering peace and stability started at home by reconciling age-old enemies.

Subsequent enlargements have bolstered peace by fostering democracy – in Greece, Spain and Portugal. Look how those vibrant democracies have flourished over the last three decades.

In the current enlargement, the prospect of membership has had a big impact. It has bolstered democracy, peace and stability across the divide that split Europe in two for fifty years.

The European Union's soft power has provided impetus for economic, social and political reforms in the candidate countries. And it has fostered respect for human rights and democratic values.

Our soft power can help to resolve armed conflicts, too. The example of Cyprus is striking. The realisation that the Greek part of the island is going to join the Union has galvanised the Turkish Cypriots. They have demonstrated in large numbers in favour of accession. I still have hopes that Cyprus may yet join us as an undivided island.

One important aspect of soft security is treatment of minorities.

In democracy, the majority rules but minority rights must be protected. None of our nation-states are homogeneous in ethnic terms, much less so in religious, ethnic and cultural terms.

Minorities have often suffered at the hands of dominant groups. They have also served as a pretext at times for intervention across borders.

The problem is particularly acute in the Balkans.

Recent events in Kosovo demonstrate clearly how precarious the situation is there. There is no room for complacency. Peace is a fragile plant that calls for constant care and nurturing. There will be no lasting solution in the Balkans if we do not offer the countries in the region realistic prospects of joining the European Union. This has worked with other countries in the past. And it will work in Kosovo, too.

The Union makes borders less meaningful, so being a minority within a single member state is less of a problem.

In our Union, everyone is – in a sense – in a minority. And in our Union, no state can lord it over the others.

Fundamentally, no religious, ethnic, cultural or other component must be able to dictate to others, but all must have equal dignity. That is why I call our Union a 'Union of minorities'.

Forging a ring of friends

In terms of fostering peace, the most important aspect is a stronger common foreign and security policy.

This also implies taking action in our region.

At the beginning I spoke of the need to underpin peace with structures that tackle the root causes of conflict.

We cannot confine our efforts to our member countries. We need to project stability beyond our borders. That means promoting political and economic reforms that can enable our neighbours to share in our peace and prosperity.

It means working with partner countries on the basis of converging interests and shared values. And a broad, long-term view of our self-interest is the key idea behind the policy we are developing for the countries on the enlarged Union's borders.

The aim is to create a ring of friends around the Union – stretching from Russia right around the Mediterranean to Morocco – and to share with them the peace, stability and prosperity we have enjoyed in the Union for the last fifty years.

We hope to include the Israelis and the Palestinians among these friends. This can only work if both these peoples can live in sovereign and independent states, secure within their borders, and at peace with each other.

When both can take part in a process of political and economic integration, this will bring lasting stability to the region and will make the world a more secure place. This will effectively guarantee *sustainable peace*.

I am aware this is a daring proposition, but I make no apology for it. There is no alternative to this now.

To be totally clear, a two-state solution would be only the first step, however gigantic. But even such a giant step would not achieve our goal of sustainable peace for the region.

We must bear in mind that we can no longer just rely on the diplomacy of states. This goal calls for much more.

The new model I have in mind would no longer treat individuals and social groups as passive subjects but make them the real protagonists of national and international politics.

It will probably take many years, but it is the only way forward.

Ultimately, we want to extend to these countries the four freedoms on which the Union is based. This will give tangible form to our commitment not to erect new barriers across Europe.

The bomb attacks in Madrid have brought home the urgency of such a policy. It is clear that until there is a settlement between the Palestinians and the Israelis, the Middle East will continue to spawn terrorism and insecurity for us too.

That is why we need a wide-ranging response. We need to convince our allies of the need to work together in a multilateral context. And to convince them of the effectiveness of soft power. It will help ensure our own security, both internal and external.

Investing in peace

We Europeans know from long and bitter experience that war is the worst of all solutions and must remain the very last resort.

And because we have always lived in close contact with other cultures and civilisations, isolation has never been an option for Europe. We know that the open societies and tolerant cultures we cherish can be the first victims of any conflict and any terrorist threat.

We have transformed the Cold War truce into true peace. On 1 May, the European Union will have twenty-five member states. Peace is now a consolidated fact for the European Union.

However, we are seeing the emergence of new threats and new challenges.

Fighting terrorism, ensuring international stability and security, keeping the world economy on an even keel, safeguarding the environment for a sustainable future are beyond the capacity of any individual state – however powerful and however limitless its resources may seem.

That goes for the countries of Europe and it goes for our allies and partners around the world. That is why multilateralism is the only option.

Tomorrow will see the emergence of new powers and perhaps new superpowers.

That is why promoting our values internationally is so important for our own long-term security.

Postscript

On leaving office as President of the European Commission in 2005, by which time he had seen the Constitutional Treaty signed in Rome on 29 October 2004, Romano Prodi returned to active political life in Italy. He served a second period as Prime Minister from May 2006 until May 2008. In September 2008, he was appointed to head a working group of the United Nations and the African Union to work for peace in Africa in pursuit of the very theme of his lecture.

Notes

1 Donald Cameron Watt, *How War Came. The Immediate Origins of the Second World War 1938–1939* (London, William Heinemann Ltd, 1989), pp. 5–8.
2 John Hume, Nobel Lecture, Oslo, 10 December 1998, © The Nobel Foundation, www.nobelprize.org/nobel_prizes/peace/laureates/1998/hume-lecture.html (last accessed 13 February 2013).
3 John Hume, Nobel Lecture, © The Nobel Foundation.
4 Thomas Hobbes, *Leviathan*, 1651, chapter XVIII.
5 John Hume, Nobel Lecture, © The Nobel Foundation.
6 Mikhail Gorbachev, Speech in East Berlin, 7 October 1989.

6

Europe as a force for creative reconciliation

President Pat Cox

Introduction

As he reminded his audience, when Pat Cox delivered his lecture on 'Europe as a force for creative reconciliation' on 26 April 2004, the reunification of the continent with the accession to the European Union of ten new members was only six days away. As President of the European Parliament, he was privileged to watch this historic development from a unique vantage point. In June 1989, when he was first elected to the Parliament, such a development was barely imaginable. The European continent was still divided, as it had been since the end of World War II, by the obscenity of the Iron Curtain. Two economic, social and, most importantly, military systems were in place, each with the capacity, but fortunately not the desire, to destroy the other. Within months of his election, this situation changed with astonishing rapidity when on 10 September the Hungarians opened their section of the Iron Curtain and East Germans, who did not need a visa to cross Czechoslovakia, seized the opportunity to move to the West. The European Union had grown out of the post-war perception that a basis had to be laid for the French statesman Robert Schuman's vision of creative reconciliation, to which Cox rightly referred as a key starting-point for European integration. After three wars between France and Germany since 1870, and coming from a country still reeling from the bitter legacies of four years of occupation, the courage of Schuman's vision for the future peace of Europe should be honoured.

As Cox recalled, there was no certainty of a positive outcome. Aspirations in Eastern Europe had been quashed before, most bloodily in Budapest in 1956, but also in Prague in 1968 and, more recently, in Poland. Indeed, once the East German government responded by closing their borders and mass demonstrations of protest took place in Leipzig, Dresden and Berlin, such a *denouement* seemed possible, especially in the light of what had recently happened in Beijing's Tiananmen Square. Such an outcome was averted by the Soviet leader, Mikhail Gorbachev, who was not prepared to condone repression. On 9 November, crowds of East Germans crossed the Berlin Wall, setting in hand a sequence of events which progressively spread across Central and Eastern Europe, bringing down the empire which Stalin had created in Eastern Europe and, in the end, the Soviet Union itself. The imminent accession to the European Union of Latvia, Lithuania, Estonia, Poland, the Czech Republic, Slovakia and Hungary on 1 May 2004, under Pat Cox's Presidency, marked nothing less than a revolution in the affairs of Europe, as he said, it was the reuniting of a continent.

A graduate of Trinity College Dublin in 1974, Pat Cox came to public notice as a regular broadcaster with Raidio Telefis Eireann (RTE). As a result of a repositioning of Irish politics in 1985, a new political party, the Progressive Democrats was formed, and he became its first Secretary General and Director of Elections. It was in the Progressive Democrat interest that he was elected to the European Parliament from the Munster constituency in 1989, subsequently standing as an Independent. From 1998 to 2002, he was Leader of the Liberal Democrat group of members. His career in Brussels and Strasbourg was crowned when he became President of the European Parliament in 2002, serving for the statutory two and a half years until 2004. Containing as it does representatives elected from all the member states of the European Union, the role of the Parliament is almost by definition a complex one, and it falls to the President to ensure its effective operation. In a very real sense, the President is the embodiment of the democratic will and aspirations of Europeans as expressed in their Parliament, and to be elected to that office through secret ballot is a particular mark of trust. In his lecture, Pat Cox noted that he could not have been elected without British votes, as well as those of others.

During his Presidency he was, as his lecture emphasised, committed to the principle of European Union enlargement. He noted that the negotiations with Romania and Bulgaria were then on track, and both countries did, in fact, join the Union in 2007. He was also optimistic about the prospects for Croatia, which had emerged out of the debacle surrounding the breakup of Yugoslavia. This country, for centuries linked with Hungary, and then part of the state of Yugoslavia which had emerged after the First World War, had asserted its independence in 1991. Would it become part of the new Europe, helping to signal an end to the bitter conflicts which had convulsed the Balkans? On 9 December 2011, Croatia signed its Accession Treaty and, subject to ratification, was due to become a member of the Union on 1 July 2013. He was more cautious over Turkey, which had first applied for membership in 1987. As a predominantly Muslim country, and with its large and youthful population, Turkey presented the European Union with both challenges and opportunities, not least since its accession would extend the EU's borders to troubled areas of the Caucasus and Middle East. In his speech Cox referred to Europe's existing cultural diversity, which added to its richness. In October 2005, the Union agreed to begin negotiations with the Turkish government, the outcome of which remains to be resolved.

On the Middle East, he observed that an American-led imperium could not be the basis for a sustainable peace, and pleaded for dialogue amongst the states bordering on the Mediterranean. Well aware that the Iraq War had exposed deep divisions in Europe, he argued that these needed to be replaced by a common purpose in foreign policy and defence. He ended with an appeal to the values of Europe, to its commitment to human rights and the rule of law, to the environment and to its record of assistance to the poorest countries in the world. While acknowledging that he could understand those who feared losing control over their own culture and values, he argued that the 'European Union is itself an illustration of this ambition to reconcile people in a common destiny, overcoming the destruction wrought by division, hatred and distrust', exactly what those who had charted its foundation would have wished.

Lecture

I want to thank you for the invitation to address the University of Ulster where John Hume holds the Tip O'Neill Chair in Peace Studies.

It is a particular pleasure in my role as President of the European Parliament to have been asked to give this address at the University of Ulster. It affords both a personal and institutional opportunity to acknowledge the political contribution of one of the European Parliament's outstanding, respected and longest serving members, first elected in the direct elections in 1979.

Just six days before the historic reunification of our continent – when on 1 May our Union will grow from fifteen to twenty-five – and just over a month before the first continental-scale European elections in June, it also provides a platform, at a unique moment of redefinition and renewal, to tell and sell the story of the Europe of values we are building – the story of the process of European integration as a powerful force for transformation and creative reconciliation.

John Hume

John Hume is one of Northern Ireland's eleven-plus generation for whom, like so many of us, education was a key to personal growth and transformation that previous Irish generations were denied. Early involvement in the civil rights movement, inspired by Dr Martin Luther King and others, matured for John into a political vocation of unparalleled influence. He is a graphic illustration, if one needed such, of the power of influence as distinct from the influence of power. With the brief exception of the Sunningdale Executive in the early 1970s he was neither a Prime Minister, a minister nor in government and yet his presence has been both constant and immense.

Tonight is neither the time nor the place and certainly I am not the person to comprehensively assess John Hume's contribution to Irish politics. Yet two outstanding features of his approach commend comment. He intuitively grasped at an early stage the importance of internationalising the Northern Ireland problem and the search for its solution. Encouraging the active engagement of the two sovereign governments, Irish and British, and of the EU and harnessing the potential and goodwill of Irish American diaspora are key achievements of John Hume's dogged political determination. For him, international engagement was essential to break the inertia of insular isolation.

A second insight was John Hume's deep understanding of the real meaning of European integration, not the common view of many in Ireland that the EU was or is about funds or markets alone, but rather he saw it as a model for conflict resolution, peace and reconciliation and constantly expressed his conviction as to its relevance to Northern Ireland.

In a speech in the European Parliament John Hume remarked that from his own experience the three principles at the heart of the European Union are the same three principles at the heart of the Agreement in Northern Ireland. 'Number 1: respect for difference – that is what all conflict is about. Difference should be respected. Number 2: institutions which respect difference, and Number 3: working together in the common interest and by doing so breaking down the barriers of the past'.

It is said come'th the hour come'th the man. For nationalist Ireland in its long and dark hour of travail John Hume was there, steadfastly flying the flag of constitutional politics, of respect for the rule of law over the alternative paramilitary law of the jungle. I am so pleased John Hume is here tonight and I want to say to you, John, on behalf of the European Parliament, how much we respect and thank you for that contribution. Inspired by European integration he tirelessly preached the message of peace and reconciliation.

Inspired by this very special colleague let me turn now to the European Union – the values it espouses and promotes in its internal and external politics – and the process of integration as a powerful force for transformation and creative reconciliation.

Transforming Ireland

It is easy to forget the Ireland of my early childhood only four decades ago.

It is easy to forget that, as recently as 1960, four decades after securing political independence, 75 per cent of Irish trade was still with the old colonial mother country, the United Kingdom. It was a very singular dependency. What did we do with Irish agriculture? We exported almost 90 per cent of it to the United Kingdom and produced cheap food along with the Commonwealth for the urban British market. What did we do with the currency? We linked it to sterling. What did we do with our surplus labour? Our emigrants flooded across to our common labour market with the UK. What did we have as a people? We had political independence but economically we were totally dependent on Great Britain alone. But in effect we were reduced to the status of a stagnant economic region of the wider British economy.

We did not stop there. How did we handle labour relations? We did so in the classic British method of the time – the bosses and the workers didn't get on. It was a process not of partnership, but of confrontation. As a people who gave up its young to emigration we had a diminished sense of our own worth. It was an era when primarily we exported our people rather than sufficient foods and services.

Much has changed in the past forty years. We invested more in the education of our young. Television opened our eyes to a wider world. Slowly and painfully we learned the need for national budget discipline and to overhaul our economic environment at home but politics and public administration too played a vital role. Leaders such as Whitaker, Lemass, Lynch and FitzGerald led us from isolation to connection, led us from the closed to the open, led us from a pervasive sense of failure to an era of opportunity. Ireland's connection to the European Union was at the heart and core of the momentous opportunity. Ireland's connection to the European Union was at the heart and core of that momentous transformation, not singular in its claim to change our circumstances but central and indispensable to it.

In my view the greatest and most creative act of Irish sovereign independence was the moment when through pooling some of our sovereignty we added real value to our small state's influence. It was this movement towards Europe with committed and enlightened leadership and conviction that paved the way for the transformation that brought us from stagnation to opportunity, from inferiority to achievement, from being a failed entity in the British regional economy to being a competitive player on the global market.

Change of context

Europe has had a transforming influence in other ways too. One of the great founding fathers of European integration, Jean Monnet, said, 'when you change the context, you change the problem'. It has taken many years for peace to take root in Northern Ireland and this is primarily due to the commitment and will of political leaders in Northern Ireland itself ably assisted and encouraged by the British and Irish governments, by the United States and the European Union. An important contextual change has been the ease and sense of equivalence with which Irish Taoisigh and British Prime Ministers have worked in the corridors of power in Europe. Old enemies and old practices over time have withered on the vine in the shared new context and so the old problems, all of which have not yet gone away, are being recast in the new order.

In the Republic we do not have the same antagonism regarding our Irish nationalism when we deal with British representatives any more. I could not have been elected President of the European Parliament without British votes among many others.

We have managed to lay to rest ghosts of history because we have been liberated by the changed context. Our independence long sought and struggled for by the dead generations was, in its early decades, claustrophobic and isolated.

Only when we contemplated, prepared and actually connected ourselves by free political will to the European project and to the wider world did this small but vibrant country begin to create the conditions in which we could flourish and flower.

Perhaps for some we may have replaced our post-colonial dependency on Britain with a new dependency on Europe funds; the old quick-fix for selling, indeed under selling, our European adventure was access to funding. European solidarity gifted €37.5 billion of support to Ireland in our first 25 years of membership. It has made an important contribution to modern Irish economic growth, but such funding still was always of secondary importance. Real Irish GNP doubled in the past decade. Structural funds accounted for a very modest proportion of that total.

The muscular economic effect of European integration in Ireland can be found elsewhere in our guaranteed open market access to the European internal market and its additional capacity to attract foreign direct investment. When we joined the EEC in 1973 total Irish exports were worth just under €5 billion a year. By 2001, Irish exports were worth more than €80 billion. Subject to competitiveness, this is sustainable bread and butter economics. It does not need a handout. The extent of our escape from economic dependency on the UK is revealed by our export statistics, as remarked earlier; in 1960 Britain took 75 per cent of Ireland's exports. That singular dependency has been transformed. Though still our largest single export market, Britain's share by 2001, had fallen to 22 per cent of total Irish exports.

The old psychology in Ireland was inferiority. There is always a risk that we may replace it by a new equally doubtful psychology of hubris. The hubris, the arrogant misplaced pride of some who minimise the supportive extent of our openness and interconnection to the wider world while accentuating the presumption that much as we did for ourselves we have done it alone and in future can do it alone. We must avoid any nostalgia for standing alone. Our national self-interest is served by intelligent interdependence, choosing the best of both Boston and Berlin, while still retaining real choices as a people. We should not risk turning off the light and turning back the enlightenment which has made us the most privileged generation of all Irish generations.

A reunited continent – this process of transformation and creative reconciliation is happening on a continental scale

When we look at this snapshot of Ireland, when we look at this process of transformation and reconciliation which has taken place in our own country, we must remind ourselves that it is a process of rebirth and renewal which is taking place on a continental scale.

When I was first elected to the European Parliament in June 1989 our continent was still divided and although the seeds of change were being sown all over Central and Eastern Europe at that time, no one could predict with any certainty what would happen. Indeed many feared that what might happen could have been something very tragic. The experience of Budapest in 1956, Prague in 1968, or the crackdown in the early years of Solidarity in Poland, all indicated that oppression might still assert itself.

As we approach the 1st of May 2004, when our continent will finally be truly reunited and we welcome ten new members into the European Union, I think it is important to remember that sense of excitement and hope which we all felt when the Berlin Wall fell in November 1989. What seemed an impossible dream back in the summer of 1989 will finally become a reality this year.

I think this is a very exciting moment, in terms of the longer, wider European history. It brings us back to the original reasoning as to why we have European integration. People trace many different points of origin, in analytical terms, as to what are the foundations for the modern European Union. But for me, it was the speech on 9 May 1950 by Robert Schuman in the French Foreign Ministry in the Quai d'Orsay in Paris that represents a point of departure, in particular his reference to creative reconciliation.

In Western Europe after the Second World War, there were people who had the courage to look at the big picture. People like Konrad Adenauer, Robert Schuman, Jean Monnet, Paul-Henri Spaak, de Gasperi and others who took the time and who had the leadership, the will and the political and personal determination to think long, think wide and to think big. They did not become lost in the micro petty details but rose above the ashes of that war, seeing hope where there was despair, opportunity where economic breakdown prevailed and seeing in the European project an ideal of reconciliation and progress. This marked them out as a special generation among all the European generations that had gone before.

Today's generation is challenged by a parallel and similar challenge. We are being given the opportunity, on a truly continental scale, though this next enlargement to do what has not been done in Europe's history in millennia – to create a new unity, not at the point of the sword, not through the barrel of a gun but through the free will of free, sovereign, independent peoples.

And that process of integration, of transformation and creative reconciliation, has a wider influence.

Romania and Bulgaria

After the current wave of enlargement, the door to the EU must not be closed. The negotiations with Romania and Bulgaria are on track. The Monitoring reports of the Commission confirmed the differentiated progress of Bulgaria and Romania in their membership preparations. The common objective of accession in 2007 is realistic, and we should not relax our commitment and determination to assist. Nor should we renege on the principle of 'own merits': a candidate state has the right to be assessed on its own merits irrespective of extraneous political considerations. Equally, our engagement requires full reciprocity of effort on the side of the candidate states: we fully expect delivery on what has been promised. It is no secret that certain sectors, particularly administrative and judicial capacity, still require special care and attention.

Turkey

The remarkable progress made by Turkey in the last year, under the leadership of Prime Minister Erdogan, surpasses the efforts made by previous governments over four decades. The enormously positive impetus of the legislative reforms under way is widely acknowledged. Turkey stepped in the direction of satisfying the Copenhagen criteria but as the Commission has pointed out, significant implementation gaps remain and more needs to be done.

Western Balkans

I visited the western Balkan region in the autumn of 2003 and took great encouragement from what I perceived as a new and positive mood, consistent with the European vocation of all the states. We need to encourage and foster the movement towards Europe. We need to encourage the states to cooperate among themselves, not only in economic and trade terms, but in their common battle against organised crime. That new network of cooperative links and working towards shared objectives will itself prove a valuable preparation for membership. We need to encourage the efforts of, for example, Croatia and Macedonia, and acknowledge progress where it has been made.

The historic decision by the European Commission last Wednesday, to recommend Croatia's membership application, sends a very positive signal about the momentum for integration of the Balkan countries into Europe. It is very good news for Croatia, and very good news for the rest of the region.

As well as our success stories there are frustrations and there are areas where we must do more.

Cyprus

As one of the first tasks of my Presidency I travelled to Cyprus on Europe Day, 9 May 2002. When I addressed the House of Representatives in Nicosia, I quoted Schuman about world peace: the part of his 9 May 1950 Declaration that 'world peace cannot be safeguarded without the making of creative efforts proportionate to the dangers which threaten it'. I asked the members of Parliament to reflect on that phrase with me. It talks about peace, it talks about creativity, it talks about efforts being proportionate to the danger. Each of those things has such a resonance in Cyprus, of all places, and each of those things has such a resonance at this moment, with a once-in-a-generation opportunity for a comprehensive settlement.

With the prospect of EU membership, the context of the Cyprus problem has radically changed. We are thirty years on from the traumas of 1974. Now we have a once-in-a-generation opportunity for reconciliation. Expectations of going backwards to some cherished and idealised past are an illusion. Presumptions that a settlement or another deal lies just around the next corner are illusory. If there is no settlement, we will deep-freeze a status quo which all the leaders of Cyprus have been pledging, over thirty years, to change.

When I was in Cyprus, I was able, thanks to the kind assistance of United Nations troops, to walk through the time-warped and weed-covered centre of Nicosia, the zone which is conventionally described as the 'Buffer'. There I saw, in a deserted café, an unfinished bottle of Cypriot wine and several glasses on a table, several overturned chairs, all covered in a thick layer of dust – untouched and un-cleaned for nearly thirty years. Is this the monument the people of Cyprus wish to bequeath to their children, grandchildren and perhaps the unborn generation after them? Do we want to leave Nicosia as the last divided capital in the reconciling Europe of 2004?

I am deeply disappointed at the failure of imagination and courageous leadership exhibited by too many at this time. This is a failure to comprehend the new EU reality of Cyprus. As I said, this is not 1963. This is not 1974. We will have failed if we have not understood the context change of Cyprus' European moment. We will have failed to understand the true import of the European idea. It will be a great pity if our legacy to upcoming generations is an unresolved conflict, when a durable resolution is at hand.

Middle East

Europe must redouble its focus on the Middle East. A US-led imperium in the region cannot be a basis for sustainable peace. Europe is best placed, philosophically, institutionally and politically, to give a lead for peace. The so-called soft security issues of bridge-building, dialogue, reconciliation and reconstruction are the harder issues to deal with, and this is the space where Europe has special experience and capacity and needs to act.

The Euro-Med partnership is, for Europe, a special arena for a dialogue of cultures. A large number of European Union citizens celebrate cultural origins, mainly from the other shore of the Mediterranean, and their different cultures and religions add richness to the European Union.

Our aim is to build a common destiny, necessarily based on each side's recognition of the other with its specific characteristics and its historic contribution to human civilisation. We want to intensify this dialogue of cultures, to diversify its forms and extend its scope. The Euro-Mediterranean partnership offers a new framework in which all issues affecting the societies on both shores form an indivisible whole. Such an ambition is necessarily based on trust and mutual respect, but also on knowledge of each other. Indeed, how can an area of development, peace and stability be built if human beings do not know one another? Mutual ignorance breeds fear. And fear causes alienation.

The European Union is itself an illustration of this ambition to reconcile people in a common destiny, overcoming the destruction wrought by division, hatred and distrust. The European Union can lay some claim to better understanding the desire for dignity and respect in diversity. We can understand those who fear losing control over their own culture and values.

Iraq

If the difficult debate on Iraq taught us anything, it exposed a gap between our aspirations and our capacity to act. At a time when we are looking to the future of Europe, we have to realise that constitutions and institutions will be merely empty vessels, if they are not animated by determined political vision and will. That is the challenge: to breathe new life into our common purpose.

The time has now come for the EU to take a step back and in all serenity to address the question of how to formulate a united and graduated response for dealing with hard cases and tough choices in the domain of foreign policy, security and defence. To do this we need to be honest with each other and recognise the fault lines which lie underneath Europe's Iraqi crisis which, if anything, have not diminished greatly since the end of the Iraq War.

Much of the debate in Europe has been rather a 'house divided against itself'. And a house divided against itself diminishes itself. We must learn and apply the lessons of how to work together to create a greater coherence, a greater presence and a greater balance in terms of international affairs.

We need as Europeans to lift more weight in important international debates. I believe that that is even more true, now, than one year ago. I think we are challenged as Europeans to begin to respond with a wider vision, and bring our message of 'creative reconciliation' with us in the wider world.

Elections

Let me turn now to the first continental scale European elections which will take place in just over a month's time and the message we must tell in our campaigns, in our dealings with the media, in debates within our parties and with our voters.

The June elections will be a unique European moment, unparalleled in terms of scale and diversity, and the first common opportunity to give members of the European Parliament a mandate for a five-year mission to deal with this new Europe – *la grande Europe*, as French commentators refer to it.

We will have elections to the European Parliament from the Atlantic coast of my Munster constituency in Ireland to the eastern borders of the Baltic states – something on a truly continental scale that Europe has never experienced before.

It is my belief that in an earlier generation, in the period of the so-called 'founding fathers' there was a permissive popular consensus regarding the question of European integration. Those people who lived through the dreadful alternative: the Europe of the old imperial days which led to the First World War, the Second World War and the ideological Europe of the Cold War were prepared to support any leadership which envisioned and delivered a new European alternative of reconciliation. But cherished freedoms once gained can soon be discounted by popular opinion. For today's and tomorrow's generation of Europeans, consent must be earned and new narratives found to express enduring ideals.

Campaign on a message which is based on realities

That is why campaigning on a message which is based on realities is indispensable. In having that debate, we must not talk about Europe in some kind of abstract form. We must avoid Euro-speak. We need to speak in plain language, about things which clearly matter to people – not the language of Euro-specialists.

We need to say, for example, that in a world facing so many security threats it clearly makes sense to coordinate our efforts rather than act separately and alone. Europe also can bring added value in fighting international crime and carries real economic weight in the increasingly globalised economy. We need to be able to act in concert because we can do more together than separately.

We also have a generation of young people who are hugely interested in issues such as the environment and sustainability in a way that their mothers and fathers and grandparents were not. And one thing we know for certain is that trans-frontier pollution will not be resolved by individual countries acting alone. Europe is a mobiliser in fields such as this.

Tell the story of a Europe of values/Europe as a force for reconciliation and transformation

Above all, we must talk – in our campaigns – about a Europe that has real meaning, about the Europe of values, not the sterility of a Europe of markets nor the intricacies of the Common Agricultural Policy. Too often and too easily, people slip into thinking that Europe is just a big market for big-time business players and that it has nothing to do with them. Europe stands for much more.

If you look at law-making in the European Parliament, much of it is about the consumer rather than about the big market players. Much of it is about sustainability and the environment. Much of it, also (including the Lisbon Agenda) is about how we can make sure we have sustainable jobs and sustainable growth in our economies. These are not the issues of big business; these are the issues of day-to-day life.

But to give Europe real meaning, we must tell the evolving story of the Europe of values we are building and its power as a force for transformation and creative reconciliation in the world.

We must talk to people about human rights and the rule of law. I am proud that Europe led the way on setting up the International Criminal Court to fight for international human rights. I would prefer any day the due process of an ICC to the absence of process in Guantanamo Bay.

We must talk about our values of solidarity and cohesion. Even though we could do more, the European Union is the largest donor community of aid to the poorest countries on earth – outspending the USA by two and a half to one every year in untied official assistance. We are the biggest donor of humanitarian food aid in the world.

We must tell the story of the Europe of values we believe in and tell the story of the successes we have had.

I am convinced that when you speak in plain language, when you talk about a Europe of values, Europe as a force for transformation and creative reconciliation and a Europe which has a direct impact on their lives – and when you speak with conviction and passion – you can get a response.

That is the challenge for Europe's politicians in the elections this June.

Postscript

Pat Cox retired from the European Parliament in 2004, but not from his interest in European affairs, which he carried forward in his work for the European Movement, and in the campaign for Irish ratification of the Lisbon Treaty.

7

Peace and reconciliation
in the modern world

Senator Hillary Rodham Clinton

Introduction

Then Senator, Hillary Rodham Clinton opened her lecture on 26 August 2004 by saying that it was a 'time of great promise and opportunity for the people of Northern Ireland', when truthfully, many of her listeners there that day would have described a much gloomier picture of an attempt at devolved government that had been stymied for almost a year, with little obvious solution to the impasse in sight. Talks were scheduled for September, 2004, in Leeds Castle; something that she referred to at several points throughout her lecture; however, it would be another twenty-one months before the Stormont Parliament was once more in session.

Worldwide, the picture was not much better: 2004 saw Islamist terrorists strike in Madrid, state violence in Darfur reach genocidal proportions, human rights abuses by coalition forces in Iraq come shamefully to light and the international debate rage over the nature and scope of US global action.

Taking as her theme (what she described as an assignment from 'The Professor'), 'peace and reconciliation in the modern world', what clearly stood out for Senator Clinton was the concept of modernity within the context of contemporary world politics.[1] Modernity, she stated, was representative of positive developments such as human rights, equality, justice and the rule of law, which were under attack from enemies in the shape of 'Neolithic forces' determined to tear that progress to the ground; so that securing peace in Northern Ireland and around the world, she declared, though 'always a noble goal, is now a strategic imperative'. As Senator for New York when the World Trade Center was destroyed by al Qaeda on the 11 September 2001, and steeped in the debate that rumbled, both at home in the United States and globally, surrounding the projection of US power, it was unsurprising that her talk took such a focus.

With the prominence of the US political debate, internationally, and the breakdown of devolution, locally, it was insightful that Clinton chose to tie the two themes together, describing how the modern world presented many more challenges for peace, but how the stakes surrounding its attainment, both in Northern Ireland and around the world, had never been higher; binding success in the province to 'regional, European and even global stability' in the struggle against extremism.

Clinton had, by then, for some time been actively engaged in the foreign policy debate at home in the United States, as per her position as New York's first ever female representative and the first First Lady of the United States to hold an elected office. However, her political acumen was in development many years prior to this date, through both her studies in Political Science at Wellesley College and Law at Yale and her experiences in the US justice system and as a political and civil activist and campaigner for her husband at both state and national levels. As both Arkansas' and America's First Lady she was, perhaps, one of the most activist in US history, taking on briefs that extended to women's rights, education and healthcare and, indeed, as a true partner to her President husband, was involved in many other issues that made up his heavy burden, including Northern Ireland. She spoke, therefore, from a position of unique insight and audience members were treated to an external view that placed local troubles within a global security context, a perspective that many may not have previously contemplated.

In an interesting foil to President Clinton's lecture, which presented listeners with lessons *for* the peace process in Northern Ireland and beyond, Senator Clinton rather drew four lessons *from* events in the province and proceeded to use these to illuminate both the ways in which the United States should conduct its affairs globally and how the people of Northern Ireland might bring themselves beyond the deadlock that they were labouring under at the time.

Her first lesson was that only with sustained and constant engagement can the US help foster peace around the world. This lesson was borne out by America's involvement in the Northern Irish process, which Clinton described as 'essential', and should remind them that the position of 'paramount power' occupied by the United States must be used to bring people together and not simply to threaten the forceful expression of that power in pursuance of a unilateral purpose.

Secondly, she described the contemporary attitude of some in the US body politic that they can and should 'go it alone' as a 'grievous historical mistake'; stating that America can never work too hard to form alliances nor have too many friends. The importance of the deep friendships between the US, Northern Ireland and the Republic were testament, she said, to the truth of this lesson, whilst current problems in the Islamic world highlighted how American ignored it at its peril.

Third, peace requires the foundation and cultivation of inclusive democracies, with particular focus on women, minorities and children. From Northern Ireland we have learned, she stated, that 'peace and reconciliation begin, not by eliminating differences, but by creating the ground of mutual respect' and commented that the people at the grass roots were often far ahead of the politicians in this respect.

Lastly, Clinton observed that peace takes time, but that in the modern world, with its fast pace and media culture, time was often the enemy of peace. Changing deeply entrenched attitudes was not easy, she acknowledged, but if too much time is allowed to go by, in such contexts, people lose hope, they lose faith in their politicians and they lose faith in the process; a clear warning to listeners not to allow their differences to take them backwards along their path.

She ended with the wonderfully paradoxical hope that Northern Ireland's politicians would soon be arguing passionately with one another: over economics, farming, healthcare, education and justice; such matters that participants in *real* democracy fight for.

Lecture

Thank you very much, Chancellor. Thank you very much, Vice-Chancellor, Kieran McLoughlin from The Ireland Funds, my dear friend and mentor in the ways of peace, Professor John Hume, all of you for the great honour that you have bestowed upon me this afternoon.[2] I like the sound of Senator Doctor. I'm not sure that my colleague and majority leader who actually is a doctor, Bill Frist, will like that very much, but, it is indeed a delight and extraordinary opportunity for me to return here to this university on such an auspicious occasion.

I listened carefully to John Hume's words, as I always do, as well as to the other speakers. And it strikes me that once again we meet at a time of great promise and opportunity for the people of Northern Ireland, for indeed this entire island, as well as countless others far beyond your shores. For me, this started during our first visit in 1995. I, of course, had followed the troubles and the challenges, the work and the difficulties that had gone on for so many years before. But when my husband and I came here, as well as Belfast, and saw the hope on the people's faces, we were even more encouraged and determined to do whatever we could, officially and personally, to encourage those who took risks for peace.

Earlier today I had the pleasure of seeing many of the leaders, including the Secretary of State and the leaders of the various parties who will convene again in September under the auspices of the British and Irish governments to continue their pursuit of this most essential and noble goal, creating the peaceful conditions in which individuals can pursue their own God-given potential, make decisions on behalf of themselves and their families, start and grow businesses, pursue education, raise children and watch grandchildren grow in the whites before their eyes. I join with so many others in hoping that the next months see continued progress on behalf of the peace process here in this wonderful and blessed place.

When Professor Hume asked me to deliver the Tip O'Neill lecture, as is often the way when dealing with Professor Hume, he gave me an assignment. It was, well, would you mind coming and delivering the Tip O'Neill lecture on peace and reconciliation in the modern world? Well, that was a mouthful. But, as is the way with those of us who receive the assignments from the Professor, I, of course, said yes. And then I got to thinking, what a subject? Peace and reconciliation in the modern world.

There are many of you in this room, including the Professor, who could lecture us and teach us far beyond anything I might contribute. It also struck me as somewhat of a paradox, peace and reconciliation in the modern world. Is there a difference between peace and reconciliation in the world of the past, in different times and points in human history when peace and reconciliation was either harder or easier? Is there something about the modern world that poses either extra challenges or perhaps greater opportunities in the pursuit of peace and reconciliation? Well, as any good student tries to do, I pondered that at some length since receiving Professor Hume's assignment.

It strikes me that the world has quite changed since 1995 when I was here and certainly when I returned in 1997, to my great honour to be asked to deliver the Joyce McCartan Lecture, and that indeed the modern world is quite at risk, the sense of modernity, the achievements of reason and the rule of law. Those are now under attack from Neolithic forces that have staked their claim to a very different kind of world. In fact, it may be argued that modernity itself, with all of its achievements on behalf of human rights and equal rights and justice, reason and the rule of law, is the real enemy of those who attacked us in New York and those who continue, as we speak even today, to plot and conspire to turn the clock back on the modern world.

Seen in that light, what's at stake here in Northern Ireland goes far beyond the potential for lasting peace, justice, opportunity, economic growth for the people of Northern Ireland. But, indeed, is a signal event in the unfolding challenge that we confront around this world today.

When we first came here, my husband and I, as he reminded you last year during his lecture, the Internet was really just starting to take root. We often marvel at the fact that when Bill became President in 1993, there were fifty sites on the worldwide web used for scientists and researchers. The explosion of information, mostly for good, has been breathtaking. The European Union had not yet moved to a single currency, the economy of our own country was still recovering from stagnation and had not yet seen the explosive growth that marked the 1990s, and so much seemed so long ago, reflecting back on less than a decade.

Today we do live in a world that has been forced closer together, the phenomenon of globalisation makes it possible for us not only to exchange information and ideas with the flick of a mouse, but also for nineteen hijackers to get on airplanes, to use credit cards, to rent automobiles and to wreak horrible destruction and tragic loss on our nation, and then to strike in many other places around our globe. The reasons you have for peace remain compelling, to create a better world for all the children of Northern Ireland, to level the playing field, to remove special privilege, to create equal opportunity. Not to guarantee results, but to guarantee chances. To reward responsibility and hard work and merit.

But now as the need for peace in Northern Ireland goes well beyond local stability, it now speaks to regional, European and even global stability. The need goes not only to the potential of the extraordinary people who call Northern Ireland home, not only here but throughout the world, but to Europe's potential, to the ability to compete and thrive and become and remain prosperous from Belfast to Budapest. I would add yet one more argument. The motive behind the push for peace now goes not only to the security in one's neighbourhood, but also to Europe's security and to global security as well.

This is not to say that one can just wipe away the important historical deeply held reasons why peace is still elusive and requires the hard boring work that Max Weber referred to as politics, 'the slow boring of hard boards'.[3] It takes time. It takes commitment. It is frustrating. What is self-evident to some seems totally foreign to others and yet it must continue, and imbedded in that is the respect for diversity while maintaining and even celebrating individual identity.

When Professor Hume accepted the Nobel Peace Prize in 1998, he said, and I quote, 'I want to see Ireland as an example to men and women everywhere of what can be achieved by living for ideals rather than fighting for them, and by viewing each and every person as worthy of respect and honour'.[4] Those of you who have worked so hard for peace and reconciliation here have so much of value to give to the world. Your experience, your wisdom, your understanding, even with its fits and starts, the peace process in Northern Ireland stands still as a model for conflict resolution in the modern world.

There are many lessons that are being learned from this process, and what has already been accomplished, far more than I have time to list or certainly discuss, but I would like to just talk about four lessons that have particular applicability to my country, but also the global context in which this struggle for peace in Northern Ireland occurs.

First, I think we have learned that only through sustained constant engagement with the rest of the world can the United States help foster peace where tensions exist and democracy is threatened. Second, we have learned that allies matter and we can never work too hard to establish them or have too many friends. Third, we have learned that the road to peace starts with the formation of democracies that are inclusive, that spreads the promise of democracy to all people in society, especially women, children, minorities. And, fourth, we have learned the paradoxical lesson that peace takes time, but that in the modern world, time may not be the friend of peace.

Now, obviously, the circumstances surrounding internal conflict differ in scope and complexity. The conflict in Africa, in the Middle East, in Eastern Europe or South America, or elsewhere, is unique, and each must be spoken to in that manner.

The complexities must be taken into account, but there are common threads and there is an overwhelming reality. Peace, always a noble goal, is now a strategic imperative. If we are to avoid the proliferation of weapons of mass destruction, particularly nuclear weapons, and to stop the spread of Neolithic fundamentalism, then we need to harvest as much peace in as many places as possible so that we may be united in the defence of our fundamental value and way of life.

When I think about these issues today, I obviously bring to this lecture the experience of September the 11th, and particularly my experience in New York. Many of you have friends and relatives in New York, so you know, first-hand, from their description, what that day and its aftermath meant.

I remember at the first annual memorial that we held at Ground Zero when all the names of all the victims were read, the disproportionate number of Irish names, Irish American, Irish citizens, you could hear it. So this is, for me, an experience that transcends our own pain and our own loss and sends a searing message to us all that we are vulnerable, that those who wish us ill are no respecter of person, of nationality, of ethnicity, of religion, of history. They aim to spread death and destruction in as large and public a display as possible. Not with the belief that they can immediately undermine or topple or even demoralise a society, but that they can breed the insecurity, the fear, that so often is a precursor to decline and despair.

On many occasions my husband has quoted the wonderful Seamus Heaney poem that you all know so well, that the hope and history did rhyme line that has meant so much to both he and I as we have struggled with you and encouraged you from afar – and longed-for tidal wave of justice can rise up and 'hope and history rhyme' – but there's another phrase in that poem that hasn't gotten quite so much attention, and that is the line that one can believe 'a further shore is reachable from here'.[5] It may not even be yet in sight, or may be only dimly perceived, but before one starts out on a journey to that further shore, one has to believe that it is there. And that's what the search for and the risk taking for peace requires. That somehow we can make it to that further shore.

With respect to these lessons that I referred to, you know, we're having a great debate in our country over American foreign policy. I don't think that has probably escaped your attention. In that debate, we are looking to define how America uses its power, how we involve ourselves in others' affairs, how we present ourselves to the world, what our values are that we continue to stand for and hopefully promote, not just fight for. It's clear to me that the way we were involved and continue to be encouraging with respect to the peace process in Northern Ireland is a lesson and one that I hope others in our country will take to heart. In part, because of the close link going back through centuries between the Irish and the Americans, there was a ready ground to tread, the four horsemen already mentioned, two of whom are still with us, had a great stake in the process.

No one fought harder for America to be supportive than Tip O'Neill. Tip O'Neill was, as my husband pointed out last year, not only a great politician, but a great man, someone who understood in his fingertips what made people tick, who could see their hopes and aspirations, their fears and insecurities, but who never took advantage of that. One can talk to his colleagues and hear the stories that go on for hours. There isn't a story of meanness, there's not a story of gotcha, there's not a story of superiority, there is this human relationship that he created with practically everyone who came within his reach.

Being a great politician, he understood the principles that are required in the politics of any democracy; that no one can get everything one wants. There is no 100 per cent resolution, not in a democracy, it is to continue working where both the majority and the minority feel they have a stake in the future and should continue to participate. In fact, he has written at length in his writings about the importance of compromise.

Well, when the American involvement began in earnest, it was with a great leap of faith and a fundamental compromise. A compromise that a longstanding policy in our country that many of you recall was quite controversial, that the United States would do business with anyone who was serious about pursuing peace, that one does not, as was memorably said by the late Prime Minister Yitzhak Rabin, make peace with one's friend. So visas were issued, meetings were set up.

There was not a visible shore that we were rowing toward, but there was a belief that one would appear. And so the American involvement was essential, in my view, and I think history will record that. It has remained essential, and I'm delighted that the United States will be present at the meeting in September.

As Thomas Jefferson, one of our founding fathers, referred to in a way that sums up this message about American involvement, we steer our ship with hope, leaving fear astern. Now this is neither the time nor the place for me to discuss differences I might hold with our current government, but I think the peace process in Northern Ireland reminds any government of the United States that our position, our paramount power at this moment in history, argues for an involvement that goes far beyond the threat or use of military power alone, that the use of our position in the world can very well help to bring people together and avoid conflict and pursue peace. I'm hoping that that lesson is learned.

The second is that allies really matter and you can never have too many. There is something of a feeling in the United States today among some that we can go it alone, that our overwhelming power and the rightness of our cause in the eyes of those who have this conviction argues that we proceed whether anyone follows us or not. I think that is a grievous historical mistake.

When we came in 1995, and my husband became the first United States President to visit Northern Ireland, that was a sign, a symbol, if you will, that the people of Northern Ireland and the Republic had an ally, had a friend. We fought together as allies in the war, John was reminding me of the great base that is here, and you were there for us immediately after September the 11th. In fact, it was the Irish who were among the first to institute a day of mourning, and we are profoundly grateful for your love and support. The Taoiseach and the Republic led the people of Ireland in that official day of mourning, and Prime Minister Blair came to Washington to show the solidarity of the British people.

So we will work to remain friends and allies, but friends and allies cannot take each other for granted. They have to be, every day, looking for new ways to forge deeper and stronger bonds. That's why I've worked very hard to continue to build up the relationships between my country and my state with Northern Ireland and the Republic. But, in addition to the personal relationships that are created and the symbolic impact that results, the importance of allies cannot be overstated in the world in which we find ourselves today.

We are engaged in a battle for hearts and minds in the Islamic world. We are in very difficult situations in Afghanistan and Iraq and they ripple out through the broader Middle East and far beyond. Not having allies to stand with you and validate you and help you reach out and make those arguments to win over hearts and minds is counterproductive, and we are finding that. Many of us warned about that early on, and now we see the importance that allies have in a battle for democracy where people are choosing sides, literally, every day.

US engagement in the world is a two-way street. We not only need to be more willing to work with other nations, but, our friends and allies and like-minded peoples around the world also need to recognise the challenges that we face. A failure to build a secure, free Iraq has troubling implications, not just for the Iraqi people, or the Americans, but for Europe, for the Islamic world and so many more.

A failure would mean even more chaos in the Middle East, more anger and opposition for the West, in the Muslim world, and, therefore, I believe we need a new commitment, not only with respect to the specifics of Iraq and Afghanistan, but on broader basis to re-write the rules of international involvement.

We need to think through more clearly, what does peacekeeping mean? What is the role of the United Nations today? Do we need new security institutions? How will we work to help the development needs? I was very impressed to learn both in my visit yesterday in Dublin and then the day before in Reykjavik, the commitment of both the Icelandic and the Irish government to increase their development aid, to recognise that we have a stake in scourges like HIV AIDS, in the failure to educate girls, in the problems of economic empowerment that stand in the way of individuals making a decent living for themselves and their families.

So this is a time for people of good faith to put aside their objections and concerns about our policy to date and begin meeting together, like those grateful did so long ago with respect to the Irish peace process, about how we will promote peace and reconciliation in practical achievable steps. The institutions that stood up so well the last half of the twentieth century are not up to the task in the twenty-first, and we need to admit that and to go about the business of revitalising them, reforming them or creating new ones because we desperately must have an international framework in which we pursue democracy, freedom and human rights.

Lesson three, with respect to inclusive democracies follows from this. You know, peace and reconciliation begin not by eliminating differences, but by creating the ground of mutual respect. The parties in Northern Ireland, as the Agreement states, are, and I quote, committed to partnership, equality, and mutual respect as the basis of relationships. This foundation is essential and is built not just by agreements or by political leaders, but by private sector leaders, by academic leaders, by religious leaders. It is built in neighbourhoods. It is built in the peacekeeping work that is done by individuals one to another.

That's why I was so impressed by the work done by Joyce McCartan, a woman who did her part to bring both traditions together. For her efforts she was often called a troublemaker, but she was not a troublemaker, she was a peacemaker, and she was brave and I miss her voice even today. There are examples all over the North of people ahead of the peace process. They are not waiting for all of the strand one and strand two issues to be sorted out, they're going about the business of working with one another and beginning the process of trusting one another.

Here in Derry, for example, a wonderful garden project was launched last March at the Foyleside centre. It includes the Cathedral Youth Club in the Fountain and the Long Tower Youth Club, Brandywell. These young people are planting seeds, growing thriving plants and, at the same time, in a metaphoric way, are planting the seeds of reconciliation. We need hundreds of projects like that because sometimes it takes the people to reinforce the vote, as John referred to, the votes in favour of peace on behalf of the agreements, that is still the message that the people have sent to the leaders and we need to heed that message and we need more people to create the conditions that will enable the leaders to act to fulfil it.

It is also important to ensure that women have a place at the table. Joyce was just one of the many women I have met in my business here who has been a peacemaker in her own way, quietly, often shunning the spotlight, not seeking it, but working person to person to create those bonds. I was delighted this morning to have the opportunity to meet with a large group of women brought together by the Vital Voices Democracy Initiative and hear from them about the issues that they are worried about.

The contrast between my first meeting with women, back in 1995, and this, was clear and extraordinarily gratifying. That first meeting with Joyce McCartan and a small group of women was largely devoted to the pain they had experienced, the losses they had seen. Every woman around that table of both traditions telling me in excruciating detail how her son went out one day and never came back, how every time her husband left for work she prayed he'd return home safely. The first question today at the City Hall in Belfast was from a woman who said, how do we do everything we want to do, combine our family responsibilities, our work responsibilities, it was a personal question about personal opportunity and growth.

We got to some of the others, but it was such a stark contrast. That in Belfast today, when I walked in to the Europa Hotel, and the manager said, we are at 100 per cent occupancy, I can remember in 1995 when we stayed in that hotel and part of it was covered with scaffolding and plastic sheets because it had been damaged so badly. When someone else told me that $800 million of private investments has come to Belfast alone, when the tourists I met were there from not just the United States, visiting friends and relatives, but from all over Europe and Australia, and the immigration to Northern Ireland, because people believe here is a land of hope and opportunity, has increased dramatically. So there is so much good news that I can see with my own eyes.

But the final lesson, the paradoxical one, that peace takes time, but time may not be a friend of peace, is what I would leave you with. Of course changing deeply held beliefs is not easy. Change is never easy, whether it is on a personal level or in a family, a business, certainly in a society. And where there is so much pain that people can rightly point to as a reason for not changing, it becomes even harder.

I thought to myself, what would have been the experience here in the North if the 3,200 people who have died in the last thirty-five years all died on the same day as nearly 3,000 did on September the 11th? Instead, it's been private and personal lives, it's been individual funerals, it's been the mourning of the wife, and the daughter, and the mother, and it's stretched over so many years.

So there's no big event, no overwhelming tragedy to point to, and yet the loss and the pain that each person legitimately feels who can tell you about someone who didn't come home is as real as the loss that we experienced, collectively, on September the 11th. If it's your husband who doesn't come home, it doesn't matter if he was the only casualty or one of 2,800 plus.

So time is an element that has to be taken into account, but I would urge those who are part of the process to think seriously about the opportunity that is provided by the meetings in September. There are tough issues to be worked out. The democratic institutions of Northern Ireland have to be discussed, how will the Assembly and the Executive be stood up, the thorny, continuing problems of decommissioning and policing and justice and human rights, of implementing the rest of the tenets of the agreement are serious ones that have to be taken and worked through. But if too much time goes by people lose hope. They lose faith in their leaders. And they lose faith in the democratic political process, which is not only, in my view, a loss for Northern Ireland, but it's a loss for democracy, it's a step backwards for showing that our way of life, our way of decisionmaking, our way of governing works in a complex modern world.

Now there is much said, conspires against these decisions being made. Some of them rooted in the soils here in Northern Ireland, and unique to the problems and the history that you know so well. But there are larger trends at work that I also think are worth mentioning. One is in the media environment that exists in our world today. Extremism, or at least the holding of absolutist views, or, in our parlance, black or white, is encouraged. If you are a modern politician in a modern media environment, as we all are today, there is no place left in the world, I think, without it, you are rewarded for being somewhat extremist, somewhat obstreperous, you're much more entertaining that way.

I have colleagues in the United States Senate who are among the most thoughtful, accomplished people in that body, but television stations don't want to book them because they are too thoughtful and too reasonable. They don't come out into television and call their opponents names or come up with sharp and witty personally destructive things to say. They come to talk about solving issues and problems. So the media environment makes it very difficult to do hard work and we have to overcome that in some fashion, as it's true for my country as it is for this society and others which unfortunately seem to be adapting to some of the worst of our media practices.

Going hand in hand with that is the idea that compromise is weakness, that if you don't hold your ground and stick to it regardless of evidence, you are somehow weak and unworthy of leadership. I have said often in the last three and one-half years that the current administration in Washington seems to intend to turn our capital into an evidence-free zone, where facts and information are viewed as troubling to the overall objection of full speed ahead no matter what the evidence might be. I can only remind us that Tip O'Neill says in his book, in the chapter entitled 'Compromise is the art of politics', that the hardest part of leadership is compromise.

People often think when you compromise you are compromising your morals and your principles. That's not what political compromise is. Political compromise is deferring your ideas so a majority can be reached. That's what makes our system and any democratic system work over the long term, and there can only be achievement through compromise if it is to be lasting achievement.

Thomas Cahill wrote a book entitled *How the Irish Saved Civilization*. It's a wonderful book. I don't want your heads to swell, but you might want to refer to it from time to time. The book is begun with a quote from Reinhold Niebuhr, 'Nothing that is worth doing can be achieved in our lifetime, therefore, we must be saved by hope. Nothing which is true or beautiful or good makes complete sense in any immediate context of history, therefore, we must be saved by faith. Nothing we do, however virtuous, can be accomplished alone, therefore, we must be saved by love'.[6] These are words that come out of our Judeo Christian tradition. They come out of our democratic experience, those of us fortunate enough to have been born in and come to age in a democracy. Those are the guiding principles that can lead Northern Ireland to a true democracy where the majority and the minority understand each has a stake in a positive and better future.

We've done so much together. I hope that the next months enable us to reach that further shore and I hope that first and foremost, for the people of the north, and for all the Irish people, wherever they may reside, who consider this beautiful island their home, their heart, but I also hope you reach that shore because we need you to. We are in a new and difficult world, whether progress continues is really up to all of us and it requires unity of purpose and commitment to stand for the fundamental principles that underlie the Good Friday Agreement.

I am very hopeful, I could not be in the business I'm in if I were not, and I hope that this time next year you'll be arguing about all the things people in democracies argue about. Are we moving too slow or too fast in economic development? What should or shouldn't be the government's role in education? How will we provide healthcare that guarantees the best possible treatment for the greatest number of people? What will the agricultural policy be? How will we ensure that policing is done in a way that creates confidence and trust? These are the problems that a democracy should argue over, but we have to get to that point and many of us are hoping and praying that day will come soon and that we can all celebrate the accomplishment together.

Thank you and God bless you.

Postscript

Senator Clinton went on to become the most popular female contender to run for the office of US President, eventually losing out to Barack Obama in the Democratic race for candidacy. Since then she has taken up the commanding position of US Secretary of State in the Obama administration from 2009 to 2013, where she was a leading advocate of the 'soft' power approach to the conduct of international affairs. She continues to advocate for peace and progress in Ireland, north and south, through nurturing good economic and political relations between the US, Ireland and the UK.

Notes

1 'The Professor', of course, refers to Professor John Hume under whose auspices, as the holder of the Tip O'Neill Chair in Peace Studies at the University of Ulster's Magee Campus, Senator Clinton was invited to speak.
2 The Honorary Degree of Doctor of Laws had been conferred on Senator Clinton on the occasion of her visit to the University.
3 *From Max Weber: Essays in Sociology*, translated by H. H. Gerth and Wright Mills, The International Library of Sociology (London: Routledge and Kegan Paul Limited, 1949), p. 128.
4 John Hume, Nobel Lecture, Oslo, 10 December 1998, © The Nobel Foundation, www.nobelprize.org/nobel_prizes/peace/laureates/1998/hume-lecture.html (last accessed 13 February 2013).
5 Seamus Heaney, *The Cure at Troy* (Derry: Field Day, 1990), p. 77.
6 Quoted in Thomas Cahill, *How the Irish Saved Civilization: The Untold Story of Ireland's Heroic Role from the Fall of Rome to the Rise of Medieval Europe* (New York: Nan A. Talese, 1995).

8

Learning the lessons of peacebuilding

Secretary-General Kofi Annan

Introduction

When Secretary-General Kofi Annan addressed his unquestionable expertise to the lessons of peacebuilding on the 18 October 2004, in mind no doubt were the many conflicts that the United Nations has confronted, both over its institutional history and also during his many different incarnations within the organisation, as well as the ongoing problems being met by nation-building operations in both Afghanistan and Iraq and the hampered efforts to stem conflict and massacre in the Sudanese province of Darfur.

Peace operations are not defined in the UN Charter. Peacekeeping developed incrementally in response to various crises starting in the Middle East in 1948. Although the first multidimensional peacekeeping operation was set up in the Congo in 1960, the superpower standoff that characterised the Cold War severely constrained the mandates of peacekeeping. However, at the end of the Cold War period, the demand for and of UN peacekeeping, enforcement and building simply exploded. The mixed successes and, some might comment, disasters of these operations then engendered their own lessons; but the UN moved on and continued its work, attempting, as an institution, to bring all of these lessons to bear.

Annan, himself, began his education in global engagement long before joining the UN. Indeed, the one key value that he left Mfantsipim School in Cape Coast with was the idea that suffering anywhere on the globe was a concern for all of the peoples of the globe. His education brought him around that globe from his native Ghana, to Europe, to the United States, where he became a true internationalist. He then worked his way up through the organisation that he came to head, learning many lessons about the right way to do things during his long career.

Joining the UN in 1962 he held a number of positions in Geneva, at the World Health Organisation and the UNHCR where that core lesson from his school days was put into action. From there he moved to UN headquarters where he held a number of posts before taking the reins of an expanding peacekeeping department as Under-Secretary General for Peacekeeping (1992–1996), at a time when the organisation was responsible for more, larger, ambitious operations than ever before in its history. His handling of events during his tenure at the Department of Peacekeeping Operations (DPKO) won him fans around the world and so when the time came to find a new UN chief he won the votes to become Secretary-General from 1997–2006, during which time he was named, along with the organisation that he served, as 2001's Nobel Peace Prize winner. Indeed, he was once described by US diplomat Richard Holbrooke as the 'best Secretary-General the UN has ever had'.[1]

During his time as Secretary-General he radically reformed the organisation, streamlining the bureaucracy, increasing efficiency and getting capital flowing again. He also dealt with many international crises and conflicts and attempted to alter international opinion with regard to humanitarian intervention and peace operations; something that he would develop further in the time that followed his delivery of this lecture, with the advent of the 'Responsibility to Protect' doctrine.

It was within this expert context that Kofi Annan situated his address, beginning, as he did, by emphasising the fact that in dealing with any conflict situation there is no 'one size fits all' solution; all are different. In spite of this pertinent fact, he told listeners, there are several lessons that can be applied in all peace operations. First of all, the UN must be aware of its own limitations. States sometimes use a UN resolution, mission or the organisation, in a more general way, as a smoke screen for their own inaction. Consequently, the Secretary-General should not commit the organisation to action that a lack of political will may doom to failure; an uncomfortable and imperfect lesson from an uncomfortable and imperfect international system.

No external party, he cautioned, can become engaged in conflict resolution or peacebuilding while physical conflict rages all around it and whilst its employees are under severe personal threat, and those missions that organisations, like the UN, *do* commit to must have clear and achievable aims and a vision of how an end-state will be decided, if not a clear vision of that end-state itself.

External parties to any conflict must truly understand the context of each trouble spot in which they become involved. The international community, Annan advised us, cannot determine what can be done, or must be done, in order to achieve and build peace if it does not understand what caused, or what is at stake in, the conflict in the first place.

He warned that the UN must take care with the expectations placed on it by all parties involved in a conflict, both within a conflict zone

102   *Kofi Annan*

and in the wider international community. As Mats R. Berdal wrote: 'too often periods of misguided idealism have given way to exaggerated periods of disappointment'; a point that the problems of 1990s peace operations which had been preceded by such euphoric optimism must have driven home, during his time at the DPKO.[2]

Linked to this lesson was Annan's avowal that building peace was a long-term commitment. Therefore, it must be impressed upon all involved that such an endeavour, of necessity, takes time. If radical changes and results were expected right away both internal and external participants may become disenchanted and disengage from the process, condemning it to failure. Additionally, peacebuilding exercises must also be approached in the correct order; building each piece of the puzzle, one on top of the other, towards a peaceful society. Attempting to do things out of sequence will not result in any lasting success.

Finally, Annan placed the onus for achieving peace firmly upon the shoulders of the people within any conflict zone: '[n]o conflict', he said, 'can be overcome by the good will of the outsiders alone'; a lesson, no doubt, garnered from his own experiences of 1990s peace operations in Bosnia, Somalia, as well as his more recent encounters in Syria.

He ended with an exhortation. The most important lesson of all is to keep on learning; to be ceaseless in the quest for improvement. He could not be more right. When lives hang in the balance, action must be apt, sober, judicious, serious, considered and united.

Lecture

Thank you, John [Hume] for that kind introduction.

My short talk today is about learning – not teaching. The question I want to examine with you is, how can outsiders best contribute to the process of building peace in war-torn societies?

Such a process must, by its very nature, be deeply rooted in local communities and local identities. Outsiders, however well-intentioned, do not know best. The people of the country or region concerned must feel that it is their process, if it is to have any hope of success. Yet I believe that outsiders can help, particularly if they learn the right lessons from their own experience, and apply them in a sensitive way.

Let me again start by saying how deeply moved and gratified I am to be giving the Tip O' Neill Lecture at this distinguished university. But, please do not take my general observations about peacebuilding as oblique comments on your own problems. You have been managing those without help from the United Nations. You have well-established mechanisms to do so. And we have an equally well-established policy of not seeking to duplicate such mechanisms.

I don't mean to imply that you have solved all your problems. There are many, I know, that you are still wrestling with. But it does seem to me that you are managing them better and more hopefully than in the past. For some years now you have been spared the large-scale violence and terror that used to disfigure your beautiful part of the country and seemed to blight its future. Your efforts to create a better world for your children have been a source of inspiration and hope to people in many other countries. If the world is to learn lessons about how to manage a transition from troubles and violence to peace, surely it can learn some of them from you – from your commitment, courage and imagination in seeking solutions and fostering trust between communities which had been at loggerheads for decades.

Which brings me back to my theme. Since the end of the Cold War, our member states have set the United Nations to work in many fractured and war-torn societies. We are no longer asked, as we used to be, just to 'keep the peace' by helping maintain a ceasefire. Now, increasingly, we are tasked with going beyond that, to engage in conflict resolution. This means tackling root causes. It means trying to help the people in those fractured societies to work together to build a lasting peace. And I believe we have learnt some valuable lessons, if only by the painful method of trial and error.

For one thing, we have learnt to approach this whole topic with considerable caution. A great Northern Irish poet [Louis MacNeice] once wrote: 'World is crazier and, more of it than we think,/Incorrigibly plural'.[3]

And that is certainly true of war-torn societies. Each has its own particularity, born of its own – often very local – history, culture and religion and ethnicity. There is no 'one size fits all'.

So there are no easy lessons and very few uncontested ones. There is now a huge literature about post-conflict peacebuilding. It deals, for instance, with secession and partition; with spoilers; with transitional justice, truth commissions and reconciliation; with elections and power-sharing; with the rule of law; with economic liberalisation, reconstruction and development; even with international administration or trusteeship. All these issues have spawned intense debate. Some would put the emphasis on eliminating root causes and dealing with spoilers. Others would give primacy to the need for swift economic growth and reconstruction, arguing that lapses back into conflict are much more common in very poor societies. The debate remains unresolved, because we are all still learning, and it may take some time before the various approaches can be reconciled.

In the last fifteen years or so, the United Nations has developed a considerable body of experience of managing and resolving conflict, as well as of peacebuilding. But we should acknowledge that our record has been mixed. Among the successes I would mention particularly are Namibia, South Africa, Mozambique, El Salvador, eastern Slavonia, Guatemala and East Timor. The failures, alas, often receive more publicity – especially those of the early and mid-1990s, Somalia, Bosnia, Rwanda and Angola. I do not think it coincidental that, in the case of failures, either there was no peace to keep or peace agreements proved fragile because the underlying causes of conflict had not been resolved. We have learned useful lessons from both our successes and failures, and are doing our best to put those lessons into practice.

What are these lessons? Let me suggest nine that are well worth considering.

• First, we should say no when we need to.

We must know the limits of what is achievable by the United Nations. We should be especially careful not to allow ourselves to be used as a fig leaf for lack of political will by the international community to deal effectively with an issue. If the Security Council seeks to give the Secretary-General a mandate which he believes to be unachievable, especially if coupled with means which he knows to be inadequate, he should say so clearly and in advance. I believe that we have learnt that lesson, uncomfortable though it may be.

• Second, know where you are going.

Our most successful experiences have started from a clear and achievable mandate. In post-conflict work, this means the clearest vision of the end-state – or at least, a clear understanding, accepted by all parties, of how and when the end-state will eventually be decided.

In your own case, I know, you have agreed that the decision must be based on the fundamental democratic principle of the consent of the governed.

In East Timor, the task of the United Nations was made much easier by the fact that the goal of independence, the interim UN stewardship and the authority vested in us during that time, were all established from the outset. The same was true, before that, in Namibia.

Contrast that with the situation in Kosovo, where there is profound disagreement about the end-state, and the method for deciding it, not only between the former belligerents but also among international actors.

• Third, know the context.

Here I return to Louis MacNeice and his 'drunkenness of things being various'.[4] The specificity of a conflict will determine what can be done and when. In Nicaragua and South Africa, we were able to help with elections, in countries that were ripe for elections. But in the Democratic Republic of the Congo, where three-and-a-half-million have died in six years of war, careful and thorough preparations are needed before elections go ahead. In post-conflict situations, elections work best when they are the result of a political consensus as to their objectives. In the absence of such consensus, the parties often feel under no obligation to honour commitments they have entered into. They don't respect the rules of the game because they haven't really acquired the rules of the game.

I wish I could tell you that the United Nations, and in particular the Security Council, was always attuned to the context – to the hard questions of what drove the killing, and what drove the end to the killing. Too often it has not been so attuned, and people in the countries concerned have paid the price. The bottom line, I am convinced, is that we need to be closer to those whose peace it is, to make or break.

• Fourth, never neglect security

This is the point closest to achieving consensus among experienced peacebuilders: most of the tasks that we call peacebuilding can only be carried out where there is already a reasonable level of physical security.

Of course, that begs the question of what level any given society will consider 'reasonable' – and also of how you get there. In some cases security can be achieved purely by negotiation or dialogue between the warring parties; in others you need a stabilisation force, with robust rules of engagement.

But it is none the less true: without security almost everything else is impossible; no effective government; no reconstruction; no return of refugees; no return to school; no elections.

• Fifth, manage expectations.

There is a moment, when the killing stops, when everything seems possible. Expectations run high.

That can be dangerous, because the road to peace often proves long and hard. The various elements of peacebuilding – transforming suspicion into trust, recrafting state institutions, reconstructing war-torn economies – can take years or decades to accomplish. During that time people's hope, and their faith in the process, need to be sustained.

So expectations need to be managed from the beginning, and throughout the process – which requires a major effort of public information and education by the peacebuilders.

In particular, it is vital to explain what the United Nations is there to do, and what it cannot do. Otherwise expectations are unrealistic, and they are inevitably disappointed. When disillusion sets in, the people can easily turn against the very peace agreement they had first welcomed,

• Sixth, stay on course – peacebuilding is a long-term commitment.

This lesson follows from the previous one. Nearly half of all peace agreements collapse within five years. Others fall into a sort of limbo of no war, no peace. In the life of almost every peace process, there comes a time – usually three to seven years out – when disillusionment is high, when the wheels seem to be turning without any real forward movement. Fatally, this often coincides with the waning of outside interest. Political engagement and financial support are drawn down, just when a process needs a second wind.

Hard-worn arguments on human rights and the reform of justice are often eroded once domestic and international attention diminishes. In Guatemala, securing such reforms, which were crucial to moving the country beyond the mere absence of warfare toward consolidated peace, was the hardest part.

In Haiti, we had a peacekeeping mission in the mid-1990s, and trained a new police force. And then we left – along with other international institutions – before a viable peace had taken root. Now we are back, with much of what we did before swept away – almost literally, as the recent flash floods have laid bare the legacy of years of misrule.

The lesson – a very important one – is that everyone needs to stay engaged: the Security Council; member states; international NGOs; and of course the former parties to the conflict; and the people themselves, who are the most essential actors in any peacebuilding process.

At least there are signs that the international community is now learning that lesson.

We are staying the course better today in places like Sierra Leone and East Timor. And we are structuring our new mission in Haiti for the long term.

• Seventh, get the sequencing right.

One of the things we have learnt, from the painful experience, is the peril of trying to do things in the wrong order. For instance: before there can be meaningful elections, there must be respect for the law, and some shared understanding of what the result will mean and how power will be distributed. We learned that lesson the hard way in Angola.

Before there can be full economic liberalisation, there must be some social stability. We have learned how disastrous it can be to introduce policies, however sound in the long term, which cause high short-term unemployment while large numbers of people still have weapons, and little or no stake in the peace-time economy. In such circumstances, surely what we need is not stringent structural adjustment but poor-friendly and peace-friendly policies on the part of the international financial institutions.

And before the international community disengages, there must be a growing economy. It should be no surprise that in the poorest countries, with little or no economic growth, like Haiti and Liberia, peace processes failed and conflicts lapsed back into violence.

• Eighth, keep everyone on the same page.

We have had massive interventions in the past which failed, or came close to it, because they were too fragmented. The system is now working in a more coherent way. We are reaching out to our colleagues in the United Nations family, to NGOs, to the broader international community and also to the local population in the countries where we work, to make sure that we are all on the same page, both in setting our priorities and in the way we carry them out.

• Finally, local populations should take responsibility – it is they who must live with the peace.

There are many situations in which it seems easier, for everyone, to let outsiders take the lead – to draft the laws; to run the elections, or the courts; to make the hard economic choices. But unless those who will live with the effects of decisions have a real part in taking them, the decisions will sooner or later be put aside.

No conflict can be overcome by the goodwill of the outsiders alone. Those who live with it understand the dynamics better than any international player. Those who live with it must be involved in the effort to end it, and must see benefits that justify the compromises and sacrifices involved.

This is a list that could go on. There are lessons, for example, about greed as well as grievance. Whatever the origins of a conflict, it often cannot be ended without cutting off the resources that sustain it – and providing the fighters with an alternative, peaceful means of earning their living. Nowadays we no longer contemplate demobilisation and disarmament – the two 'D's' – without adding an 'R', which stands for reintegration into the civilian economy. Without this, it is a virtual certainty that new weapons will be acquired and violence will resume. And there is also, of course, the need for reconciliation, which cannot work unless the victims of atrocities feel that they have obtained justice, or at least a full acknowledgement of past wrongs. Absent such a reckoning, there is a lingering sense of unfinished business, and in the long run this can be destabilising.

Let me end by saying that the most important lesson of all – for me personally, and for the United Nations as an organisation – is that we must always be listening and looking out for new knowledge. Ladies and gentlemen, let us learn those lessons. And let us employ them in our future peace operations, as we work together to try to make the world a better and safer place, for our own sakes and for our children.

Postscript

Kofi Annan has remained actively engaged in global issues since his tenure at the United Nations ended in 2006, with his involvement in educational and not-for-profit work on leadership, the environment, humanitarianism and the mediation and resolution of conflict. He created the Kofi Annan Foundation in 2007 to progress universal efforts towards peace, security and sustainable development. In 2008 he assisted in bringing to an end civil unrest in Kenya and in 2012 he was appointed as Joint Envoy to Syria by the UN and the Arab League.

Notes

1 Holbrooke, Richard, 'Foreign Policy. The FP Top 100 Global Thinkers', Special Report, December 2009, www.foreignpolicy.com/articles/2009/11/30/the_fp_top_100_global_thinkers?page=full (last accessed 26 February 2013).
2 Berdal, Mats R., 'Fateful encounter: the United States and UN peacekeeping', *Survival*, 36:1 (1994), 48.
3 Louis MacNeice, 'Snow', *Collected Poems* (London: Faber and Faber Limited, 1966).
4 MacNeice, 'Snow'.

9

Europe's role in world peace

Dr Garret FitzGerald

Introduction

Few politicians had a greater claim to speak on the subject of 'Europe's role in world peace' than Dr Garret FitzGerald. Perhaps his academic training at University College Dublin, from which he graduated with a BA in History, French and Spanish, and became President of the French Society, was an indication of where his interests would turn. During his formative university years in the Second World War, Ireland was largely isolated from the rest of Europe, but he took an avid interest in the course of events, recording his excitement at being able to follow on an underground radio from Paris the historic events of the city's liberation on 25 August 1944. A career as a research and statistical officer with the national airline Aer Lingus meant that economics increasingly engaged his attention, leading to an academic appointment in the subject at UCD in 1959, subsequently gaining his PhD. As his interest in economics grew, he had come to question the continuing worth of the protectionist policies that the country had followed since the 1930s. Increasingly his attention was drawn to the newly established European Economic Community (EEC), which became the European Union on 1 November 1993 when the Maastricht Treaty, which had been concluded the previous year, came into effect. In 1959, he became Chairperson of the Irish Council of the European Movement, editing and writing its news bulletin, and welcoming to Dublin the first President of the Commission, Dr Walter Hallstein.[1]

From 1965 onwards, he was increasingly to the fore in the country's political life, at first as a Fine Gael member of the Seanad, and then from 1969 as the party's representative from Dublin South East in Dail Eireann. His entry into active politics coincided with Ireland's attempts, along with those of the United Kingdom and Denmark, to gain entry to the EEC. He devoted a chapter of his 1972 book *Towards a New Ireland* to an exploration of what membership would mean for the country, especially the implications for relations between the Republic and Northern Ireland.[2] The opportunity to pursue Ireland's future within the EEC came the following year when he was appointed Minister of Foreign Affairs in the Fine Gael–Labour coalition government of Liam Cosgrave. Only a few weeks previously, on 1 January 1973, Ireland, together with the United Kingdom and Denmark, had formally joined the Community.

It was a critical time in Anglo-Irish relations, with the complex negotiations leading to the Sunningdale conference of 6–9 December 1973, in which he was fully involved. The Sunningdale Agreement, which involved the British and Irish governments, the Ulster Unionist Party, the Social Democratic and Labour Party, and the Alliance Party, sought to link the newly established power-sharing executive in Belfast and the Irish government in a Council of Ireland. The new dispensation did not survive the Ulster Workers Council strike the following May. Its failure resulted in the end of devolved government until the implementation of the structures which came into place after 1998.[3] Even so, he was also concerned with wider EEC issues, including relations with the United States, and involvement in the critical and contentious politics of the Middle East, where Ireland put its weight behind some recognition of Palestinian aspirations, which lay at the heart of the region's problems.

The climax of his political career came in the 1980s, when he headed two coalition governments, from July 1981 until the following February, and then again from December 1982 to June 1987. As Taoiseach, he was at the centre of two major political initiatives, the New Ireland Forum and the 1985 Anglo-Irish Agreement, which set a new context for constitutional nationalist aspirations in Ireland. The lecture he delivered on 15 December 2005 was the mature reflection of a political veteran whose interest in, and commitment to, European affairs had begun in his student days during the Second World War, which reflected his academic background in history and economics, and which was informed by his experience of international affairs at the highest level.

Informed as it was by his wide reading of history and economics, Dr FitzGerald's lecture surveyed what he rightly described as 'Europe's inglorious history of war', relating this to the ruined state of the continent in 1945, and how its states learned the lesson that they had to work together through the mechanism of the European Union. He focused particularly on what he called Europe's seven value reversals; namely, a commitment to international law; supra-national supervision of human rights by the Strasbourg Court; the creation of a European Zone of Peace and the dedication of European national armies to peacekeeping and peacemaking; the substitution of aid for colonialism; the abolition of capital punishment; global ecological action; and the International Criminal Court. In several of these initiatives he contrasted European attitudes with those of the United States. He traced the steps by which Europe had gradually moved towards a common foreign policy, meeting the challenges created by the collapse of Soviet power in Eastern Europe. He argued that the reason why the long-standing rivalries of the region did not erupt was because of the attractive power of the EU, the exception, of course, being what he described as 'the Yugoslav Debacle' in the western Balkans. The deep divisions amongst European states over the Iraq War had resulted in moves for a common approach to post-war Iraq. He identified ten peacekeeping missions which the EU had undertaken in a range of countries in Europe, Asia and Africa, and raised questions about the validity of Ireland's concept of neutrality. Despite demographic and other pressures, his message was the essentially positive one that the 'result of all this rapidly developing peacekeeping and peace enforcement activity is that Europe is now an extraordinary positive force in the world'.

Lecture

Introduction

Europe was heavily engaged in spreading war outside its own boundaries from at least the early sixteenth century – and, recalling the Crusades some would say from the late eleventh century – until the middle of the twentieth century. Only during the past half-century has that unhappy process been turned on its head, so that today we can, with credibility, speak and write about Europe's role in spreading peace.

First, what brought about this reversal of roles?

Second, how is Europe exercising this new and beneficent role: by example, or by action – or both?

Third, how can we hope that this new role for Europe will develop in the decades ahead – bearing in mind that in terms of its share of world population and economic strength this small continent of ours clearly has a rapidly diminishing weight in the world.

Europe's inglorious history of war

Although for several millennia Europe's civilisation in many respects lagged behind those of China and Japan, from the sixteenth century onwards a combination of technological developments and the crude energies of our continent's peoples, mainly Indo-European in language and culture, served to stimulate a move towards European world dominance – which until early in the last century was fed by competition between rival hereditary leadership families – monarchs – persistently and violently disputing European primacy within Europe.

As western technology's destructive capacity grew exponentially, these attempts by one or other of Europe's families, or later major powers, to secure domination first of Europe and then of as much as possible of the globe came increasingly to threaten western civilisation.

First the Habsburgs of Austria and Spain, then Louis XIV, then Napoleon Bonaparte sought to control Europe, in a series of conflicts that eventually overflowed to the world outside Europe. Finally Germany, so long divided, came together under Prussian leadership, and then most disastrously under Hitler, whilst in Russia the expansionist Czars were replaced by Lenin and Stalin.

Europe's global role peaked around the start of the last century – until displaced by the United States, the economy of which had been growing at a phenomenal rate throughout the nineteenth century. At the end of which it began to assert itself externally, winning colonies for itself – never admitted to be such, of course – through the 1898 Spanish-American War, although outside of the Americas it did not seek a global role until after the Second World War.

At around the same time Japan and Russia – the latter also a European player – were in the process of emerging as major industrial powers, challenging each other in the West Pacific. China, however, was still dormant, prostrate under the yoke of rampant European colonialism.

Thus, 100 years ago Europe was still supreme, but its power had a self-destructive potential. With the growth of military technology, many centuries of rivalry between its major powers for dominance within the European Continent was starting to carry a lethal potential.

The stability of the European state system was not enhanced by the survival into the modern age of the monarchical system, for although the role of monarchs was by that time subject in most European countries to some element of democratic control in domestic matters, especially finance, this was much less true of foreign and military policy, which remained a matter for the then Executive rather than the legislature – as has indeed remained the case even since the disappearance of monarchs with executive roles.

Moreover, a new source of weakness within the European system was starting to appear in some countries around that time, namely demographic changes through which eventually Europe's population – even at that time quite a small proportion of that of the globe as whole – was going first to stabilise and in the twenty-first century to decline in absolute terms.

The process by which a Europe, the economic strength and military power of which was already in 1900 coming under long-term threat, moved dramatically from world dominance, exercised selfishly, to a far more constructive and positive role in the world a century later, has been quite an extraordinary one. Unfortunately it required two destructive and lethal intra-European wars – the second of which brought our continent to the point of near self-destruction – to force the western part of our little continent to pull itself together and set out consciously to reverse the dangerous tide of its history, in a way that came to re-shape radically its global role.

Impact of the Second World War

In 1945 Europe emerged physically and morally shattered from the most lethal of all these conflicts to face the fact that the post-war world was to be dominated by two, initially isolationist extra-European superpowers: the Soviet Union and the United States. That traumatic shift in global power led to the belated recognition of the futility of attempts by one part of Europe to dominate others, finally forcing a radical reversal of its trajectory towards self-destruction.

In its first manifestation this reversal was quite narrowly focused on forestalling any further conflict between France and Germany by securing a pooling of what were then seen as the key sinews of war: coal and steel. No one then realised where this move would eventually lead – and indeed several decades were to pass before the consequent peace-generating capacity of the Economic Community was to display itself.

Within the following two decades the attractive power of the European Community of six Western European former wartime enemies that grew out of the Coal and Steel Community pulled into its orbit three other West European democracies – Britain, Denmark and Ireland. Then, between 1975 and 1985, it pulled back into the democratic fold three Southern European dictatorships – Greece, Portugal and finally Spain – thus starting to spread throughout Southern Europe a Zone of Peace.

In parallel with this process, during the 1950s and 1960s, Europe's colonial empire had dissolved – not always peacefully. In Kenya and Congo/Zaire, in Vietnam and Aden, in Malaysia and Algeria, and in Portuguese Africa amongst other areas, European colonial powers at first sought vainly to hang on to colonial power that in some of these cases gave them control of important natural resources, but eventually they reluctantly came to terms with a new kind of world composed exclusively of independent sovereign states. Gradually Europeans came to accept that their future role outside their own continent would be one no longer of domination and exploitation. Instead they came to accept a future role of providing aid for the economic development of these former colonies. This may at first have been largely for neo-colonial reasons, but increasingly, as time passed, more generous motives came to the fore, and gradually secured strong support from their own peoples.

Whilst there certainly have been cases of collusion by former colonial powers with corrupt dictators willing to sell out their people's natural resources, these former European colonial states, together with other states that had no such role, or only a minimal involvement, e.g. Denmark and Sweden, have increasingly committed themselves to assisting the emergence of democratic systems in these countries.

Europe's seven value reversals

Let me list briefly – approximately in chronological order of their actual emergence – seven key reversals of history for which Europe has been responsible during the past fifty years to dramatically turning on its head its generally malevolent past global role.

Of course, as we live in an imperfect world, some of these achievements have been far from perfect – but that should not prevent us from realising what remarkable progress our continent has made since 1945, or the extent to which this progress has differentiated Europe from most other parts of the world, including other democracies such as the United States, and has thus offered it the possibility of playing a hugely positive role in the future of our globe.

1. Commitment to international law. Contrast Europe's commitment to international law with the dismissive stance of the US over the World Court's ruling on its mining of Nicaraguan ports. And note Margaret Thatcher's refusal to agree to a US request that she support the Israeli bombing of the PLO in Tunis – she told me herself that her response to President Reagan at that time was: 'What would you say if I bombed the Provos in Dundalk!' – and the extreme reluctance or her acceptance, only under great pressure, of a role in the US bombing of Libya as a quid pro quo for US support on the Falklands War.
2. Acceptance of a supra-national supervision of human rights by the Strasbourg Court. Contrast this with the current unwillingness of the US even to accept the Geneva Convention.
3. Creation of a European Zone of Peace and the increasing dedication of European national armies to peacekeeping and peacemaking – with, however, several notable failures, such as Srebrenica and Rwanda. After 1989 this Zone of Peace spread to Eastern Europe, except the western Balkans. It has also had an indirect influence on Russian policy with Georgia and the Ukraine although not yet in Chechnya. Contrast this with the US invasion of Iraq without UN

authority – and its earlier hasty withdrawal from Somalia. (This Zone of Peace is a key issue to which I shall return in the latter part of my address.)

4. Substitution of aid (transfers from rich to poor) for colonisation, albeit with in some cases a neo-colonial element in the form of tied aid, and military equipment sales. Contrast European and US civil aid – in relation to its GNP, Europe's civil aid is four times greater than that of the United States.

5. Abolition of capital punishment: rejection for EU membership of any country which keeps this penalty. Contrast this with the retention of the death penalty in many US states.

6. European initiative on global ecological action. Europe has been the undoubted leader in this attempt to save future generations from global warming and, by its absolute refusal to be diverted from this task last weekend, forced the start of a US climb-down on this issue.

7. International Criminal Court: a European project which the US rejected and has attempted, but failed, to sabotage. Note the possible future impact of this on war.

This record of historic European initiatives is far too little recognised in Europe, where mistakes and setbacks of the EU are given huge media prominence and where extra-European admiration and enthusiasm for its global role is largely unknown.

Common European foreign policy

For over thirty years the EU has aspired to developing a common foreign policy: seeking agreement amongst its member states on as many specific areas of foreign policy as possible. This was always bound to be a slow process, for the Union's member states have had very different histories. Nevertheless, they have come closer together on many issues as they have been forced to address different external challenges over recent decades – for example, the persistent Middle East crisis, US intervention in Central America in the 1980s, the Yugoslav crises of the 1990s and various African crises in the 1990s, as well as the threat of international terrorism in the present decade.

This convergence of member states' approaches to foreign policy has not been widely noticed, simply because good news of that kind is not news, whereas when member states disagree on some issue, as is bound to happen from time to time, that makes headlines.

Let me give several examples of the process of gradual policy convergence. When thirty-two years ago I became Minister for Foreign Affairs, the Community, as our European Union was then called, was deeply divided on the issue of the Middle East. Six of what were then nine members of the European Community saw the Palestinian issue as primarily a refugee crisis, failing to recognise that Israel would never find peace until the Palestinians, who had lost everything in the course of successive Arab/Israeli wars, were given space in which to establish a state of their own. At that time only France, Italy and Ireland recognised that reality.

It was only in 1980, at a crucial Foreign Ministers' meeting in Venice, that these six countries finally came to share the analysis of the French, Italians and Irish. Three years later, the Community also reached a common position on a second issue, making a statement implicitly critical of the US militarisation of Central America.

With democracy established throughout Western Europe, and de-colonisation completed, the European Union, as it had now become, faced after 1989 a new opportunity and challenge in and after 1989 – when the Soviet Union and its Eastern European empire suddenly collapsed. It immediately became evident that the attractive power of the European Union, already demonstrated within Western Europe, was going to operate powerfully in Central and Eastern Europe also.

Now, it had always seemed possible that if and when Soviet domination of this half of Europe ended, old conflicts that divided these states might break out again. After all in the first half of the twentieth century Romania and Hungary had quarrelled for decades over Transylvania, which had changed hands several times; Romania and Bulgaria had conflicting claims to the Dobrudja near the mouth of the Danube; Hungary and Czechoslovakia had shared claims to southern Slovakia; Poland and Czechoslovakia disputed ownership of Teschen; Carpatho-Ruthenia had changed hands several times between Czechoslovakia, Hungary and the Ukraine; and Lithuania's present capital Vilnius had been taken by Poland after the First World War. Not to speak of all the territorial quarrels within Yugoslavia and between it and its neighbours – Albania, Bulgaria, Hungary, Austria and Italy.

Once Soviet power in the region collapsed there was every likelihood that some or all of these disputes would flare up again. In the event nothing of the kind happened -- outside the western Balkans. Why? Quite simply because the attractive power of the European Union – and in the shorter run of NATO also – far outweighed old territorial ambitions throughout almost all of this region. The pulling power of the Union's Zone of Peace proved irresistible. And, more recently, we have seen how the Union's influence has helped peaceful revolutions in Georgia and the Ukraine and has started to affect the way Turkey handles its Kurdish problem.

The Union's special strength is its broad spectrum of instruments, ranging from international development cooperation (the Union and its member states are responsible for well over half of all civil development aid), trade policy, diplomacy, political dialogue, migration policy, economic leverage, and the whole range of civilian and military instruments of crisis management, which are mutually reinforcing.

To an extent which we still fail to recognise, large parts of the world now associate Europe with a philosophy of humanity, solidarity and integration. The EU is seen as a model of the way to approach international affairs. It has become the prime inspiration for the African Union, Mercosur in South America, the Central America Free Trade Association, Asean in East Asia and the Gulf Cooperation Council.

Recently, fearful of US impatience with Iran's nuclear policy, the EU's three largest states have sought – so far without much success it has to be said – to defuse this new potential crisis by diplomatic measures – a policy that has secured the support of its EU partners. There have also been a number of peacekeeping initiatives in relation to Africa – in Sierra Leone and Zaire – that have won support from all the states of the Union.

Thus the pressure of events, and also in some instances what have been seen by Europeans as worrying developments in US policy, have gradually brought into existence a range of common EU foreign policy positions.

Even the spectacular European failure to agree a stance on Iraq several years ago eventually served to create great pressure in favour of a common approach to the post-war problems of Iraq, in a move to improve a damaged US–Europe relationship – and in the hope of recovering some influence over what has been seen as worrying US unilateralism.

Failure of attempts to improve EU foreign policy structure

It is not surprising that in parallel with these multiple developments the EU came to see a need to improve the structures through which it develops these common policies. In recent years we have seen the emergence of a foreign policy personality, Javier Solana, acting in parallel with the External Relations Commissioner. The hitherto abortive European Constitution made provision for the merger of these two roles, by 'double-hatting' one person to fulfil both functions. With the rejection of this Constitutional Treaty by two of the founding member states it may be desirable to devise some ad hoc means of making this cumbersome joint system of foreign policy decisionmaking work better.

The Vice-President Foreign Minister who was to have been appointed under the new European Constitution was to have been assisted by a European External Action service, which would have brought together

elements of the European Commission's External Relations Directorate-
General and of the Council Secretariat, and would have been reinforced
by diplomats seconded by the Foreign Ministries of member states.

The appointment to the EU Washington Delegation of a senior
European politician, John Bruton, with experience both of the European
Council and also of the Presidium of the Convention that recently
drew up the draft of the European Constitutional Treaty, may have
foreshadowed the hoped-for future development of such a new kind of
European diplomatic service. Because of Ireland's exceptional relationship with the US Congress, not matched by most other European states,
this appointment has already been reported to have secured for the EU
greater access than formerly to parts of the US political system.

Irish critics of the gradual evolution, by unanimous accord, of
common EU positions on aspects of foreign policy might be challenged
to say which of the elements of a Common EU Foreign Policy that have
so far emerged they disagree with – and why. What I myself have found
striking is in fact how closely the common policies that have developed
over the years correspond to Irish aspirations and values.

Peacekeeping since the 1950s

Of course, since the 1950s individual European states, Ireland amongst
them, have played an active, one might say a leading role in UN peacekeeping.

One of the first of these missions was to separate Israeli and Egyptian
forces in the Sinai after the withdrawal of invading British and French
forces in 1956. Irish troops participated in this force. And Irish troops
were of course also actively engaged in the Congo for some years in
and after 1960, when Congo/Zaire became independent but came close
to collapsing and for a period the commanding general was Irish. Irish
administrators were also actively in the process of keeping that huge
country united, and restoring peace there in the early 1960s. Conor
Cruise O'Brien was the UN administrator in Katanga in 1961, where
my brother Pierce was his Finance Officer – later being responsible for
evacuating 30,000 Balubas from Katanga to the South Kasai Province.
A year earlier another of my brothers had been administrator of the
Kivu Province.

Since then there have been many UN peacekeeping missions, in a
large number of which Irish troops have played a part – most notably
the Lebanon, and currently Liberia.

In recent years, however, the UN has increasingly tended to delegate
peacekeeping, and now peace enforcing, activities to regional bodies –
amongst which the EU has been foremost. The role in peacekeeping of

the EU as an institution – as distinct from that of its individual member states – derives from its 1990s experience in Yugoslavia, when it notably failed to agree on an approach to the break-up of that country. At the outset the EU states were deeply divided over how to react to the collapse of Yugoslavia. Germany and Austria, where Roman Catholic opinion was strongly supportive of breakaway Croatia and Slovenia, favoured early unconditional recognition of these new states whereas other EU members, recalling the massacres that had happened in this region during the Second World War, and concerned in particular about Croat extremism, favoured a more cautious approach – but eventually felt obliged to fall in line following unilateral action in this matter by Germany and Austria.

The Yugoslav debacle

When Bosnia fell apart, France and Britain intervened in a limited way to protect humanitarian convoys of aid to the civil population. But the vulnerability of their forces as they carried out this humanitarian task inhibited them and other European states from direct intervention in the massacres that followed, with the result that Europe was quickly seen to be ineffective in peacekeeping in its own backyard. The European states also lacked both the will and also the capacity to safeguard isolated communities: they simply did not have the helicopter lift capacity to move 1,000 troops 100 miles – and at a crucial stage the US refused to risk its helicopter forces in such an exercise. Then the EU ended up having to depend on United States air power to end Serb attempts to expel the Albanians from Kosovo.

It was the humiliation, and indeed shame, of that Yugoslav debacle that finally forced the European Union to develop not just a belated common policy on the Balkans, but a much wider European Security and Development Policy. As a result the Union is now well-equipped to prevent and handle conflicts, not only in Europe itself but wherever trouble arises, with the result that it now plays a major role in the global arena as a champion for peace and security The humiliation of these experiences, and of having to rely on the United States both to resolve the Bosnian problem at the Dayton Conference and later to halt Serb repression of Albanians in Kosovo, led to the emergence of the proposal to establish a European Rapid Reaction Force to deal with any future emergencies of this kind. The first of its unfortunately named 'Battle Groups' has been set up and a unit has been established to coordinate civilian and military operations.

At around the same time the UN in Rwanda failed to act to prevent genocide, and became increasingly conscious of the inadequacy of its arrangements to enforce peace in such critical situations.

In crisis situations in East Timor (in which Ireland took a special interest), Sierra Leone and Zaire, individual states – Australia, Britain and France – proved best-placed to intervene to save life and restore order, acting with the authority of the UN. In Africa the Organisation of African Union (OAU) has also proved able to provide forces to restore order in parts of West Africa, and forces from some of its states are currently engaged, so far with limited success, in Darfur in the western Sudan, with some European back-up.

So recent years have seen a major shift in the centre of gravity of peacekeeping. World opinion has become increasingly disenchanted with the concept of according absolute respect to national sovereignty, even where a national government is unwilling or unable to protect its own people from massive human rights abuses which may approach the scale of genocide. A new willingness to endorse international intervention in at least the gravest of such cases, combined with a recognition that direct action by the UN may not be the most effective method where peace enforcement rather than peacekeeping is needed, have led to a major shift towards UN-authorised regional action, undertaken by institutions such as the EU or OAU, in some cases with technical back-up from NATO.

EU peacekeeping

The rapidity with which the EU's role in peacekeeping has developed has been quite remarkable. Let me list a dozen projects currently under way in eight countries of Europe, Asia and Africa:

1. Operation Concordia in Macedonia in 2003, which took over from a NATO force and prevented a civil war breaking out between Macedonians and the Albanian minority, and which has since been replaced by a police mission. The EU role here has been helped by Macedonian hopes of eventual EU membership.
2. EUFOR and EUPM (military and police) in Bosnia and Herzegovina.
3. EUJUST THEMIS, a rule of law mission in Georgia.
4. ARTEMIS, a peace enforcement mission in Bunia in Congo-Zaire; EUPOL, a police mission in Kinshasa/Congo-Zaire; and EUSEC, also in Zaire.
5. ACEH in Indonesia, trusted and greatly appreciated both by the Indonesian government and by the Aceh rebels, which monitors the peace agreement between them.
6. AMIS, providing funding, logistic and planning support to the African Union force in Darfur, which is currently having great diffi-

culty because of the hostile attitude of the Sudan government.

7. EUPOL in Palestine, a mission of support for the Palestinian police, and EUBAM in Rafah, policing the exit and entry point to Gaza, the work of which has secured the appreciation of both the Palestinians and the Israeli government, hitherto hostile to the EU.

8. EUJUST-LEX in Iraq, an integrated Rule of Law Commission, training high level officials in the judiciary, police and prisons.

Through its European Neighbourhood Policy the EU helped to resolve the electoral dispute that threatened last year to split the Ukraine in two. It has also taken action in relation to the Uzbekistan dictatorship by embargoing exports of arms to that country and re-orientating EU funds towards support for human rights and democracy.

Neutrals and peacekeeping

Far from pulling back from involvement in regional peacekeeping actions, neutral states such as Finland, Sweden and Austria, as well as Ireland, have become very actively engaged in EU peacekeeping in Europe and further afield, which is being carried out in close liaison with the UN, with which there is now a formal arrangement for this purpose.

Irish neutrality is unlike that of the other three European states in that it has not involved any commitment to self-defence: we lack any air defence whatever; our naval forces are confined to fishery protection; and our army's role is effectively limited to peace support, crisis management and humanitarian relief operations abroad, as well as internal security (in respect of which the army has at times in the past been overstretched), and also, it has to be admitted, providing local employment by keeping open barracks in an unnecessarily large number of towns throughout the country.

For external defence against possible threats from rogue states we in Ireland have been content to rely on NATO, in whose activities, however, we have chosen to play no part. Non-participation in NATO seems to be the core value of Irish neutrality, combined with the 'triple lock' on Irish involvement in peacekeeping, which limits our involvement to operations authorised not merely by the government and the Oireachtas and also by the United Nations.

Because of this latter provision the Irish army has not been able to participate in the EU mission in Macedonia, for UN support for this mission was vetoed by China because Macedonia had made the mistake of formally recognising the government of Taiwan. Irish non-participation in this particular mission was particularly unfortunate, because this is seen as having performed an especially important function in preventing

the outbreak of civil war between Macedonians and Albanians. This
raises a question as to the validity of a concept of neutrality than can
have such a strange and indeed perverse impact on Irish capacity to fulfil
an important peacekeeping role – a concept that must seem eccentric to
our European partners.

Europe's future role in world peace

The result of all this rapidly developing peacekeeping and peace enforcement activity is that Europe is now an extraordinary positive force in the
world. It has the possibility of influencing the US eventually towards a
similar approach – drawing on opposition within the US to American
abuses of power. And it has a potential influence also on Russia and
China.

But all this depends upon Europe acting cohesively, and gaining and
keeping its moral leadership. In the longer run only a cohesive European
effort to promote globally its new value system offers a hope of influencing the US to develop similar values. The same is true in relation to
Russia and, eventually, China.

And time is running against Europe. On present form, within forty
years demography will have reduced Europe's workforce by one-quarter.
Economic growth cannot be sustained without a reasonably stable
workforce. Immigration cannot solve it either: the present temporary
influx from Eastern Europe to Ireland is a one-off phenomenon, for the
demography of these countries is even more skewed to older people
than that of Western Europe. And, beyond a certain point, immigration
from outside Europe can prove disruptive and could weaken Europe's
potentially positive role.

For Europe to exert the kind of positive moral leadership that the
world needs at this juncture, it needs to act coherently especially
during the quarter century ahead. Its capacity to do so has clearly been
weakened in recent times by poor political leadership, by persistent
economic failure in the major continental economies reflecting failure
to tackle structural weaknesses in labour market policy in particular,
and, above all, by the inadequacy of the Stability and Growth Pact – all
stability and no growth.

But the EU's potential role in spreading peace should not be underestimated: I believe that its example will in time spread beyond Europe's
boundaries – especially as this example is reinforced by its active role in
peacekeeping in other continents, and by the seven specifically European
values that it espouses, which have the support of some extra-European
states such as Canada but are not always shared by other liberal democracies.

Postscript

Dr FitzGerald, who held the degree of Doctor of Laws *honoris causa* from the University of Ulster, died on 19 May 2011.

Notes

1 Garret FitzGerald, *All in a Life: An Autobiography* (Dublin: Gill and Macmillan, 1991), *passim*.
2 Garret FitzGerald, *Towards a New Ireland* (London: Charles Knight & Co. Ltd, 1972).
3 T. G. Fraser, *Ireland in Conflict 1922–1998* (London and New York: Routledge, 2000), pp. 60–2.

10

Security in the twenty-first century

Senator John F. Kerry

Introduction

When Senator John F. Kerry spoke on the key issue of security on 5 March 2006, it was at a critical time in international affairs, not least in terms of the bitter conflicts in Iraq and Afghanistan for which no end then seemed in sight. He brought impeccable qualifications to what he had to say. His father was a Foreign Service Officer in the post-war period when the United States, faced with the challenges of the Cold War, had through the Marshall Plan and the NATO alliance forged a network of states that proved equal to the challenges of the time. While his own childhood exposure to other cultures and societies opened his mind, it made him no less a patriotic American, underpinned by his strong Catholic faith. As a result, the young John Kerry knew war at the sharp end, serving two tours of duty in Vietnam: that most controversial of conflicts. His outstanding combat record as commander of a gunboat in the Mekong Delta earned him a Silver Star, a Bronze Star with Combat V and three Purple Hearts. With equal courage, in April 1971 he testified before the Senate Foreign Relations Committee, asking the unanswerable question: 'How do you ask a man to be the last man to die for a mistake?' His opposition to the Vietnam War was as patriotic and principled as his participation in it had been. In short, he knew the perils of both war and peacemaking.

Elected as a Senator from Massachusetts in 1984, he maintained and broadened his interest in international affairs through his membership of the Senate Foreign Relations Committee, of which he was later to become Chairman. In 2004, Kerry became the Democratic Party's standard bearer against incumbent President George W. Bush. In his book, *A Call to Service. My Vision for a Better America*, which he published in 2003, he criticised what he saw as the 'harsh conservative unilateralism', which he believed the country had been following, pointing instead to America's assets, her values, alliances and 'the multilateral organizations we largely created'.[1] These were themes he developed in his lecture.

His analysis was all the more nuanced since he had recently returned from an extensive tour of the Middle East and South Asia, which had taken in both Iraq and Afghanistan. He focused upon two outstanding issues, each central to an understanding of security; namely, America's relations with the Islamic world, so often the fount of mutual mistrust and misunderstanding, and the weapons of mass destruction which had threatened the future of humankind since their first appearance in 1945. What he had to say speaks for itself, an eloquent plea in the first instance for mutual tolerance and understanding between the West and the Muslim world, the very principles which had sustained the peace process between the two communities in Northern Ireland. But he was also at pains to remind his audience of the need for the West to understand the internal dynamics of the Islamic world and the conflicts within it. Conscious of the central importance of a resolution of the Israeli-Palestinian problem, which had long confounded well-intentioned peacemakers and caused untold misery to thousands, he emphasised its significance, well aware that the recent incapacity of Ariel Sharon, who had just set in hand an imaginative realignment in Israeli politics, and the success of Hamas in the Palestinian elections held at the end of January, had made the path to peace no easier.

On what he identified as the other major threat to human security, the spread of weapons of mass destruction, he called for America's long-delayed ratification of the Comprehensive Nuclear Test Ban Treaty of 1996 to be concluded. This, he argued, would send out the right signal about the country's commitment to non-proliferation. His most immediate concern was clearly the Iranian nuclear programme, the disputed nature of which was to vex relations between the two countries in the years ahead. His lecture ended with a plea for the kind of multilateralism which had sustained American diplomacy throughout the perils of the Cold War era. That 'all ships rise on a rising tide' was a fitting peroration for a former naval officer.

In retrospect, Senator Kerry's lecture may be seen as a plea for a more subtle American approach to the burning issues of security in the Middle East and South Asia. It preceded the celebrated, if unsuccessful, amendment he introduced in the Senate with Wisconsin Senator Russ Feingold on 22 June 2006: 'To require the deployment of United States Armed Forces from Iraq in order to further a political solution in Iraq, encourage the people of Iraq to provide for their own security, and achieve victory in the war on terror'. It was also indicative of the kind of thinking on international affairs which might be expected of a future Democratic administration.

Lecture

What a wonderful privilege to be part of the Tip O'Neill lecture series here at the University of Ulster. I had the pleasure of working with Tip in Congress, and had the even greater pleasure of calling him a friend. He campaigned for me, and I for him – and I am privileged that every one of his children has helped me over the years. Tip didn't just tell us that all politics is local – he showed us. I will never forget when I was a young prosecutor in Cambridge, Tip came by to campaign. It was a joyous, raucous visit. Amazingly, Tip called everyone he met by their first name. He was incredibly proud of his Irish roots, and all of us were proud of him for his decades of public service to his country and the world.

I would also like to extend a special thanks to my friend John Hume for inviting me to speak here today. I don't need to tell anyone here about the accomplishments of John Hume – you live them every day. With his courage, sacrifice and creativity – his vision for peace and prosperity – his uncanny ability to find optimism in the midst of great adversity – he exemplifies the kind of leader we need to meet the extraordinary challenges of this new century. But I can tell you this from the gracious-ness and patience he showed in scheduling my visit here today: it's clear that the qualities that were the hallmark of his public life continue to serve him well now.

When John Hume accepted his Nobel Peace Prize in 1998, he told a story that remains as powerful today as when he first told it eight years ago. He said:

> On my first visit to Strasbourg in 1979 as a member of the European Parliament, I went for a walk across the bridge from Strasbourg to Kehl. Strasbourg is in France. Kehl is in Germany. They are very close. I stopped in the middle of the bridge and I meditated. There is Germany. There is France. If I had stood on this bridge 30 years ago, after the end of the Second World War when 25 million people lay dead across our continent for the second time in this century, if I had said: 'Don't worry. In 30 years' time we will all be together in a new Europe, our conflicts and wars will be ended, and we will be working together in our common interests', I would have been sent to a psychiatrist.[2]

Well, who knows, he may yet have to see that psychiatrist – but the fact is he's always been driven by a great sense of optimism for the possibilities the future could hold, and we all admire him greatly for that.

This January, I took a trip of my own where I saw first-hand the importance of applying this lesson of hope and perseverance to the challenges we face today. I saw emerging democracies in Afghanistan and Iraq struggling to overcome terrorism and sectarian strife as they work to create a better future. I saw Israel's democracy persevere despite the incapacitation of its leader. I saw high-tech companies thriving in India in the midst of great poverty. In Pakistan, where tensions between a secular leader and a restless Islamist movement run high, thanks to the response of the world I saw 9,000 children emerge from the devastation of a massive earthquake and go to school for the first time.

I saw open societies and closed societies, rich and poor, high tech and low tech, secular and religious. Everywhere I turned, there were disconnects. So many people desperately trying to connect to the rest of the world to make a better future, while so many others desperately cling to the past, doing everything in their power to prevent connection to anything unfamiliar.

These disconnects map the fault lines of today's conflict and future conflicts. It is in these fault lines that radical Islamists recruit their followers by playing to stereotypes of western civilisation. But it is here that the critical challenges of our time are defined: winning the struggle against terror and stopping the spread of weapons of mass destruction.

Frankly, we should start by better understanding what we are up against. The war on terror – as it is so often called – even exploited – is really a far bigger challenge than the words suggest. Terror is only a tactic. The bigger struggle we are engaged in is much more than a military operation in Iraq and Afghanistan, and it started long before 9/11. It is, above all, a much more complicated undertaking than some have made it sound. In fact, our long-term security is today as it has always been, dependent on addressing the multi-layered fabric of life which motivates those who use terror.

The truth is that we are caught in the middle of a decades-old internal struggle in the Islamic World. It is fundamentally a war within Islam for the heart and soul of Islam, stretching from Morocco east to Indonesia. In regions where the mosque remains the only respected alternative to autocratic state structures, there is no credible secular alternative. And no centre of moral authority has emerged to stop those who would murder in the name of Islam.

So ultimately, this is a struggle for the transformation of the Greater Middle East into a region that is no longer isolated from the global economy, no longer dependent on despotism for stability, no longer fearful of freedom and no longer content to feed restive and rising populations of unemployed young people a diet of illusions, excuses and dead-end government jobs.

To succeed, we must have a strategy that does everything possible to increase the internal demand for transformation in the Greater Middle East, especially its Arab core. This means we must become significantly more engaged in leveraging transformation – we must wage a more effective war of ideas and ideologies. But make no mistake, in the end, this war must be fought and won within the Islamic world. So we have a huge stake in finding partners in the Arab world who are willing not only to lead the transformation of the Middle East, but to re-establish the broad and unchallenged moral authority needed to isolate and defeat terrorists.

We must also, finally, liberate not only ourselves, but the Middle East itself from the tyranny of dependence on petroleum, which has frustrated every impulse towards modernisation of the region, while giving its regimes the resources to hold on to power. The international community of democratic nations cannot afford to continue funding both sides of the war on terror. We must end the empire of oil. And these efforts have to be truly international – all linked to the rapid emergence of new energy technologies, in order to ensure that growing economies like China and India don't just replace us as the enablers of Middle East despots.

These are daunting challenges. To wage this war with any credibility in the Muslim world, we must work to address the impression that we have done too little to achieve real progress in bringing peace to the Middle East. The victory of Hamas in the Palestinian elections makes the prospect of establishing a democratic Palestine at peace with Israel seem even more distant. But we must not lose sight of the fact that lasting peace there is key to denying Islamic extremists a recruiting tool and denying repressive regimes an excuse not to address problems at home.

History is replete with examples of conflicts that at times seemed endless and intractable. But history also teaches us that if the desire for peace stays strong, it is always possible to prevail. There are lessons of perseverance and determination for peace to be learned from your experience here in Northern Ireland. You know better than anyone how long and arduous this process can be. The citizens of Northern Ireland have proven that progress is possible for those with the courage to seize it.

We have also learned from experience that successfully meeting great challenges like winning the war on terror requires more than just one nation changing its policies. Great American presidents from Roosevelt to Truman to Kennedy understood that success requires a community of nations working together, drawing strength from shared sacrifice and steadfast commitment to our shared ideals. We must once again forge great alliances of common purpose that increase our collective strength and amplify our collective voice, so that we defeat any form of tyranny in a battle of ideas. That means strengthening and reforming not weakening and walking away from the ability of the UN to play a forceful role in troubled places like Iraq and Darfur.

Literally, the West must reclaim its moral leadership. To be successful in this battle of ideas, we must undermine the jihadist propaganda about the West. All allied nations have to pay greater attention to how our words and deeds are understood in the Middle East, because our good intentions are doubted by the very people the terrorists seek to turn against us. And these efforts must be bolstered with tangible investments, not just in foreign aid, but in the Arab people themselves in the form of schools, hospitals and other institutions that give people a voice and a stake in civil society.

All of the allies, from Europe to the Americas to Asia, must work harder to strengthen our commitment and enhance our efforts to integrate the Middle East into the global economy. This is the only way to stop economic regression, spur investment beyond the oil industry, and spark trade, investment and growth in the region. It's the only way to turn young minds and energy away from terror.

In addition, all our allies must join together to counter the teaching of hatred in Madrassas throughout the Middle East. We must press regimes more consistently and effectively to teach tolerance in schools and broaden educational opportunities throughout the region. And we must work with moderate Muslims, especially clerics, to permanently discredit the belief that the murder of innocents can be justified in the name of God, race or nation.

This will be difficult, but it can be done. There is a serious fight going on right now for the soul of Islam. As is so often the case, an extremist minority has captured the attention of the world. But despite what you see on the news, this isn't a one-sided fight. In 2004 in Amman, Jordan, senior Islamic leaders and leading moderate statesmen like King Abdullah of Jordan came together to preach religious cooperation and non-violence. In July of 2005, moderate Muslim clerics again came together in Amman and issued a formal fatwa, or religious edict, against terror.

That may not sound like much to us, but the terrorists apparently took this threat from moderate Muslims very seriously. In the weeks and months after the 2005 Amman fatwa, Muslims were attacked from Amman itself to Sharm el Sheikh to Pakistan. In fact, the overwhelming majority of recent terrorist victims have been Muslims. And the voices of moderation responded again this past January at the Hajj pilgrimage, where Saudi Arabia's leading cleric condemned the use of terrorism in the name of Islam.

Obviously, the struggle for the future of Islam isn't a fight the West can win alone – but we can offer critical support as we spread our democratic message. To do that, democratic values and openness should be championed not simply as western values but as the universal values that they are. Democracy spreads with patient but firm determination, led by individuals of courage who dream of a better day for their country. Viktor Yushchenko had that dream in Ukraine. Hamid Karzai in Afghanistan. And Lech Walesa in Poland. We need to create the conditions where this dream can become a reality in the Arab world.

Above all, we must remember, democratisation is not a crusade. If it is seen as the result of an army marching through Muslim lands it will fail. Perhaps more importantly, that's not the way democracy works. Creating a democracy requires more than an election, as the defeat of the ruling Fatah party by Hamas in the Palestinian elections further illustrates. The challenge requires building transparent, accountable and functioning democratic institutions that will enable democratically elected governments to provide basic goods and services to their people.

In the end, these steps can open a region that for too long has been closed to opportunity and progress. And they will help to modernise governments and create societies that can better meet the needs of their citizens, respond to their grievances and provide a more hopeful alternative to the dark ideology of terror. That would be a real battle of ideas – a battle I believe we can win if free nations fight together.

Taking these steps is the key to effectively addressing the root causes of terror, and beginning on a path toward long-term victory. But terrorism is not the only threat to our security. We must also do a better job stopping the spread of weapons of mass destruction and preventing the transfer of those weapons to terrorists.

It was a notable moment in the 2004 presidential campaign when President Bush and I agreed that terrorists armed with nuclear weapons posed the greatest security threat of the twenty-first century. To meet this challenge, we are going to have to be strong – but also smart. The most obvious example of this potentially devastating nexus is Iran, where the world's leading state sponsor of terrorism has defied the world by moving forward with its nuclear programme. A nuclear armed Iran clearly poses an unacceptable threat to global security. To make sure that never happens, America must lead an unrelenting collective effort that matches the urgency of the threat.

To be smart, however, we must also correct the inherent flaw in the nuclear Non-Proliferation Treaty that allows nations such as Iran to advance their illicit nuclear weapons capability under the cover of permitted civilian nuclear programmes. The fact is that once a country can create its own nuclear fuel, it can probably build a nuclear weapon. To prevent this, America and other nuclear powers must establish international control of the nuclear fuel cycle by creating a reliable, affordable and accessible bank of nuclear fuel. This will allow us to provide reactor fuel to states that conform to non-proliferation agreements while keeping that fuel under strict international safeguards.

America can also provide more determined leadership in preventing the proliferation of nuclear weapons by setting the right example ourselves. By advancing negotiations on a global fissile material cut-off treaty; foreswearing the development of new nuclear weapons; and ratifying the Comprehensive Test Ban Treaty, we can send the right message to the world about our commitment to creating a more effective global non-proliferation regime.

To meet these great challenges of terrorism and proliferation, we must reinvigorate alliances so we can marshal the collective will and resources of America and our allies. The United States has been at its best when working together with other countries in an international system of global reach and power that links the security and welfare of all free nations around the world. It was this system that won the Cold War and made possible the incredible progress of the last sixty years. It is an approach that restores traditions that have passed the test of time – and that is the message I take home with me after traveling the world from India to Pakistan to Iraq to Israel.

So as John Hume once said, 'The challenge now is to grasp and shape history: to show that past grievances and injustices can give way to a new generosity of spirit and action'.[3] We have a long way to go before we have met the great challenges of the twenty-first century. But with inspired leadership and unwavering commitment, I believe that together we can create a world in which wars are rare; a world in which America and her allies are protected by alliances forged in common interest and purpose; and a world in which order is preserved by the will of democratic nations who understand that all ships rise on a rising tide. And as we have learned from John, even though it may sometimes feel like we should have our heads examined, we must never stop believing that day will come.

Postscript

On his return to the Senate, John Kerry became Chairman of the Senate Committee on Foreign Relations. In January 2013, President Obama appointed him Secretary of State.

Notes

1 John Kerry, *A Call to Service: My Vision for a Better America* (New York: Viking, 2003), p. 35.
2 John Hume, Nobel Lecture, Oslo, 10 December 1998, © The Nobel Foundation, www.nobelprize.org/nobel_prizes/peace/laureates/1998/hume-lecture.html (last accessed 13 February 2013).
3 John Hume, Nobel Lecture, © The Nobel Foundation.

11

Between facts and fantasies: sources of anti-Americanism

Ambassador Mitchell B. Reiss

Introduction

When Ambassador Mitchell B. Reiss addressed the subject of 'Between facts and fantasies: sources of anti-Americanism' on 21 May 2006, he approached this highly topical, and controversial, issue from the distinctive perspective of having combined personal experience of diplomacy and peacemaking with a rigorous academic background and training. It is a distinctive feature of American political life that talented individuals can combine careers in the academy with public service at the highest level. Woodrow Wilson had, after all, been President of Princeton before being elected President of his country in 1912. It is not hard to think of other examples in more recent times. It is a tradition which other countries might usefully adopt, it might be thought.

When Reiss delivered his lecture he was President George W. Bush's Special Envoy for the Northern Ireland Peace Process, a position he had held since 2003. Born in Ohio, he graduated *cum laude* from Williams College in Massachusetts, proceeding to a Master's degree from the Fletcher School of Law and Diplomacy at Tufts University, and a certificate from the Academy of International Law at The Hague. He earned a Doctorate in International Relations from Oxford University and a Juris Doctorate degree from Columbia University. Armed with these impressive academic credentials, he joined the faculty of the prestigious College of William and Mary, Virginia. The Bush Presidency saw him involved in the active work of foreign policy formation and diplomacy, becoming Director of Policy Planning at the Department of State under Secretary of State Colin Powell, before being appointed to his role in Northern Ireland.

His lecture, however, focused not on the current situation in Northern Ireland, but instead on the critical issue of anti-Americanism and what this phenomenon, as well as its multiple sources, might mean for the pursuit of peace, stability and security in an undeniably unipolar world. His topic was particularly relevant, since the United States, as part of a

NATO mission, had been engaged in conflict in Afghanistan since the aftermath of the 9/11 attacks of 2001, and then in 2003 had mounted an invasion of Iraq, which had resulted in the removal of Saddam Hussein. The latter operation, as he acknowledged, had aroused widespread protests across Europe and key allies, notably France, Germany and Turkey, had refused to take part in, or support, it.

Hussein's regime was viewed by the Bush administration as a threat to the peace and stability of the region, having engaged in an eight-year war with Iran, occupied Kuwait by force, suppressed its Kurdish and Shi'a populations and was believed to have Weapons of Mass Destruction. Many Europeans, however, saw the war instead as a manifestation of unilateralism, stimulating the rise of anti-American sentiment and, accordingly, bringing into focus a debate on how the cause of international peace might best be served. From a European perspective, Reiss told listeners, if polling data was to be believed, America itself represented the greatest threat to peace in the contemporary world. However, prospects for the universal endeavour for peace were, conversely, seriously compromised by this continued spread and virulence of global anti-American sentiment. Sustained anti-Americanism, he warned, would have serious implications for the way the US conducted its affairs, including in such areas as 'fighting poverty and disease ... preventing the spread of nuclear weapons ... ending conflicts around the world' and in 'regional and international security and prosperity'.

Acknowledging the various sources of anti-Americanism in personality, philosophy and policy differences, as well as what he described as a 'cluster of systemic differences' including unipolarity and globalisation; he also observed a shift in the conceptualisation of existing models of international law and the United Nations Charter, which outlaws the use of force except in self-defence.[1] He noted the erosion of the Westphalian principle of the integrity of states within their own borders, leading to the increasing acceptance of the idea that powerful states could intervene in the internal affairs of others. This changed situation, he argued, had raised questions over pre-emption, legitimacy and the use of force – an analysis that he extended beyond the prospect of an imminent terrorist attack to include implications for humanitarian intervention; pointing out that divergence on those security issues meant that we currently had no answer to the question of how to act 'when states breach their "responsibility to protect" their own citizens and, indeed, actively abuse them?'.

Having reviewed the sources of anti-Americanism and the various policy differences and debates he came back to the key problem with which he sought to engage: 'if others mistrust us or actively work against us ... it will be more difficult [for America] to secure the peace and spread prosperity', and Reiss reminded his audience of what he believed they were already assured: 'when the United States retreats from the world, bad things happen'. The lessons of the twentieth century taught us that the United States needed to remain engaged with the rest of the world, and he conceded that although the US was pre-eminent in global power, it still needed its friends and allies politically, culturally and economically. As such, it needed to work harder to explain its policies and to reach out to others. Criticism was healthy, he said, but asked his listeners to remember that when global crises erupt, it was not 'Brussels or Tokyo or Moscow' that people called, but Washington. The US was, and would always be, 'an enormous force for good'.

Lecture

Thank you very much for that kind introduction. I'd like to thank the Chancellor, Sir Richard Nichols, the Vice-Chancellor, Professor Richard Barnett, the Provost of the Magee campus, Professor Tom Fraser, Provost Alan Sharp and the University of Ulster for inviting me to your beautiful campus. And I'd like to thank the students here in the audience, especially those who are here voluntarily. The good news is that your professors have assured me that none of what I say will be on your exams.

It's a great honour and a real pleasure for me to be with you this evening to deliver the Tip O'Neill Memorial Lecture. Not least because there's a personal connection. For part of my life, Tip O'Neill was actually my Congressman.

But there's another reason why I'm so pleased to be with you this evening. And that's John Hume, the current holder of the Tip O'Neill Chair in Peace Studies, and one of the greatest statesmen in Irish history. If Americans know only one thing about Northern Ireland, the Troubles and the peace process, it is John Hume – the causes he's fought for, the principles he's embraced and the passion and grace he's demonstrated. John, along with his wife, Pat, personify what Abraham Lincoln once called our 'better angels'. Last year the United States Senate paid special tribute to John as 'one of the greatest advocates of peace and non-violence in our time' and as a 'courageous leader of exceptional achievement ... in the cause of peace in Northern Ireland'.[2] We know that John has made enormous contributions to Derry, to Ireland, to Europe and to the larger international community – through his unflagging support for civil rights and non-violence, his respect for diversity and his emphasis on constitutional nationalism. When – not if, but when – the full promise of the Good Friday Agreement is realised and we achieve a lasting peace in Northern Ireland, it will be due in large measure to the courage and vision of John Hume, who always, always looked forward and showed us the way ahead. As much as John has been devoted to his beloved homeland, he has also been a great friend of the United States. So I know that John shares a concern about an issue that troubles many Americans, both those in Washington, DC and increasingly around the United States. That issue is anti-Americanism – the anger, resentment, envy and fear that an increasing number of people around the globe feel towards America.

We're all familiar with the anecdotal evidence. The day after the November 2004 presidential election that gave George Bush another four years, Britain's *Daily Mirror* runs a banner headline: 'How Could 59,054,087 People Be So Dumb?' Michael Moore's critical commentaries on American life, with titles like *Dude, Where's My Country?* and *Stupid White Men*, are runaway best sellers in Europe. In London, plays such as 'The Madness of George Dubya' and 'Guantanamo Baywatch' attract sell-out audiences. The playwright, now Nobel Laureate, Harold Pinter, instructs a London crowd that the United States is a 'monster out of control'.[3] In Germany, Gerhard Schroeder's re-election campaigns in both 2002 and 2005 tried to deflect attention from poor economic growth, high levels of unemployment and huge budget deficits by attacking the Bush administration and the United States. But these were nothing in comparison with Schroeder's Minister of Justice, who publicly likened President Bush to Adolf Hitler. Throughout much of the Muslim world, staged, anti-American street protests, complete with the burning of American flags and effigies of President Bush, are common events.

Now, as Americans, we understand that life isn't always fair. We know that the United States is often the target of criticism because many governments and regimes wish to distract their own people from home-grown failures: their unwillingness to deliver basic goods and services, to allow free speech and fair elections, to provide for a decent education or develop a free market that creates meaningful jobs. The American political scientist, Professor Michael Mandelbaum, has recently written that:

> Blaming the United States for disappointments and dislocations in other countries ... deflects the responsibility for these ills from the people who might well seem more appropriate targets for blame: the governments of the countries affected. Those governments use the United States as a political lightning rod, drawing away from themselves the popular discontent that their shortcomings have helped to produce and that could, if directed against them, remove them from power.[4]

As Tip O'Neill might have said, 'all anti-Americanism is local'. As Americans, we also understand that the world may even be hypocritical. I am sure I am not the only one here this evening to find curious the fact that there have been massive protests against the United States for its involvement in Iraq, but nary a one against the decades of misrule and mountain of human rights abuses that Saddam Hussein inflicted on the Iraqi people. That there have been no street rallies condemning Osama bin Laden and al Qaeda despite the thousands of innocent lives they've destroyed and the threat they continue to pose. Or, to shift the focus slightly, that the Arab world is more outraged by a few cartoons in an obscure Danish newspaper than by the slaughter of 300,000 Muslims in Darfur.

Of course, we also know that not all criticism of the United States is spurred by anti-Americanism. In fact, criticism is the hallmark of any healthy, vibrant, liberal society. But criticism should be specific and targeted, based on facts and hard evidence, and not use double stand-ards or selectivity. Anti-Americanism is something very different, more like criticism on steroids. As the American academic Paul Hollander has written: anti-Americanism is 'a freefloating hostility or aversion'.[5] It 'is a deep-seated emotional predisposition that perceives the United States as an unmitigated and uniquely evil entity and the source of all, or most, other evils in the world'.[6]

To be sure, anti-Americanism has been around in one form or another for some time. Some of us are old enough to remember the massive demonstrations throughout Western Europe against the Reagan admin-istration's foreign policies during the 1980s. But the current strain of anti-Americanism *feels* different. It seems more intense, and more serious in its implications.

Polling data supports that feeling. Recent public opinion polls have found that strong anti-American feeling is pervasive in the world – including among some of America's most trusted friends and allies. A Eurobarometer survey conducted in EU countries in October 2003 found that the US was seen as the greatest threat to world peace, along with Iran. Even in the UK, 55 per cent of respondents said that they viewed the United States as a 'threat to global peace'. A Pew Trust research poll in 2005 concluded that:

> anti-Americanism is deeper and broader now than at any time in modern history ... the rest of the world both fears and resents the unrivaled power that the United States has amassed since the Cold War ended. In the eyes of others, the US is a worrisome colossus: It is too quick to act unilater-ally, it doesn't do a good job of addressing the world's problems, and it widens the global gulf between rich and poor. On matters of international

security, the rest of the world has become deeply suspicious of US motives and openly skeptical of its word. People abroad are more likely to believe that the US-led war on terror has been about controlling Mideast oil and dominating the world than they are to take at face value America's stated objectives of self-defense and global democratization.[7]

If these feelings herald a long-term trend, then they have serious implications across the spectrum of life in the United States – from how it conducts its business relations, to how it promotes democracy, to how it fights the war on terror. I would argue that they also have serious implications for you, and for anyone interested in fighting poverty and disease, for preventing the spread of nuclear weapons, for ending conflicts around the world, and for regional and international security and prosperity.

What I want to do this evening is talk about the *sources* of anti-Americanism in the world. Why do people dislike us? Why should this worry Americans? Why should it concern America's friends and allies? And what can we do about it?

Sources of division: real or apparent?

There are four distinct sources of anti-Americanism in the world. These may be termed: personality, philosophy, policy and systemic. Let me address each one in turn.

1. Personality

First, personality. We all know that we live in a celebrity culture, where the latest fashion style or rock group or sighting of Angelina and Brad makes the headlines. The same is unfortunately true in foreign policy. Much of what passes for foreign policy debate these days focuses largely on personalities. If only President Bush and other world leaders under-stood each other better, liked each other more, this thinking goes, then all would be right with the world. Often conversations about concrete policy differences end up focusing on personalities. Almost always there is the sense that all our policy differences would disappear if only the personalities changed.

For many people, this sentiment can be reduced to a single person, President George W. Bush. Put simply, many foreigners don't like him. For example, the cover of a leading German magazine depicts President Bush as a modern-day Rambo, complete with rippling muscles and bandoliers. The critics also caricature his intelligence, despite his graduating from Yale and Harvard Business School. And unlike Ronald Reagan – and much worse in the European mindset – President Bush is an openly religious man. Reagan spoke only of an evil empire and people took it to be a figure of speech. President Bush speaks of an entire axis of evil and they suspect he means it literally. It's worth pointing out that the President's religiosity, his optimism, his moral certainty, are all traits that make President Bush, and indeed any American politician, popular domestically. These are traits that many foreigners, especially Europeans, find objectionable.

If this was the sole reason for anti-Americanism, then the problem would be easy to solve. The election of a new American President would make these feelings disappear. Unfortunately, I think the problem is more complex and deeply rooted.

2. Philosophical differences

A second and more important source of anti-Americanism is philosophical.

Philosophical differences with the United States come in two flavours: condescension towards the nature and character of American society and opposition to US attitudes on the use of force in an anarchic international system. It is nothing new for non-Americans, especially Europeans, to criticise American society. The relationship of the citizen to the state – the social contract between citizen and state – is different than in Europe. The crime rate, especially the murder rate from handguns, frightens and appals. Social injustice and inequality, especially for African-Americans, continues to plague our society, as we all saw in the aftermath of Hurricane Katrina.

In addition, American culture is often dismissed or denigrated, as if everything important to know about our country can be learned by watching *American Idol* or *Pimp My Ride*. We've all heard the joke: What is the difference between the United States and yogurt? The answer: Yogurt has real culture. But how accurate a picture of the American reality is this? More than any other country, Americans enjoy greater personal freedoms and have greater control over important decisions in their lives. We have more rights when it comes to free speech, more opportunities for continuing education, and more latitude to try and fail at starting a business, and then try again. And American culture is viewed as an oxymoron. Such high-brow dismissal of all things American as crude and crass somehow forgets to mention, or even to recognise, that the United States is home to some of the world's greatest museums and orchestras, world-class colleges and universities, and leading-edge hospitals and medical research. Or that 70 per cent of all Nobel Prize winners have been American. It ignores the fact that there must be something intrinsically attractive about a place that continues to act as a magnet for millions of people the world over to visit and live.

There is also a philosophical difference over the nature of international relations in the twenty-first century. The United States and our friends and allies overseas increasingly do not share the same world view. We do not see international institutions the same way. And we do not view the use of force the same way. The author Robert Kagan has identified this divide in his book, *Of Paradise and Power*. Simply put, America is from Mars, Europe is from Venus. Kagan describes a broad ideological gap between the US and Europe because of Europe's unique historical experience of the past fifty years, culminating in the past decade with the creation of the European Union. The United States is aggressive in defending its prerogatives as a sovereign state, as compared with European efforts to suppress sovereignty in light of two devastating world wars. The European desire to exercise power through transnational negotiation and cooperation stands in contrast to the Bush administration's view that international law and the United Nations are often unreliable; and that the defence and promotion of a liberal order still depends on the possession and use of military force.[8]

These deep and important philosophical differences are not likely to disappear anytime soon. They give rise to debate and argument and can easily spill over into more generalised and toxic feelings of anti-Americanism.

3. Policy differences

A third source of anti-Americanism is fundamental differences over specific policies. When we think about policy disputes, the Iraq War overshadows all the rest. The war in Iraq was clearly a watershed issue. There is no need to belabour the point here. Beyond the decision to go to war in Iraq, we have other policy differences. Arguments over Kyoto and global warming, our strong support for Israel, opposition to the International Criminal Court and the Comprehensive Test Ban Treaty, and the death penalty, are just a few that top the list. But it is important to note that many of these policies enjoy bipartisan support in the United States; they are neither Democratic nor Republican issues. And it is also possible that some of America's positions may look better a few years from now, as President Reagan's then-controversial decision to base Pershing II and cruise missiles in Europe in the 1980s led to sweeping arms control agreements with the Soviet Union.

Again, there have always been policy disputes between America and its friends and allies. I need go no further than to note that this year commemorates the fiftieth anniversary of the Suez War, where the United States prevented two of its closest allies, Britain and France, from seizing strategic advantage in a weak, Middle Eastern country.

4. Systemic divisions

To be sure, these three sources of anger – personalities, philosophical differences and policy disagreements – have long been fodder for anti-American attitudes overseas. And historically, anti-Americanism, as much as it can be measured, has waxed and waned over time. What is really new today is a *cluster of systemic divisions* – shifts of the global tectonic plates, so to speak. These changes in the international system are, to my mind, the most important and least analysed sources of our difficulties.

First, the collapse of the Berlin Wall and the demise of the Soviet Union changed profoundly the nature of the international system and the nature of the transatlantic relationship. The bipolar world that had grown out of the debris of World War II became a unipolar world. No longer is power balanced and countered among roughly equal states. The US stands alone, the undisputed heavyweight champion of the world. This means that the United States now attracts all the blame for a variety of global problems, for anyone with a grievance. Consider the paradox: the United States is blamed for being too strong. At the same time, it is faulted if it does not use its strength to solve all the world's problems.

There is another consequence of the United States being the world's 'hyper-power', to use the unflattering term of a former French Foreign Minister. As Princeton University Professor John Ikenberry has observed, 'The end of the Cold War ... eliminated a common threat that tied the United States to a global array of allies, and it has meant that the United States does not need these allies in the same way as in the past. But it also means that other states do not need the United States as much, either'.[9] During the Cold War, we all banded together to contain and defeat communism. A shared fear of the Soviet threat was the 'glue' at the core of the transatlantic relationship and America's alliances around the world. Today, there's far less common purpose. The global war on terror simply doesn't apply the same amount of 'glue'.

Second, there is underway a fundamental questioning and rethinking of the legal underpinnings of war and peace, and the use of force. 9/11 was the catalyst that led many scholars and foreign policy practitioners to question how well the pre-9/11 system of international law and the UN Charter could operate in a post-9/11 environment. The concepts of pre-emption, imminent attack, legitimacy and the use of force are all being re-examined and reinterpreted. And it is not just the United States that is doing so. The European Security Strategy and the High-Level Group appointed by the UN Secretary General, Kofi Annan, each acknowledge the threats of Weapons of Mass Destruction, terrorism and failing states.

But if we agree on the threats, we disagree over the policy prescrip-
tions. According to the UN Charter, a state can use force only in self-
defence after it has suffered an armed attack. In other words, states
have to await an actual attack before they can act. Is there any responsible policymaker who would recommend waiting if he knew that
some state or terrorist group was about to use nuclear, chemical or
biological weapons? Some commentators argue that there is an exception if a threatened attack is 'imminent', which would allow a state to
go first. But there is no consensus on this issue, and there is even greater
disagreement over what might constitute the threat of imminent attack.
If there is no consensus on these fundamental questions of world order,
then the United States runs the risk of inviting the world's hostility
every time it uses military force without prior UN Security Council
approval. It is important to note that the debate over when the use of
force is legitimate reaches well beyond the US war against Iraq. It also
pertains to humanitarian interventions to prevent wholesale slaughter
and genocide. What happens when states breach their 'responsibility to
protect' their own citizens and, indeed, actively abuse them?

This question suggests a third systemic change worth noting. A trend
that has developed over the past few decades is the erosion of state sovereignty. Under the Westphalian system, states have long been free to do
as they liked within their own borders without interference from outside
actors. In recent years, however, this has given way to the increasing
acceptance of intervention in the internal affairs of states. In the words of
John Ikenberry, sovereignty is increasingly *contingent*. This means that
eroded norms of sovereignty have created a new 'licence' for powerful
states to intervene in the domestic affairs of weak and troubled states. That
is, the norms of state sovereignty have less 'stopping power'. There are
fewer principled and normative inhibitions on intervention. Moreover,
eroded sovereignty has not been matched by a rise of new norms and
agreements about when and how the 'international community' should
intervene. After all, who speaks for the international community? This
erosion of the norms of state sovereignty has ushered in a new global
struggle over the sources of authority in the international system.

These questions of world order, war and peace, the use of force and
state sovereignty would be interesting, but hardly compelling, without
the presence of a fourth new factor on the international scene – the rise
of unprecedented, unmatched and unrivalled American military power.
The British historian, Paul Kennedy, has commented that 'Nothing has
ever existed like this disparity of power; nothing … Pax Britannica was
run on the cheap, Britain's armies were much smaller than European
armies, and even the Royal Navy was equal to only the next two navies

– right now all the other navies in the world combined could not dent American maritime supremacy'.[10] Kennedy actually underestimates the extent of American military might. American defence spending is now larger than the rest of the world's military spending, combined.

Europe collectively cannot come close to duplicating US military power. Although the non-US members of NATO have 1.25 million men and women under arms and another 1 million in reserve, they have only 55,000 readily deployable troops. The Europeans lack the means to transport troops to battlefields beyond Europe's borders, they lack advanced equipment, and they lack independent intelligence assets to support the troops they do deploy. This relative military weakness is certainly not because of a shortage of courage or martial spirit. Rather, it reflects a conscious decision by European officials that they would rather spend public funds on social programmes. But one result of this choice is that Europe retains only modest ability to shape international affairs, which in turn leads to resentment of the United States.

In this post-9/11 world, where previous ideas about world order and the rules about war and peace are increasingly being called into question, only the US has the military power to engage in large-scale uses of force around the world. For many, the uncertainty over the new rules of military engagement, the erosion of the norm of state sovereignty and the rise of American military might all coalesce into a generalised anxiety over how the United States wields its power. 'The powerful can be dangerous', notes Professor Mandelbaum. 'They can bully, dominate, and if they choose, crush those who are weaker. In a world in which all other countries are weak by comparison, beneath the dislike and disapproval of the United States that public demonstrations manifest and opinion polls record lies another, more potent feeling: fear'.[11] Or, expressed more simply, no one likes Goliath.

If American military power doesn't worry people, then the economic reach of the United States does. This is a fifth source of anti-Americanism: globalisation. It is no secret that many find globalisation enormously disruptive and threatening to traditional cultures and long-established ways of life. Whether it is the unsentimental demands of free-market capitalism, instant global communications, our control of plant, animal and human characteristics through genetic engineering, our potential ability to play God and build new structures atom by atom, the doubling and even tripling of human life spans and the ensuing social pressures these create – all these elements of globalisation are redefining our lives. It can be, and often is for many people, disturbing and disorienting.

Of all the countries of the world, the United States is most closely associated with these elements and, more generally, with the forces of modernity. The United States is the poster child for globalisation. The US has developed economic policies that make it especially well-positioned to take advantage of the forces of globalisation. The international economic system was designed by the US after World War II, the US dollar is the world's currency of choice and the US market is the world's largest, richest and most open. For all of these reasons, anti-globalisation efforts single out the United States; anti-globalisation protests are often indistinguishable from anti-American rants.

Sixth and finally, there is a global demographic shift taking place. The post-war generation in Europe, Korea, Japan and Australia is leaving centre stage. The impact of the passing of the generational torch cannot be underestimated. Previously, governing elites in Western Europe and the United States all shared the historical experience of World War II and the Berlin Airlift. Europeans had positive feelings towards the United States, rooted in America's wartime bravery and power, as well as in its post-war generosity. Older Koreans and Japanese also experienced first-hand America's compassion in rebuilding their homelands. That generation is now almost entirely gone from the scene. With them leaves a reservoir of historic goodwill towards the United States that is irreplaceable. Instead, there is a younger generation in power today in Europe and Asia who came of political age while protesting the Vietnam War and what they viewed as American imperialism. Those who are 'reflexively pro-American' are far fewer and less able to counter the voices of anti-Americanism.

To recap, there are important systemic changes that promote and encourage a greater prominence and higher profile for the United States in world affairs, due largely to American military, economic and diplomatic primacy. They require the United States to play a larger role than before as a provider of regional and international security, at a time when many of the old rules are changing, but new ones have not yet become settled and widely accepted. These systemic changes cannot be wished away. Indeed, they are already upon us. The question is not whether they exist, but what we do about them.

Why should Americans care? Why should our friends and allies care?
Why should Americans care if we're liked or not? After all, we know that foreign policy is not a popularity contest. Policies that are controversial today, such as Iraq, may look better in a few years. And that perhaps our unpopularity is just the price that must be paid for being the world's most powerful country. Still, we do care. Partly that is because of the normal, near-universal human desire to be liked, or at least not misunderstood or hated. We still believe in John Winthrop's description

of America as a 'shining city on the hill', and want others to view us that way as well.

But there are other, larger reasons for caring about the rise of anti-Americanism that comes with a sense of responsibility as the world's only superpower. If others mistrust us or actively work against us, we know that it will be more difficult to secure the peace and spread prosperity; that it will be more challenging – diplomatically, financially and militarily – to sustain and promote a liberal international order that benefits hundreds of millions of people around the world.

And that's why you should care: because the history of the last century demonstrates that when the United States retreats from the world, bad things happen. The US rejected the League of Nations and turned inward in the 1920s and 1930s, contributing to the Great Depression and the onset of World War II. After the Vietnam War, a weakened and inward-looking America prompted countries to develop their own nuclear weapons programmes, emboldened Islamic fundamentalists to attack American interests, allowed Vietnam to invade Cambodia and the Soviet Union to occupy Afghanistan. And to those who say this couldn't happen today, that America couldn't pull up the drawbridge and retreat behind the parapets, please note that recent opinion polls in the United States reveal a preference for isolationism not seen since the end of the Vietnam War. It is hard to imagine any scenario in which an isolated, disengaged United States would be a better friend and ally, would better promote global prosperity, would more forcefully endorse democracy, social justice and human dignity, or would do more to enhance peace and security.

What can be done?

Given these philosophical differences, policy disagreements and systemic changes, what can the United States do to revive its image in the world? First of all, we need to do a much better job explaining and defending our choices. For a country that virtually invented modern communications, we don't do a very good job of telling our story. For example, everyone knows that the United States hasn't joined the International Criminal Court, but how many people know that the US has committed close to half a billion dollars to international criminal tribunals in the last decade? Everyone knows of our strong support for Israel, but how many people know that United States has contributed more funds to the Palestinian people than any other country, more than the entire Arab world combined? Everyone knows we went to war against Iraq without a second UN Security Council resolution, but how many people know that the US is the single largest donor to the United Nations and the International Atomic Energy Agency? Or that the US is the number one donor to developing countries? That the US does a better job than Europe or Japan in terms of opening its markets to products from developing countries? That the US has increased assistance to sub-Saharan Africa by more than 250 per cent in the last five years? That the US AIDS relief effort is the largest health initiative in history?

I could go on, but you get the idea.

So we can and should do a better job of explaining ourselves. But this won't completely solve the problem. We need to do more.

A way forward

In the past few years, the sad truth is that the United States has created new enemies and behaved in ways that have antagonised even its friends. We simply must do a better job of reaching out to others. This means first of all that the United States must remain engaged with the rest of the world. It should not indulge the temptation to live in 'splendid isolation', because it would not be so splendid. For one thing, it would devastate the American economy. Foreign direct investment stood at over $1.5 trillion last year and was responsible for close to 7 million jobs. Without foreign visitors, America's tourism industries and our nation's universities would both suffer mightily. Turning away those who risk life and limb to come to America's shores in search of a better life would also betray our heritage as a nation of immigrants. From the arts to the Academy, from the sciences to the sports fields, foreign nationals enrich every aspect of our civic life.

We need to be engaged with the rest of the world because America can't meet the challenges of the twenty-first century by itself. Just as in World War II and during the Cold War, we need friends and allies. No one country can defeat the transnational threats we face today. Terrorism, infectious disease, environmental pollution, weapons of mass destruction, narcotics and human trafficking – all these can only be solved by cooperating with other states. America must remain connected to the world.

Second, Americans need to accept that the United States will not always be popular, but that it remains an enormous force for good. When crises erupt in the West Bank or Waziristan, in Bogotá or Beijing or Belfast, people still get on the phone and call Washington, not Brussels or Tokyo or Moscow. Just a few weeks ago, Washington was instrumental in helping reach agreement for the Darfur region of Sudan that will hopefully end a bloody and violent conflict.

Third, as powerful as the United States is today in military, economic and diplomatic terms, as powerful as it will be in the future, Americans must always be mindful that we cannot impose our values on other peoples and other countries. The good news is that we don't have to. Our values aren't simply American values, they are universal values. The ideas and ideals that guide American political life are our greatest strength. They also remain the greatest hope for all the peoples of the world. Liberty and the natural rights of man; intellectual, religious and economic freedom; limited government and the rule of law; tolerance and equality of opportunity – these principles will keep America powerful, they will continue to serve as our touchstone and compass, and they will continue to inspire others to dream of a better world.

Finally, I want to ask you to keep criticising us. I know some of you will need no encouragement. For the students here this evening, use the excellent education you are receiving at the University of Ulster to think critically, to break through the blizzard of information and think for yourself. To come visit the United States and see for yourself. To help us identify and correct our shortcomings. This is the only way we can improve and get better.

And when you're not helping the United States, help improve your own society. Northern Ireland is now close to realising John Hume's vision of a compassionate, just and integrated society. Help the politicians. Encourage them. Push them. Even challenge them. And as you do so, please know that the United States government and the American people will be right there beside you, standing shoulder-to-shoulder, as you go forward towards realising the full promise and potential of this great country.

Thank you very much.

Postscript

When his term in Northern Ireland, for which he received the Foreign Affairs Award for Public Service, ended in 2007, Ambassador Mitchell Reiss returned to senior appointments at the College of William and Mary, including Diplomat-in-Residence. In 2010, he published *Negotiating with Evil: When to Talk to Terrorists*,[12] and also became President of Washington College in Maryland, one of America's oldest foundations. He was also an advisor on foreign policy to the leading Republican politician Mitt Romney, continuing his record of combining academia with an involvement in public affairs.

Notes

1 As well as, as sanctioned by the Security Council, to restore or maintain international peace and security or punish aggression.
2 Senate Resolution 54 – Paying Tribute to John Hume, Congressional Record, 151: 15 (14 February 2005), S1356–S1357, www.gpo.gov/fdsys/pkg/CREC-2005-02-14/pdf/CREC-2005-02-14-pt1-PgS1356-4.pdf (last accessed 18 March 2013).
3 Simon Schama, 'The Unloved American. Two centuries of alienating Europe', *The New Yorker*, 10 March 2003, www.newyorker.com/archive/2003/03/10/030310fa_fact?currentPage=4 (last accessed 1 August 2013).
4 Michael Mandelbaum, *The Case for Goliath: How America Acts as the World's Government in the 21st Century* (New York: Public Affairs, 2005), p. 150.
5 Paul Hollander, *Anti-Americanism: Irrational and Rational* (New Brunswick, NJ: Transaction, 1995), p. 7.
6 Paul Hollander, Edited with Introduction, *Understanding Anti-Americanism. Its Origins and Impact* (Edinburgh: Capercaillie Books Limited, 2005), p. 18.
7 Trends 2005, 7, Global Opinion. The Spread of Anti-Americanism, The Pew Research Center, Washington, DC, 2005, pp. 106 and 109, www.pewglobal.org/files/pdf/104.pdf © 2012 Pew Research Center (last accessed 16 July 2013).
8 Robert Kagan, *Of Paradise and Power: America and Europe in the New World Order* (New York: Alfred A. Knopf, 2003).
9 G. John Ikenberry, 'The Security Trap', *Democracy: A Journal of Ideas*, 2 (Fall 2006), www.democracyjournal.org/2/6481.php?page=all (last accessed 16 July 2013).
10 Paul Kennedy, 'The Eagle Has Landed', *Financial Times* (London), 2 February 2002, p. 1.
11 Mandelbaum, *The Case for Goliath*, p. 147.
12 Mitchell B. Reiss, *Negotiating with Evil: When to Talk to Terrorists* (New York: Open Road Integrated Media, 2010).

12

All peace is local

President Mary McAleese

Introduction

Mary McAleese was inaugurated President of Ireland at a ceremony in Dublin Castle's historic St Patrick's Hall on 11 November 1997, having successfully campaigned for the country's highest office on the nomination of Fianna Fail. It was a mark of the respect that she had earned during her seven-year term that in 2004 she was the sole candidate for the office, serving for a further seven years, the most that the Constitution allows. In 1997, she had made history by becoming the first person from Northern Ireland to be elected. The office of President, or *Uachtaran na hEireann*, was created in the 1937 Constitution, replacing that of Governor-General, its status, powers and responsibilities being set out in Articles 12, 13 and 14. As head of state, the President takes precedence over all of its citizens and is Supreme Commander of the Defence Forces. In matters of policy the President acts on the advice of the government, appointing the Taoiseach and other ministers on the nomination of the Dail. As a constitutional head of state, the President carries the responsibility of representing the country and all of its people.

In lecturing on 'Lessons of the peace process', President McAleese was informed by her personal experience when, at a formative period in her life, her home area of north Belfast was engulfed by some of the worst of the conflict, as rioting broke out in August 1969. Over the following years that area of the city had to endure more than its share of suffering. Her turning of Tip O'Neill's celebrated phrase that 'All politics is local' into 'All peace is local' was especially apt. Although her career was to lead to the President's residence in Dublin's Phoenix Park, *Aras an Uachtarain*, her reputation was made in the very different world of academia. Graduating in law from Queen's University Belfast in 1973, two years later, at the enviably youthful age of twenty-four, she was appointed to the Reid Chair of Criminal Law, Criminology and Penology at Trinity College Dublin. Returning to her old university in 1987, she became Director of the Institute of Professional Legal Studies. Her university career reached its summit in 1994 when she became Pro-Vice-Chancellor at Queen's University, and the first woman to serve in that role. Her academic career did not, however, shut out involvement in public affairs. In 1984, she was a member of the Catholic Church Episcopal Delegation to the New Ireland Forum, set up under the premiership of Dr Garret Fitzgerald (*qv*). In 1996, in the wake of the widespread disturbances which had broken out over parading, the British government set up the Independent Review of Parades and Marches chaired by Dr (later Sir) Peter North. Here, too, she was a member of the Catholic Church delegation over an issue of acute importance to the stability of society at that time. A sense of public service also saw her involvement with such diverse bodies as Northern Ireland Electricity and the Irish Commission for Prisoners Overseas.

The lecture which she delivered on 4 December 2006 followed shortly after the historic St Andrews Agreement of 13 October, which had established a path for political progress towards the restoration of devolved government and its associated institutions, although when she spoke its terms were still to be ratified formally by the Democratic Unionist Party and Sinn Fein. The lecture opened, she explained, with the paradox implicit in Tip O'Neill's celebrated dictum that 'All politics is local'; namely, that while each conflict has its distinctive local personality, the human element is common to all. What can peace processes share with each other, particularly given that, as she pointed out, 'we are among the fortunate few who have an imminent possibility of putting conflict permanently behind us'?

Her lecture pointed to the number of obstacles that had to be surmounted in the course of the peace process in Northern Ireland, and how many different inputs had been necessary. The lessons, she explained, were the salutary ones that it was easier to enter a conflict than to exit from it, that there were 'no quick, easy solutions', and that successive Rubicons had to be crossed. The process had been a complex one, in which the European Union had helped by allowing Ireland and Britain to improve their relationship through cooperation in its affairs, and in which the Americans had been committed to seeing the triumph of politics. Negotiations, she affirmed, had to be inclusive, embracing the full political spectrum. A peace settlement meant each side having to give up something, of 'conceding a little and gaining a little'.

President McAleese also focused attention on other conflict zones in the world where people were watching to see if the politics of partnership and peace would succeed in Northern Ireland. In short, her address echoed what had been the theme of her Presidency, 'Building

Bridges'. On 11 November 1998, together with Queen Elizabeth II and Belgium's King Albert II, she had dedicated the Island of Ireland Peace Tower, where men of the 36th Ulster Division, largely recruited from the pre-1914 Ulster Volunteer Force, and the predominantly Nationalist 16th Irish Division had fought and died together at the Battle of Messines in 1917. 'The latest lesson from these fraught years of peacebuilding', she concluded, 'is that there is a time for moving on and we are well and truly there'.

Lecture

Good evening, everybody.

Thank you for your warm welcome, and my special thanks to John Hume for his invitation to me to speak to you this evening

Tip O'Neill, in whose honour this lecture series was established, told us that 'All politics is local'. It's a truth that says every conflict has its own complex local personality which makes it difficult for outsiders to fully comprehend but also paradoxically says that the human psychology at work in politics is essentially the same everywhere and so we may have something to teach and learn from one another. And that is what I want to cast a look at – what is shareable and what, too, do we need to remember

Northern Ireland is regularly compared in the media to other situations of conflict from Palestine, to Sri Lanka, the Basque Country, South Africa, Cyprus, the former Yugoslavia and beyond. In a more substantive way, there is a growing academic discipline around comparative conflict resolution – exemplified by the International Centre of Excellence for Conflict and Peace Studies here in the University of Ulster – although not many are so fortunate to have such a distinguished and experienced a Chair as the international statesman John Hume. It was John's legendary persistence as a champion of peace and his Europeanising and internationalising of the debate about Northern Ireland that helped promote today's new global reality in which more and more politicians, civil society leaders, students and professionals are engaging in dialogue across these situations, discussing each other's experiences and deepening their knowledge of conflicts, how to manage them, how to avoid them and how to get out of them. Judging by the global success rate there is a very long way to go but judging by our own situation we are among the fortunate few who have an imminent possibility of putting conflict permanently behind us

There are those who would dismiss the value of comparisons between conflicts, saying each is too unique to be of use elsewhere, that it is naïve or even arrogant to think our experience can be transferable. But the truth is, of course, that our own peace process did not occur in a hermetically sealed bubble but happened in a local, European and international context from which came many sources of inspiration, support and experience, some obvious, some subtle – but all of which impacted emphatically on our journey to peace, justice and equality

Those who drove the Northern Ireland peace process were often warned about the futility of their efforts by a litany of armchair observers and commentators and it is true that it sometimes did look as if we were going one step forward only to go two steps back

Eight years on from the Good Friday Agreement, even the sceptics would acknowledge that we have progressed to two steps forward and one step back which if you do the maths is quite a considerable advance. Two clear warnings we can send to other places of conflict – and keep well to the front of our own minds as a caution against relapse – are firstly, that entering conflict is a lot easier than exiting conflict and secondly, there are no quick, easy solutions. At times the pace has been so slow that it has felt as if people had to be persuaded one at a time. And yet looking back at where we started from and where we now are, there is a lot to be grateful to the peacemakers for.

- Considerable progress has been made in making Northern Ireland a more equal society socially, politically and economically, guided by the precepts and principles of equality and human rights. The changes in policing and in employment laws, to take two important examples, have set the scene for the development of a fully inclusive society.
- The IRA armed campaign has ended, its arms have been decommissioned and its leadership now supports the exclusively political path. The military presence is at its lowest in thirty years and as watchtowers are demolished and bases closed the apparatus of war has almost disappeared.
- Loyalist paramilitaries, while regrettably not yet over the decommissioning line, have nonetheless evolved considerably in their thinking and among them are leaders who are anxious to make a positive contribution to the new, re-imagined Northern Ireland, which is beginning to emerge.
- Bridges have been built between North and South, economically, politically, culturally and humanly, completely altering the nature and temper of dialogue between both parts of this island.
- Cooperation between the two governments has never been better and is exemplified by their role as stewards of the peace process.

- While the tediously heavy lifting required to finally put in place
  a power sharing administration is evidence of lingering, though
  hopefully diminishing, political difficulties, the fact that both the
  DUP and Sinn Fein have asserted their willingness to engage in a
  new administration is just as important evidence that the distance
  left to be travelled is relatively short and the issues at least clear.
  One side has to commit to power sharing and the other to policing.

So what lessons have we learned that might be of some use to others
faced with that dangerous intermingling of divided politics, religion,
ethnicity and violence?

The first thing we acknowledge is that there is no neat universal
solution, no one size fits all answers, for wherever people attempt to
build peace, while the challenge will be the same there will be differences
of context, memory, ambition, personality, resources and outcome.

We can say about ourselves though that the wider context was and
remains crucial and that what happens in far off places does have a
tangible impact. As I said at the beginning, what happened here did
not happen in a sealed vacuum. Northern Ireland had known sectarian
conflict and paramilitarism from its inception. The most recent episode,
known as the Troubles, began in the ferment of the American and
European 1960s civil rights movements and the rising expectations of
the local baby boomer generation, the first to benefit from widened
access to third level education, that generation so memorably described
by another Nobel Laureate of this city, Seamus Heaney, as having 'intel-
ligences brightened and unmannerly as crowbars'.[1] It ran in parallel
with the largely peaceful end of South African apartheid, the Oslo Peace
Accords, the end of the Cold War and the liberation of much of Eastern
Europe and the Baltic States in velvet revolutions – which proved
that long-frozen situations could thaw, and thaw rapidly, and that
non-violent political efforts had a formidable power. These examples
were real factors in building the all-important sense of momentum and
possibility for justice and peace in our own situation.

Another important international context was membership of the
European Union which gave Ireland the opportunity, an opportunity
it used brilliantly, to transform itself into one of the world's most
prosperous and globalised economies. Today's Ireland is socially, politically and culturally light years away from the Ireland of thirty years
ago. It is a confident, multicultural, problem-solving, can-do country,
a significant player in Europe, the United Nations and in world affairs.

The European Union can also be credited with being the prompt for
one of the most crucial dynamics in the peace process and that is the

hugely improved relationship between Ireland and Britain which began to change as they grew in friendship and trust around the Union table. In a remarkably short period of time the historically fraught relationship gave way to a deep and genuine mutual respect which made it possible to work collegially towards solving the Northern conflict culminating in the Good Friday Agreement.

Support for successive peace initiatives came from around the world but nowhere more effectively than from the United States where Irish America had long been mobilised in opposition to discrimination against Catholics by people like Hugh Carey, Daniel Patrick Moynihan, Ted Kennedy and of course Tip O'Neill himself. Successive American administrations became actively involved in constructing the peace process and there is no doubt that without Presidents Clinton and Bush and the saintly Senator Mitchell we would not be as far down the road as we are. Their unwavering opposition to violence and determination to see politics triumph were matched by an even-handedness in dealing with all sides which greatly facilitated the attempts to mediate compromise.

By the time the Good Friday Agreement was hammered out there was a long legacy of failed efforts from which to learn. The overwhelming validation of the Agreement by those who share this island gave it a huge moral status in addition to its legal authority as an international treaty. The Agreement tackled the conflict on a series of interlocking fronts addressing all the relationships and issues which had been problematic. It settled the vexed question of the constitutional status of Northern Ireland, allowing that it would stay within the United Kingdom unless and until a majority decided otherwise. It detailed the arrangements for power sharing within Northern Ireland and prescribed the inter-governmental arrangements between North and South and between Ireland and Britain, thus putting a fresh new coherency at the heart of these previously awkward relationships. Crucially the Agreement's overarching context was a commitment to the building of a society based on true equality, fairness and justice for all the people of Northern Ireland.

Fully inclusive negotiations was another clear feature of our experience. In charting the history of the peace process, attention has rightly been given to the moment of recognition that durable peace required Sinn Fein to be brought into the process. No one should be under any illusion about the risks that were taken and the enormous political and moral courage that was involved in articulating and finally achieving this. The name of John Hume towers above all others and the Agreement is clear confirmation that he led in the right direction, understanding as he did so clearly that the peace dividend had to be real in its effects across the full political spectrum from loyalism and unionism through to nationalism and republicanism.

Another important lesson learnt was to avoid the paralysis of the politics of the last atrocity. Time and again paramilitary outrages threatened to close negotiations down but intelligent peacemakers knew that there was no future in giving such a comprehensive veto on peace to the men of violence. The talking had to continue no matter what, if politics and peace were to prevail.

At various times contentious issues looked set to derail the process – the structures of power-sharing, crossborder cooperation, policing and criminal justice reform, prisoner releases, decommissioning, contentious parades and more. But with careful choreography small gestures of generosity were elicited from all sides and as each of these small steps filled in the long arrears of trust, they brought us closer to the possibility of taking bigger steps.

We learned that there was no one Rubicon but rather successive Rubicons, each vital in its own way but never more than the one that lay ahead. We learnt how important it was to get all the likely trip wires on to the table rather than have them ambush proceedings just as agreement looked possible.

We learnt to think inventively and laterally, breaking new ground with borrowed mechanisms like d'Hondt. Workable models, sequencing, care around language, all provided us with a resource base of cautionary tales and inspiration for ourselves and perhaps others.

But not one step would have been possible if the political parties and civic society had not committed, no matter how tentatively, to the process and if they had not stayed with its bumpy course through thick and thin. So courageous leadership was key and still is. Similarly none of this would have been possible had not the people of Northern Ireland, for all their woeful loss and brokenness, committed to peace and reconciliation as their gift to future generations.

Through fighting and death and injury and fear they debated and argued and listened and disputed, often with the help of the media, church groups and others, and somehow, somewhere along the way, the peacemakers reached critical mass. People began to look more analytically at their own stories and listen more thoughtfully to the story of the other. They started to look for points of connection with the other rather than points of conflict. Cross-community initiatives, cross-border initiatives, helped by the International Fund for Ireland and European funds, opened people from opposing communities up to each other in ways that had not happened previously. Many key groups in civic society gave great example as they explored ways to reach out to one another, to tackle sectarianism, to encourage simple friendships. And many organisations, official and unofficial, which had been structured on a cross-community or cross-border basis and which drew together people from all backgrounds, hung together through the most difficult of times bearing effective witness to the importance of not giving up. There was a growing realisation that peace would cost each side; that there would be sacrifices as well as gains but that ultimately 99 per cent of something was better than 100 per cent of nothing. In these very human processes of disappointment and reluctant acceptance, of conceding a little and gaining a little, lie insights that are very shareable with other communities who are further back down the road to peace and in need of reassurance that the journey ahead is worthwhile.

As the poet said, peace does come dropping slow. And here we are just a whisper away from devolution and a new government and a new dawn. The DUP and Sinn Fein have both indicated a willingness to make it happen and to make it work. That is welcome news for all of us who share this island and especially for the long-suffering citizens of Northern Ireland. It is no consolation but hopefully may be some kind of memorial of vindication for all those scandalously lost, wasted and broken lives. And there is another constituency watching to see if the politics of partnership and peace will make it across the line here. That constituency is in Darfur, Iraq, Afghanistan, Lebanon, Myanmar, Congo, Palestine, Israel and all the other places where there is only fear and hatred and violence and no end in sight despite a clamour for peace and stability. And then there is the constituency that is our children and our grandchildren.

Recent events confirm to us that the peace process is still a work in progress. How could it be otherwise when you consider that the conflict it is attempting to resolve is more like four hundred rather than forty years old. But this is the most liberated and the best educated generation ever to inhabit this island. It has the brainpower to know the past was a mess and the skill to clean the mess up effectively. It has the heartpower to recognise the loss and waste that came out of conflict and the passion to heal and to reconcile.

Northern Ireland played Ireland's starring role in the first industrial revolution. It has a strong entrepreneurial tradition, a rich multifaceted culture drawing on the deep wells of Irish, British and Scottish tradition. But just at the point where its most educated generation ever appeared, it slid into the Troubles and so has never until now had the chance to reveal its fullest potential, harnessing all its talent, in a unified civic society, working together in peace and partnership. In the South, though access to free second level education came twenty-five years later than in the North, there is no mystery as to what that education revolution unleashed into Irish society, for the Ireland built as a result is today the success story par excellence of the European Union. But both jurisdictions inhabit one small divided island and we have yet to see what could be accomplished if both jurisdictions worked comfortably and respectfully together for the advancement of this region and for all its inhabitants. The potential is enormous. The business communities north and south have been powerhouses of fresh energy and pragmatic thinking, seeing as they do the many benefits to be gained for both jurisdictions by working collegially.

Through the pressures for peace from so many constituencies we now have this hard-earned, miraculous chance to see what a fresh, new culture of cooperation within Northern Ireland, between North and South, and between Ireland and Britain can accomplish.

A wise man once said, if you are given the opportunity of a lifetime make sure you take it in the lifetime of the opportunity. Let's hope the opportunity will be taken and that soon, very soon, Northern Ireland will become a byword for the triumph of politics.

The latest lesson from these past fraught years of peacebuilding is that there is a time for moving on and we are clearly well and truly there.

Postscript

As the Constitution demanded, on 11 November 2011 Mary McAleese left office, but in the previous May another important bridge had been put in place when she welcomed Queen Elizabeth II to Dublin. The two heads of state joined in ceremonies at the Garden of Remembrance at Parnell Square and the Irish National War Memorial at Islandbridge. With the first visit of a reigning British monarch to independent Ireland, times had moved on, as in her lecture she had counselled that they should.

Notes

1 Seamus Heaney, 'From the Canton of Expectation', *The Haw Lantern* (London: Faber and Faber, 1987), p. 47.

13

From peace to reconciliation

Foreign Minister Dermot Ahern, TD

Introduction

Coming as it did at a pivotal time in the political fortunes of Northern Ireland, Foreign Minister Dermot Ahern's lecture 'From peace to reconciliation', on 3 April 2007, provided a unique range of insights into what had, by any reckoning, been a historic series of events. A solicitor by profession, by 2007 he was a highly experienced politician, having represented County Louth for Fianna Fail since 1987. After serving as a Minister of State at the Department of the Taoiseach and then at Defence, in 1991 he became Government Chief Whip in the Dail. During the 27th Dail, he chaired the British-Irish Parliamentary Body, which had been set up in 1990 to bring together representatives from the parliaments in Dublin and London. He then held the portfolios of Social Welfare and of Communications, Marine and Natural Resources before being appointed Minister for Foreign Affairs on 13 September 2004.

His appointment to Foreign Affairs came at a time when the political institutions in Northern Ireland, set up under the terms of the Good Friday Agreement and the Northern Ireland Act of 1998, seemed to be faltering. The Northern Ireland Assembly and the Executive had been suspended twice, the first time on 11 February 2001, and then again on 14 October 2002. There were two significant developments, however. On 26 September 2005, the Independent International Commission on Decommissioning confirmed that the IRA had put its armoury beyond use, the last of four acts of decommissioning which had begun in October 2001. In politics, a series of Assembly and Westminster elections saw power shift on the Unionist side from the Ulster Unionist Party (UUP) to the Democratic Unionist Party (DUP) and on the Nationalist side from the Social Democratic and Labour Party (SDLP) to Sinn Fein. The question of the hour was whether an agreement could be brokered between the DUP and Sinn Fein, which would enable devolution to be restored. Agreement to that end was accomplished at a meeting convened by the

British and Irish governments at St Andrews in October 2006. In the St Andrews Agreement the two governments reaffirmed their commitment to the principles of consent, inclusivity and the equality agenda. Crucially, the political parties committed themselves to the operation of a power-sharing government and the north–south and east–west bodies, and to support for the police and the courts.

The St Andrew's Agreement paved the way for political breakthrough. On 28 January 2007, an extraordinary Sinn Fein *Ard Fheis* in Dublin passed a resolution committing the party to supporting the Police Service of Northern Ireland, the Policing Board and the District Policing Partnerships and on 24 March, the DUP's executive agreed to participate in a new Executive in May. Two days later, the Reverend Ian Paisley, leader of the DUP, and Sinn Fein President Gerry Adams confirmed that they would enter into government on 8 May. The reconstituted Northern Ireland Executive consisted of the DUP, Sinn Fein, the SDLP and the UUP, later joined by the Alliance Party. The Reverend Ian Paisley of the DUP and Martin McGuinness of Sinn Fein became First and Deputy First Minister.

When Dermot Ahern spoke on 4 April, then, the historic event of 26 March was only days old, and he acknowledged that in providing the 'solid basis for genuine, sustainable power-sharing government in Northern Ireland', it had achieved what few had thought possible. He counselled that there were still crucial issues to be tackled. The loyalist paramilitaries had yet to decommission, but on 3 May the Ulster Volunteer Force announced that it was assuming a civilian role and on 11 November the Ulster Freedom Fighters said it was standing down.[1]

Recognising that what was happening was not an end in itself, Ahern turned to three themes which the incoming Northern Ireland Executive and the Irish government would have to address. The first of these was the creation of an infrastructure that would sustain prosperity across the island. The issue of sectarianism needed to be addressed, still ingrained as it was, and he appealed for those engaged in parading disputes to engage. This was an important message since serious problems over parading had emerged in various locations from 1995 onwards, and while, as he observed, constructive moves had been made in Derry, the situation in some other locations remained to be resolved. Finally, he exhorted his listeners to ensure that 'the peace process must leave no one behind', and that the work of reconciliation would take decades.

While emphasising the importance of the next steps, he acknowledged that it was 'a time full of hope and expectation', which events in Derry had pioneered. Conscious as he was that 'we remain deeply mindful of the terrible suffering of the more recent past', he was convinced that the meeting of 26 March had seen 'a shift in the political paradigm of Northern Ireland, when the parties grasped the opportunity of a lifetime and committed themselves to support and participate fully in a partnership government and in all of the institutions of the Good Friday Agreement'. Moving from peace to reconciliation would require continuing dedication to the 'common values of democracy, equality and the rule of law'.

Lecture

I am honoured to be here tonight at the invitation of John Hume, a man to whom Ireland owes a great debt.

This is a time full of hope and expectation for Northern Ireland. It is therefore a great privilege for me to share some personal reflections on the political process with you tonight and to cast an eye forward to the collective challenges ahead.

John Hume

Long before we had a political agreement, we had a political process. It is difficult but vitally important to recall the realities of Northern Ireland at the height of the Troubles. For twenty years violence was met by retaliation, each successive mindless act entrenching individuals, polarising communities and choking hope.

Derry saw the worst of the troubles. But it was also here that the first important steps were taken towards imagining a better way. Few had the courage and the bold imagination to set about patiently giving shape and reality to that better way. John Hume is one of those few. John Hume had an instinctive grasp of what was required. He knew that the way ahead would be difficult and lonely. For that we will always be in John's debt.

Though the SDLP will nominate just one minister to the incoming Executive, it has been central to making this government happen. Not alone because of John Hume. We should be thankful that those who accompanied him and who followed John, in particular Mark Durkan, were equally ready to take difficult but absolutely necessary steps knowing full well that those very steps exposed them to political criticism from both flanks. The party's decision to join the Policing Board in 2001 is a case in point. That decision was vital to embedding and accelerating the implementation of the Patten reforms.

It has often been said that in recent years support has shifted decisively away from the middle ground. Subsequent events have shown that this was too simple a reading. In reality, Sinn Fein and the DUP were each embarked on a process that has brought them far from their previously entrenched positions.

Today the middle ground has become, thankfully, the only viable political space in Northern Ireland. That is a very significant part of John Hume's legacy.

Irish America

It is also Tip O'Neill's legacy, and that of many friends of Ireland who followed him. The roll is too long to call in full but the contributions of Bill Clinton, George Mitchell, Ted Kennedy and his fellow horsemen, George Bush, Hillary Clinton, successive US diplomats and special envoys, will always be honourably linked to this process. Its success will be their success too.

The Tip O'Neill Chair here at Magee is funded by the American-Ireland Fund which has contributed enormously to peace and reconciliation on the island of Ireland. It is right that we express our appreciation for their magnificent work and our confidence in their future strategy.

I was pleased, therefore, that the government was recently able to announce an endowment to The Ireland Funds of €10 million (£7 million approximately) over the next five years which I hope can be matched by private sector support.

America's genius for optimism helped keep this process alive through its darkest days. And America brought two great insights that helped make the process work.

The first insight was Washington DC itself: the role that political acknowledgement by the administration and by Congress could itself play in sustaining the process. Year after year, doors have opened in Congress and the White House, sometimes to encourage, sometimes to cajole, but always with an open-handed generosity. Without that diplomatic track, I do not believe we would be where we are today.

The second insight was the economy: the role that economic growth and job creation could play in tackling the economic roots of extremist politics. Tip O'Neill saw that immediately. So, too, did Congress, which began voting significant funding as early as 1986 – when unemployment was 16.8 per cent – in support of job creation. These efforts were marked not only by generosity but also by imagination. Through US intervention, for example, venture capital was deployed for the first time ever in Northern Ireland and the border counties to help small companies to grow and to build lasting jobs.

John Hume too was one of the first to recognise the particular importance of the social economy – an insight that was directly responsible for the growth and consolidation of the credit union movement in Northern Ireland.

These initiatives dovetailed with the potential for future economic growth and development unlocked by the negotiation of the Good Friday Agreement in 1998.

In the years since then, Northern Ireland has seen unprecedented prosperity. Unemployment is at historically low levels. Investment from abroad is steadily increasing. The property market is rising. Long-awaited urban regeneration is taking place. The landmark Harland and Wolff crane now has many companions on the Belfast skyline.

The prosperity is now underpinning the peace.

Community leadership

Many of those who drove progress at community level will gather at the Royal Hospital in Kilmainham in two weeks' time to share experiences and look ahead to some of the challenges facing them.

Many are from Derry – indeed many of the most inspiring stories of quiet heroism within divided communities are Derry stories. Uniquely, Derry brokered the first and arguably the most imaginative agreement on parading – the Derry Initiative.

At last year's conference, I had an opportunity to meet with Alistair Simpson, former Governor of the Apprentice Boys, and to discuss this with him. Not surprisingly, he made clear that this local success could not have been brokered without John Hume.

Monday 26 March

It is a great honour to follow President Mary McAleese in this lecture series at John's invitation.

I was struck by a comment she made in her remarks here last December. She recalled the words of a wise man who said: *if you are given the opportunity of a lifetime, make sure you take it in the lifetime of the opportunity.*

If ever the lifetime of an opportunity was nearing its end, it was on Monday 26 March.

The meeting between the DUP and Sinn Fein at Stormont on that day achieved what few believed possible a few short months ago – a solid basis for genuine, sustainable power-sharing government in Northern Ireland.

No one could see the pictures we saw that morning and hear the words that were spoken without feeling real hope for the future.

It was a moment which left many commentators surprised. In that moment, we saw the habits of recent history overturned.

In 1985, faced with the reality that politics in Northern Ireland appeared to have entered a *cul de sac*, the British and Irish governments took shared political responsibility for the process through the Anglo-Irish Agreement. There were short interludes: bad ones where politics seemed driven by events; good ones where the parties assumed responsibility in the Executive following the Good Friday Agreement. For over twenty years, however, responsibility has more or less remained with the two governments.

That responsibility gave rise to a political partnership which I believe has been unparalleled anywhere else in Europe during these years. It assumed its strongest form in the political relationship forged over ten years by Bertie Ahern and Tony Blair.

Had our current efforts to secure devolution been unsuccessful, the government had long resolved to strengthen their partnership even further. That was never a threat. It was born of the simple recognition that, throughout this process, when hopes were dashed and things got tough, that relationship grew only stronger.

The only way that could ever change was if the parties collectively took responsibility themselves.

That is what happened on Monday 26 March when the parties agreed a revised date for devolution and Ian Paisley and Gerry Adams sat down together to agree a way to share power.

On the day we saw a shift in the political paradigm of Northern Ireland, when the parties grasped the opportunity of a lifetime and committed themselves to support and participate fully in a partnership government and in all of the institutions of the Good Friday Agreement.

Challenges ahead: a programme for partnership

As I said at the outset, this is a time full of hope and expectation for Northern Ireland. It is a time to ponder the challenges ahead.

For our work is not yet done.

Restoration of the power-sharing institutions on 8 May, as now agreed by the parties, will mark major progress, but it will not be the end of the road.

It will be a critical stepping stone to the creation of a society in Northern Ireland where questions of identity, culture and tradition are no longer identified with discord and division, but are seen through a prism of tolerance, generosity and mutual respect.

There will be challenges in the period ahead as we seek to ensure that restoration of the institutions in May can pave the way for true reconciliation, so that the vision of a new beginning for Northern Ireland articulated in the Good Friday Agreement is realised.

Tackling those challenges will require a new partnership between the new Northern Ireland Executive and the Irish government.

I want to reflect tonight on three important issues for that collective agenda.

The first is *building prosperity*.

North–South cooperation has already delivered tangible benefits to all parts of this island. It has enabled creative and innovative all-island thinking in many diverse policy areas. Revitalising border communities and harnessing synergies in energy and transport are just some examples.

We are working within the framework of the North West Gateway Initiative to enhance the development of this part of the country, for the benefit of communities on both sides of the border.

Only yesterday, the new all-island free travel scheme was introduced. An all-island electricity market will soon be a reality.

I used the facilities at the City of Derry airport earlier this evening – the Irish government's contribution to its development was an investment which clearly makes sense.

At this critical moment in the peace process, we must acknowledge that we will never reach our full economic potential on this island without much closer North–South cooperation.

This year, for the first time, our National Development Plan proposed significant Irish government investment in projects and initiatives of mutual benefit North and South.

We want to take that Plan forward now in partnership and in agreement with the new Northern Ireland Executive and with the British government.

We will make available €580 million (£400 million) to fund an unprecedented package of infrastructure investment. One of the key elements in the package will be the development of a dual carriageway standard road to Derry and Donegal. That will remove the single greatest impediment to the development of this region.

It will be the biggest and most important cross-border project ever on this island.

That is just one element of the package. We look forward to working with the new ministers in the Executive, including through the framework of the restored North–South Ministerial Council, to implement the imaginative and ambitious policies that we need to rise to the challenge of building future prosperity on the island.

The second issue I wish to focus on is *tackling sectarianism*, one of the toughest and most urgent challenges for both governments.

Sectarianism is arguably one of the gravest and most pernicious threats to society on this island. Yet it is an unacknowledged crisis, making headlines only when it kills.

This year, my department set aside a specific budget within the Reconciliation Fund to support good projects in communities seeking new and more effective ways of addressing sectarianism. If necessary it will be increased. No good project should be turned away for lack of practical support.

Notwithstanding the progress make on the political front, dealing with the legacy of division remains one of our greatest challenges. Often we see this played out around contentious parades – an issue that has the potential to raise tensions that have wider implications for stability well beyond the area involved.

There is now a renewed obligation on everyone involved in parading on both sides not to allow contentious situations to escalate, but to encourage discussion, practical engagement and cooperation.

The third focus of our efforts should be ensuring that *the peace process must leave no one behind*.

We need to give serious consideration to our approach in dealing with the challenge of building lasting reconciliation on the ground in local communities.

Throughout the peace process, this important work has been sustained by generous international assistance, particularly from the US and the EU but also from Canada, Australia, New Zealand and others.

Current levels of such assistance will not always be available. This is understandable as the gains of the peace process are increasingly consolidated and as our economy on this island continues to prosper.

It is clear to me, however, that the work of reconciliation and of rebuilding communities will take not years but decades.

What are the toughest challenges ahead? How do we address them? How do we resource them? How do we ensure those resources are well spent?

There are many questions we need to reflect on carefully, if we are to pursue the goal of reconciliation without bias or discrimination and for the benefit of all.

Some time ago, the Taoiseach explicitly invoked the sentiment of a tide of opportunity rising all boats in connection with loyalist transformation.

I cannot let tonight go without reiterating his message.

Just as the Provisional IRA have yielded to the will of the Irish people and brought their war to an end, so too must we see an end to loyalist aggression and violence. I know that many within Loyalism wish to play a constructive part in the new landscape of relationships emerging. We recognise they need space, encouragement and support to move beyond their recent past. As we have said before; those seeking genuine efforts at transformation will see a positive and open response from this government.

The time is right for finally grasping such opportunities.

Closing remarks: a shared future

In short, the programme for partnership must build a shared future, not only for the community in Northern Ireland, but more broadly on this island.

This can only be founded on acknowledgement of our shared past.

Through decades of conflict, that past has sometimes been reduced and simplified to a parody of its complex self. Yet the past can bring us together just as surely as it has previously divided us.

The commemoration last year of the Easter Rising and the Battle of the Somme are a powerful reminder of what can be achieved.

For long, the Boyne has divided us into two traditions. It can equally unite us in a shared history. So too should the events whose anniversaries we will mark in coming months and years: the battle of Messines, the Flight of the Earls and the Plantation of Ulster.

As we ponder our next steps, it is vital that we remain deeply mindful of the terrible suffering on the more recent past.

A peaceful future can be the only fitting testimony to all those who suffered tragically, as was acknowledged by Ian Paisley and Gerry Adams on Monday 26 March, and as Mark Durkan has consistently expressed.

In the words of Ian Paisley: 'We must not allow our justified loathing of the horrors and tragedies of the past to become a barrier to creating a better and more stable future for our children ... With hard work and commitment to succeed ... we can lay the foundation for a better, peaceful and prosperous future for all the people of Northern Ireland'.[2]

John Hume's approach to shaping a new future on this island was driven by a love of this country, a deep abhorrence of sectarianism and of violence, and a fundamental belief that the viable solution to the political problem should have at its core common values of democracy, equality and the rule of law.

These common values are at the heart of the peace process. They have been central to our efforts to-date to achieve the full potential of the Good Friday agreement and the consolidation of a peaceful society.

They will be no less important now as we move on.

Notes

1 Thomas G. Fraser, 'Northern Ireland: the search for a democratic settlement', in Vanessa E. Shields and Nicholas D. J. Baldwin (eds), *Beyond Settlement. Making Peace Last after Civil Conflict* (Madison Teaneck: Fairleigh Dickinson University Press, 2008), pp. 210–23.
2 Statement by Dr Ian Paisley, Democratic Unionist Party, 26 March 2007.

14

Moving out of conflict

Dr Maurice Hayes

Introduction

When Maurice Hayes lectured on 'Moving out of conflict' on 4 June 2007, his title seemed especially apt, since the devolved administration which had come into existence as a result of the St Andrews Agreement was scarcely a month old. While it might have been tempting to dwell upon the political implications of what had been, by any measure, a remarkable transformation of the political dynamic, he was sufficiently immersed in the complex fabric of Northern Ireland affairs to reflect more broadly on how society might be able to move ahead. He had long been of the view that reconciliation would be the work of a generation. He brought a distinctive perspective on events, that of a distinguished public servant who had served at the heart of government, but who was also a scholar of Irish life and culture, as fluent in the Irish language as he was in English. The complex cultural background of society in Northern Ireland, and how it related to a sense of British and Irish identities pervaded his lecture, the theme of which was how he saw Northern Ireland might progress.

Although born and raised in County Down, his family came from County Waterford and County Kerry, both now in the Republic of Ireland, settling after the First World War in Downpatrick, where his father became Town Clerk. In 1955, Hayes, too, became Town Clerk of Downpatrick, having been educated at De La Salle College in the town, and then at Queen's University Belfast from which he gradu-ated with a degree in English. The imagery of Seamus Heaney, Michael Longley and John Hewitt can be seen in his lecture. The intimacy of the Northern Ireland conflict, where virtually everyone knew, or knew of, a victim, can be seen in the fact that Longley's poem, *The Civil Servant*, concerns the murder of a friend. During his years in Downpatrick he was confronted with the hard realities of post-war reconstruction, not least over housing, but was careful to preserve the historic fabric of the town. At a time when few in Northern Ireland thought much about community relations, he fostered civic weeks which would bring the two communities together, a portent of the work that he was later to pursue on a larger stage, and which his lecture highlighted.

In December 1969, at a fateful point in Northern Ireland's history, on the initiative of the leading Unionist politician Brian Faulkner, also a County Down man, he chaired the newly created Community Relations Commission. In October 1973, he joined the Northern Ireland Civil Service, just before the Sunningdale Conference in December produced a template for political progress based upon a power-sharing executive and a Council of Ireland. During the short life of that Executive he was part of its secretariat, observing the workings of government from the inside. He witnessed at first hand the collapse of the Executive as a consequence of the Ulster Workers Council strike of May 1974. The end of the Executive resulted in the long period of direct rule from Westminster, which put new burdens on civil servants.

For thirteen years Maurice Hayes worked in the civil service, ensuring that key developments in health and social policy, including measures to normalise life for the handicapped, were pushed forward; a career which culminated as Permanent Secretary of the Department of Health and Social Services. On leaving the civil service in 1987, he was appointed to the offices of Northern Ireland Commissioner for Complaints and Northern Ireland Parliamentary Commissioner for Administration, or, as he preferred more simply to call it, Ombudsman. Public service did not end with his retirement. Nominated by the Taoiseach, he served in the Seanad in Dublin, and became a director of Independent Newspapers. A critical appointment was to the Independent Commission on Policing in Northern Ireland, chaired by Chris Patten, and set up as a result of the 1998 Good Friday Agreement. Reporting in September 1999, the Commission's recommendations formed the basis on which the Police Service of Northern Ireland came into being in November 2001. He chaired The Ireland Funds, the international charity which provided the funding for the Tip O'Neill lecture series, and in 2003 was awarded the degree of Doctor of Letters (*honoris causa*) by the University of Ulster.

Central to his analysis of how society might move out of conflict was the overlap of nationalities in Northern Ireland, he said, pointing to his native Downpatrick with its English Street, Irish Street and Scotch Street as an example of the complex society the two communities had inherited. A failure to manage the two contrasting British and Irish cultures and traditions had, he argued, sustained the conflict, and the new dispensation under the Good Friday Agreement presented the opportunity to address it. Should Northern Ireland draw a line under the past and move on, as the leaders of France and Germany had done after 1945, he asked? Society owed something to the victims of the conflict, since the problems of memory, truth-finding and reconciliation remained. Reconciliation, he counselled, was far down the line, and what had to be reached was 'peaceful co-existence, the building of trust, and finally toleration of differing accounts of the past – one community's heroic defenders being the other community's vicious attackers'. A clear message was that diversity was to be cherished rather than feared, that history and geography had given rise to a complex and rich society. A period of calm, a generation or two he thought, was needed so that the political parties could concentrate on working on common problems, not least those of the economy and social structures, so that difference and diversity could be accommodated, as they had been in post-war Europe. The achievement of a lasting peace would have to be built patiently over time. Linking the building of peace at home to the evolution of the European Union, he hoped, finally, that through this practice of inclusive democracy, the people of Northern Ireland would find it 'possible to recover from the legacy of competing nationalisms, which have bedevilled Europe since the nineteenth century and before, and left deep scars on the Irish psyche'.[1]

Lecture

It is an honour to have been asked to contribute to your series of lectures, not only because it invokes the name of Tip O'Neill, a legendary champion of democratic values and good government, and the presence of Professor John Hume, who holds the eponymous chair, but because of the eminence of the speakers who have preceded me, and the loftiness of the themes they have embraced.

The more local and immediate subject I would like to discuss is how this society, fractured in so many ways, yet potentially united by so many common concerns, can manage the painful transition from violence to whatever better condition might replace it. How do we as a society move on to build the peace and heal the scars left by the conflict?

We do so at a time of relative hope, when the parties have agreed to work together in government, a range of functions has been devolved and local people, responsible to local electors, have their hands on the levers of government. All the signs are that they are determined, this time, to make a go of it. It is a time to rejoice, and to pay tribute to all those who, over the years, have had a hand in reaching the settlement which now seems to be available – not least to John Hume, who generated much of the energy, most of the hope in dark times, and most of the seminal ideas which are now being reified.

What is needed now, more than anything, is a period of calm, of constructive consolidation as the parties work together on common problems and gain the trust necessary to move from a situation where politics is seen merely as the extension of the war by other means (thereby turning von Clausewitz on his head) to a society where difference can be accommodated and diversity positively cherished.

For those who wish to nod off now, that is the essence of the message I wish to deliver: make haste slowly, or as my Kerry mother would put it, 'Walk aisy when your jug's full'.

Only too often in history, the settlement of a conflict has merely been to sow the seeds of the next one. Versailles is a case in point – the swingeing penalties inflicted on Germany led to the rise of Hitler and an even more terrible Second World War. Contrast this with the magnanimity of the Marshall Plan which laid the foundations for peace in Europe for sixty years, and the vision of statesmen like Monnet, de Gasperi, Schuman and Adenauer which led to the formation of what was to become the European Union, and made war between European states, which had been enemies for centuries, unthinkable. It is not irrelevant to our theme that these were the men who inspired the young John Hume. Neither is it irrelevant that economists should advocate something of the nature of a Marshall Plan, as a peace dividend, to underwrite the new structures of government here.

There is, too, for us, the burden of Irish history, a tragically cyclical pattern of refusal to accept a settlement as final on the one hand, pitched against demands on the other that everything should be final and irrevocable. There is a mindset, too, which sees everything short of utopia as unfinished business, and the will of a democratically expressed majority either as wilful stupidity or pusillanimity on the part of the electorate, or as a betrayal of the soul of the nation, whose real interest and destiny are to be protected by the incorruptible few.

It is this spirit which has led to splits, to breakaways, to the fission of splinter groups. It is this which historically, on both sides, Republican and Unionist, has evinced a tendency to turn on those who have taken leadership roles and have seen the need to move from entrenched positions towards accommodation and compromise for the common good, to be denounced as traitors and replaced by others who then have to begin the same weary learning-curve.

There are those, too, who are happier in the cocoon of conflict – they know who they are and what they are and who they are fighting against. To change these dispositions is to threaten them in their personality and in their identification and role in the community. Like many people who have been prominent in wars, they fear being lost in the anonymity of the peace.

They take a perverse pride, too, in the longevity and consistency of their quarrel, in which all sense of proportion is lost. In Churchill's memorable phrase, after outlining the world-shattering events of the Great War: 'As the deluge subsides and the waters fall short we see the dreary steeples of Fermanagh and Tyrone emerging once again. The integrity of their quarrel is one of the few institutions that have been unaltered in the cataclysm which has swept the world'.[2]

There you have it, eight hundred years (or is it nine now?), three hundred (or four?), eighty, thirty, take your pick – ours is the biggest and best and longest conflict of all. And yet look around the world, especially after 9/11 (where more were killed in thirty minutes than in thirty years in Northern Ireland) or Iraq, where more are killed in a month, not to mention Kosovo, Darfur, Rwanda or Sri Lanka.

What history, and the Troubles, have produced is a victim culture, in which all are simultaneously victims, some other party is always to blame and it is up to someone else to do something about it.

Seamus Heaney catches it in *The Cure at Troy* (which I believe can be read as a version of the Hume–Adams talks, the dialogue between the physical force and the parliamentary traditions in modern Irish history):

> ... all of them glad
> To repeat themselves and their every last mistake,
> No matter what.
> ... self-pity buoys them up.
> People so staunch and true, they're fixated,
> Shining with self-regard like polished stones.
> And their whole life spent admiring themselves
> For their own long-suffering.
>   Licking their wounds
> And flashing them around like decorations.[3]

There are, of course, real victims, all 3,697 of them, by one count, and ten times that number injured, and all those, family and friends and relations who suffer in silence, who bear the physical and psychological scars of conflict. I make no hierarchy of victims; there are no good dead or bad dead, just those who are, in most cases, unnecessarily dead. I make no distinction between victim and perpetrator, the perpetrators, in many cases being victims, too, with a long life to live remembering deeds they now regret.

One of the features which distinguishes low intensity conflicts from more conventional warfare is that in the greater conflicts, after a truce, the dead are buried, prisoners are exchanged and the combatants leave the battlefield and go home, In our case we live in the battlefield, the warriors on both sides are at home, the memories remain, the sites of slaughter are signposted and perpetrators and victims rub shoulders in the marketplace.

The very intimacy of the struggle, and the pain it causes, are shown in Michael Longley's poems. One, *The Civil Servant*, concerns a man I knew well, a magistrate, actually, but a man of great compassion and a passion for justice:

> He was preparing an Ulster fry for breakfast
> When someone walked into the kitchen and shot him:
> A bullet entered his mouth and pierced his skull,
> The books he had read, the music he could play.
> He lay in his dressing gown and pyjamas
> While they dusted the dresser for fingerprints
> And then shuffled backwards across the garden
> With notebooks, cameras and measuring tapes.
> They rolled him up like a red carpet and left
> Only a bullet hole in the cutlery drawer:
> Later his widow took a hammer and chisel
> And removed the black keys from his piano.[4]

Lost Lives, that monumental listing by David McKittrick and his colleagues of all those who died as a result of the Troubles also spotlights both the universality and the particularity of victimhood, and the random and condign visitation of death. It was a book which won, among many other awards, the Belfast version of the Pulitzer Prize: it was the most stolen book in Belfast.

If I may quote from a review I wrote at the time:

> They are all there, the victims, the grandfather and the babe in arms, the octogenarian and the twins in the womb, the last viceroy of India and the Pakistani char-wallah, the lawyer and the litigant, tinker, tailor, soldier, sailor, rich man, poor man, beggar man, thief. There is too the appalling roll-call of disaster, the sites of slaughter which dot the Ulster countryside in a litany of shame and suffering. There are indeed clusters, in West Belfast and South Armagh, in the murder triangle of Mid-Ulster and the multiple interfaces of North Belfast. There is the Abercorn Restaurant, the Four Steps Inn, McGurk's Bar and Graham's Bookie's shop, the Shankill Fish shop, the Miami Show band, Kingsmills, Teebane, Ballygawley, the Mountain Lodge, La Mon, Loughinisland, Claudy, Greysteel, Narrow Water, Enniskillen, Omagh, Bloody Friday, Bloody Sunday, bloody every day, the bloody punctuation marks of the story of thirty years of strife.

What, then, to do with victims? Bodies like Eolas and Healing Through Remembering are producing thoughtful and useful documents in order to stimulate discussion, but as yet (and properly) with no pat answers. Many would prefer to draw a line under the past and move on. Politically it would be the easiest thing to do, no recriminations, no backward look, just move on – as France and Germany did in Europe under the leadership of wise and visionary statesmen, until in the fullness of time trust could emerge, new friendships develop and old animosities be forgotten.

There is a lot to be said, in our case, too, for drawing the line, in order to let politics and mutual trust develop. The present democratic institutions are a delicate graft on a rootstock riddled with memories of sectarian struggles, deeply rooted in centuries of animosity. There is a real danger that the graft might not take if there is too much scrabbling in the underground looking for evidence of the bad husbandry or the criminal neglect of yesteryear. The general political will that the institutions should be made to work, should be allowed to do so, could easily be frustrated if we insist on picking at the sores of old wounds, raising old ghosts, revive old animosities and suspicions, and most of all shattering the burgeoning trust which is a prerequisite for peaceful coexistence and cooperation.

Louis MacNeice's father, the then Bishop in Belfast, said as much in 1935, preaching on the Sunday before the Twelfth, in an attempt to prevent riots which bloodily ensued:

> It would be well to remember and to forget, to remember the good, the things that were chivalrous and considerate and merciful, and to forget the stories of old feuds, old animosities, old triumphs, old humiliations ... Forget the things that are behind you, that you might be better able to put all your strength into the tasks of to-day and to-morrow.[5]

Sadly few listened to him then, as few would listen now. Forget the sins of our own side, yes, forget the wounds we inflicted, but not the hurts suffered or those who inflicted them. We had this in the release of prisoners in the wake of the Good Friday Agreement, which might have seemed to herald a new beginning but for the persistent demand to pursue and punish every last policeman, and in the torpedoing of the legislation which would have permitted the return of those on the run, because it would provide similar treatment for security forces, and in the persistent demand for serial sworn public inquiries which would provide 'closure' (whatever that might be) or 'truth', which is as elusive now as it was for jesting Pilate two thousand years ago.

I do not believe that the Saville Inquiry will unearth the essential truth, the definitive account of the events on Bloody Sunday, which are so deeply incised on the psyche of this city. I can think of many better things to do for the families of victims and survivors for £200 million. And if Bloody Sunday, why not inquiries for every other atrocity beginning at Abercorn and ending at Omagh?

And yet, we do owe victims something, if only the opportunity to be listened to, to tell their story. The most immediate need is to help with the disappeared, to find the bodies, some account of the circumstances of their deaths and the possibility of a proper burial. There are other practical things which could be done too, but the problem of memory, of truth-finding and reconciliation remains. Much of this is the work of years.

Reconciliation in the fullest sense is far down the line. The best that can be hoped for is peaceful coexistence, the building of trust and, finally, toleration of differing accounts of the past – one community's heroic defenders being the other community's vicious attackers.

One thing is certain, there is no ready-made model which can be taken down off the shelf in some far-off think-tank and applied like a sticking plaster to the local situation. Whatever does emerge must be custom-built and must evolve from the variables of culture and history. The likelihood is not of a single great initiative, but a variety of small individualised initiatives as communities come to terms with the past and reach towards a shared understanding of where society might go in the future – which might be the most we can hope for by way of reconciliation.

I do not believe that Northern Ireland is ready for the full formalism of a Truth and Reconciliation Commission on the South African model – indeed I know that there are mixed views in South Africa about its utility there.

What is striking, over the years of the Troubles, is the degree to which those most grievously afflicted by some outrage or other have been the first, and most eloquent, to call for no retaliation and to make moves to build the peace. I think of Gordon Wilson, who held his dying daughter's hand in the rubble of the Enniskillen bomb, then dedicating the rest of his life to reconciliation, or Joyce McCartan, who lost three sons, one killed by loyalists, one by republicans, and one by the security forces, as well as seventeen members of her extended family, who spent herself in the search for peace through mutual understanding.

They remind us of the words of the woman in O'Casey's play *Juno and the Paycock*, describing herself and her loyalist neighbour: 'on either side of a scales of sorrow, weighed down by the bodies of our suffering sons'.

All this requires a sort of heroic stoicism, as exemplified in Michael Longley's poem 'Ceasefire'.

> I get down on my knees and do what must be done
> And kiss Achilles' hand, the killer of my son.[6]

There is, I believe, a real role here for the arts. There are difficult
subjects, charged with emotion, personally and communally stressful,
which we can deal with more easily in a poem or dramatised or fiction-
alised than in the rawness of memory or real life. The artists may not
establish the facts, but they may drive down to a substratum of existen-
tial truth which will make sufficient sense of a terrible sequence of events.
Indeed this is what Aristotle had in mind in defining *catharsis* as a prime
role of drama – the purgation of the emotions by vicarious experience.

Of course, all this has to take place in a political context. Political
settlement of a kind may help reconciliation: conversely if people could
learn to trust each other the politics would be much easier. That can best
be done by people working together to solve the social and economic
problems of security, survival, employment and well-being which beset
both communities. Which is as good an argument as any for devolved
government.

Perhaps the most pessimistic diagnosis of our situation was that made
by Richard Rose thirty years ago: 'The problem is, there's no solution'.
He posited it as a clash between what he called 'the great Unbargaina-
bles' of religion and identity, and concluded resolution is not possible.[7]

Of course, if you postulate it as a clash between polar opposites in
absolute terms, no resolution is possible. And yet no problem which
results in a continuance of human suffering can be left simply to fester.
The work of politics and the challenge to politicians is to work at it
until other times and other circumstances enable it to be reformulated
in terms in which it is capable of resolution.

And for that we do not need zealots – men and women with eyes
blazing, an incorrigible conviction of their own rightness, of their
solution as being the only one possible, and an insatiable desire to
impose it on others along with their own values, norms and practices.

Arthur Koestler described what was necessary in other terms:

> What we need is an active fraternity of pessimists. They will not aim at
> immediate radical solutions because they know this cannot be achieved
> in the hollow of the historical wave; they will not brandish the surgeon's
> knife at the social body because they will know their own instruments are
> polluted. They will watch with open eyes and without sectarian blinkers
> for the first sign of the new horizontal movement. When it comes, they
> will assist at its birth, but if it does come in their lifetime they will not
> despair. And meantime their chief aim will be to create oases in the inter-
> regnum desert.[8]

We are, too, in the semi-desert in which we find ourselves, approaching a post-nationalist age. Nationalism as a political creed is the bastard child of the Enlightenment, developed in nineteenth-century Europe. It can arguably be held to have led to two major wars in the last century and numerous colonial adventures. Nationalism, as distinct from patriotism, tends to define itself in terms of what it opposes rather than what it embraces. It is essentially an oppositional and conflictual doctrine. Irish nationalism, in particular over the last century and a half, tended to express itself as Anglophobia and, through most of the twentieth century, as Catholic. Which did not leave much room for those who were not Catholic (and Gaelic) and those who felt themselves to be British and wished to preserve that part of their cultural identity.

Northern Ireland has been described, classically, as the place where Britishness and Irishness overlap, a sort of locked in zone of transition between two polities, two cultures, two traditions. It is the failure to manage this which has created and sustained the conflict, and which we now have the opportunity to address.

Perhaps we are at a stage where diverse and often competing identities can be accommodated on the island. Europe is emerging, not as a superstate but as a union of states where the more stridently aggressive expressions of national interests are suppressed and modulated in the interest of the wider good in a globalised world, and at a time too when regionalism has become a motor for growth, and great cities reassert their salience as economic and cultural poles of growth. At the same time the redefining of the elements of the United Kingdom is deconstructing the traditional version of Britishness, and forcing people into new and less competitive alignments.

At the same time, too, for most purposes, the border has virtually disappeared, shrunken to a line on the map, of significance only to the political geographer, the constitutional lawyer and the law enforcement officer. There is free movement of people and labour; qualifications, by and large, are mutually recognised; there is free movement of capital despite the difference in currency

It was in the variable geometry of this matrix that the Good Friday Agreement (or its variant title the Belfast Agreement) was moulded. Leaving aside for a moment the arrangements for governing Northern Ireland, which, thankfully, appear to be falling into place, there is a radical change in the articulation of the main political and constitutional relationships between the two sovereign states. The twin pillars of Sunningdale, and of policy since then, of power-sharing and the Irish dimension are retained and restated.

More important in the long run was the enshrinement in legislation, and in the political culture, of what had for long been an implicit element of policy, the principle of consent – that there could be no change in the constitutional status of Northern Ireland without the consent of a majority of the electorate there (a reassurance to Unionists) and an undertaking by the British to facilitate such a change when the majority called for it (a guarantee to Nationalists).

The Good Friday Agreement crucially recognised the overlap of nationality by providing that people in Northern Ireland could regard themselves as British or Irish or both, and that all traditions were entitled to equal respect. For the first time, it recognised that nation and state could be separate entities, that national self-identification could run across borders, and did not necessarily require a coterminous state to defend it, and that the symbols of each group and their values should have equal respect and protection. It was recognised too that there was an east–west axis as well as a north–south one. The development of this part of the model was made easier as a result of devolution within the United Kingdom.

One of the difficulties of an agreement like this is that Unionists tend to see it as an end point while Nationalists see it as a process, as a staging-post en route to a united Ireland, which is what Unionists do not want. In part this reflects a clash in theological backgrounds. For evangelical Protestants, salvation is a single salvific event, for Catholics it is a pilgrimage with stopping-off points on the way. One requires stasis, finality: the other movement and potential.

There are some who believe that unity will be achieved as if by magic once the majority in favour reaches 50.1 per cent. This, however, would produce only the mirror image of the present problem with a substantial recalcitrant minority being forced to accept Dublin rule. There obviously cannot be a situation where even the smallest proportion of dissentient voices can prevent forever a change, which the vast majority desire, but there is also a limit to the amount of dissent which a polity can endure without breaking down. But to say that when the pointer on the electoral swingometer reaches a minimal point past half way all is changed utterly is surely to oversimplify what must always be a very difficult and complex set of inter-relationships. The essence of the principle of consent is that assent should be freely given. The essence of a secure and stable democracy is that all must be able to feel part of the whole, to share in a common identity without undue sacrifice of individuality, either as persons or communities, and where the melding of traditions produces the added value of richness in diversity rather than a clash of civilisations.

A modern democratic society is more than a mere counting of heads. An electoral majority is a form of convenience in arriving at decisions not a licence to oppress. The history of Northern Ireland illustrates the dangers of an oppressive majority which disregarded a sizeable minority except when it was necessary to put it in its place.

Indeed the Downing Street Declaration of December 1993 included an acceptance by the then Taoiseach, Albert Reynolds, that 'the lessons of Irish history, and especially of Northern Ireland, show that stability and well-being will not be found under any political system which is refused allegiance or rejected on grounds of identity by a significant minority of those governed by it'.[9]

The modern trend is towards consociational democracies where government is by consultation and consensus. In increasingly multicultural and pluralistic societies the pattern is likely to be of mutating majorities as various interest groups coalesce and disperse depending on the dominant issue.

The corollary to the principle of consent is not a licence to dominate those who do not consent. A situation which brought into a united Ireland the best part of a million reluctant and possibly disaffected Unionists, who still valued their British heritage, would be a recipe for continuing unrest, if not immediate disaster, and would be unlikely to be welcomed by the citizens of the Republic who would have to find, at least in the short term, and failing a radical transformation of the Northern Ireland economy and its dependence on the public sector, the cost of replacing the transfer from the British Treasury which underpins social services in Northern Ireland. It could also provoke a level of conflict and violence, which would envelop the whole island and inhibit tourism and inward investment.

A further problem with an all-change approach when the needle touches 50 per cent plus x is that it leads to destabilisation as one side counts the days to takeover and the other sees its worst fears being realised. There is a strong sense of inevitability in the demographic trends, and concentration on numbers is likely to reinforce the link between ethnicity, if not religion, and voting patterns. Unionists are likely to view this, as Carson expressed it in an earlier generation, as a sentence of death with a stay of execution.

If the essence of the exercise is, as John Hume has often argued, the uniting of people rather than territory, it is more important to get rid of the causes of division in the minds and hearts of people. If the object is to ensure as far as possible that people of different traditions can live together on the island in reasonable harmony, then the particular constitutional envelope in which they do so becomes less important, if it leaves room for innovative forms of governance as time mellows attitudes, as immigration makes societies more diverse and as the external environ-

ment changes. The Good Friday Agreement, in recognising that national
and group identities could flow across boundaries, and that the hard
edges of nationalisms could be dulled, is a useful point of departure.

One of the difficulties is that we are prepared to accept people, and
indeed to be generous to them, as we want them to be, not as they see
themselves. Harry West once declared that he had no difficulty having
Catholics in government as long as they did not have the political views
most Catholics seemed to have. Catholics *qua* Catholics were all right,
not Catholics as Nationalists or Republicans.

Similarly Nationalist Ireland can deal more easily with Protestantism
than with Britishness. The invocation of Wolfe Tone by Republicans to
reassure Unionists of their *bona fides* is a case in point. His desire to
unite Catholic, Protestant and Dissenter, while laudable, was merely
a means to an end, to break the connection with England. He is not
always a reassuring icon for those who value the British connection as
the part of their identity they are most reluctant to lose.

The main cause of conflict in the North for over a century now has
been the clash of competing nationalities and the insecurity of both
groups arising from the lack of certainty for one group and too much
for the other. There has also been the concept of the double minority
– of Unionists, a majority in the North fearful of becoming a minority
in a united Ireland, and Nationalists, a minority in the North hopeful
of joining a national majority. Recent events have accentuated fears.
Unionists see the tide running against them while Nationalists have
the growing self-confidence of those who think they are winning. In
addition there are, on both sides, bitter memories and the scars of thirty
years of conflict, which will take a generation or more to heal.

One approach might be to put the constitutional issue in baulk for a
period while people, in getting on with the ordinary business of living
and managing the place together, learn to accommodate to each other
and to trust, so that when the time comes to change gear on the constitutional arrangements, it is something which happens because it has
grown out of those relationships, and marks the direction in which it is
natural and sensible for most people to choose to go. This would require
a degree of vision and patience from those who then happen to be in
the numerical majority.

In this way people could use the structures of the Agreement constructively and with imagination, developing the North–South links organi-
cally to cater for the expanding range of functions, which the economies
of scale will dictate should be managed on an all-island basis.

Once people cease to be fixated on a single destination, the possibilities become infinite for organic growth at a rate, which all the constituent

elements can adjust to and accommodate. What the Northern Ireland conflict needs is to be taken out of the pressure cooker of immediacy, which puts stress on everyone. It might take a generation or two – a short time in historical perspective, but if by taking the pressure off people either to rush to the consummation of their constitutional dreams, or to frustrate those of others, then a sounder and more lasting arrangement based on consensus could emerge, then it would be time well spent. Meantime, the energy which could then be diverted into building up the economy and social structures in the North would be well spent too.

It may not satisfy the constitutional purists or the absolutists, it may indeed be confusing, but as the old schoolteacher says in Brian Friel's play: 'Confusion is not an ignoble condition'.[10]

I was lucky enough to grow up in a small town in a mixed area in County Down where people generally got on well together. The three main streets, English Street, Irish Street and Scotch Street, met in the centre at the Town Hall corner (a local poet remarked that the Welsh, having St Patrick, needed no street).

This confluence always symbolised the origins of our differences, the strength that each gave to the whole, and the possibility of convergence and confluence. Today one would have to add a Chinese strand, an Estonian, Latvian, Polish and Bulgarian as new people come in to enrich the mix with their own energy, initiative and cultural heritage.

John Hewitt, the Ulster poet, in typifying the mix of blood-lines, identities and traditions in the North of Ireland, invoked the metaphor of a knotted ball of twine:

> Kelt, Briton, Roman, Saxon, Dane, and Scot,
> time and this island tied a crazy knot.[11]

The way to unloose a knot is not to pull it tighter, but to ease the tension so that it may be unravelled, the single strands teased out and disentangled until all breaks free. After which, of course, the threads are not lost, but can be rewoven and reassembled in a more complete and coherent pattern.

In this way, too, it might be possible to recover from the legacy of competing nationalisms, which have bedevilled Europe since the nineteenth century and before, and left deep scars on the Irish psyche. The European Union in the present draft constitutional treaty is a union of nation-states, but it is more than that and may develop into something unique. In recent years we have seen trends towards decentralisation in what were highly centralised states like France and Spain. The same is happening more slowly in the United Kingdom. Great cities are becoming dynamic poles of growth and regions are asserting their individuality. It is in this creative tension between the supra-national and the local that new structures will emerge which will accommodate a different and richer concept of unity on the island and relationships with the other island. This could go further to recognise the complexity and the richness created by history and geography, the interaction of peoples in peace and war over centuries, than existing models based on erasing or sustaining lines on maps while leaving the divisions in the minds of men unchallenged, or in putting all within a single undifferentiated framework of governance which looks back to the early twentieth century rather than forwards into this.

So, like Gatsby, believing 'in the green light, the orgastic future, that year by year recedes before us. It eluded us then, but that's no matter – tomorrow we will run faster, stretch out our arms further ... And one fine morning – So we beat on, boats against the current, borne back ceaselessly into the past'.[12]

Notes

1 Maurice Hayes, *Minority Verdict. Experiences of a Catholic Public Servant* (Belfast: The Blackstaff Press, Belfast, 1995), *passim.*
2 Winston S. Churchill, *Hansard*, 150 (16 February 1922), column 1270, quoted in J. J. Lee, *Ireland 1912–1985, Politics and Society* (Cambridge: Cambridge University Press, 1989), p. 46.
3 Seamus Heaney, *The Cure at Troy* (Derry: Field Day, 1990), pp. 1–2.
4 'The Civil Servant', from *Collected Poems* by Michael Longley. Published by Jonathan Cape, 2006. Reprinted by permission of The Random House Group Limited. US rights permission by Wake Forest University Press. We are grateful to Michael Longley for his permission to publish this.
5 *Belfast Telegraph*, 8 July 1935.
6 'Ceasefire', from *Collected Poems* by Michael Longley. Published by Jonathan Cape, 2006. Reprinted by permission of The Random House Group Limited. US rights permission by Wake Forest University Press. We are grateful to Michael Longley for his permission to publish this extract.
7 Richard Rose, *Governing Without Consensus: An Irish Perspective* (London: Faber and Faber, 1971).
8 Arthur Koestler, *The Yogi and the Commissar* (London: Macmillan, 1965), quoted in John Darby, *What's Wrong With Conflict?* (University of Ulster: Centre for the Study of Conflict, 1994), p. 14.
9 'The Joint Declaration of 15 December 1993' (Downing St. Declaration), www.dfa.ie/home/index.aspx?id=8734 (last accessed 25 February 2013).
10 Brian Friel, *Translations* (London: Faber and Faber, 1981).
11 'Ulsterman', *The Collected Poems of John Hewitt*, edited by Frank Ormsby (Belfast: The Blackstaff Press, 1991), pp. 489–90.
12 F. Scott Fitzgerald, *The Great Gatsby* (London, Chatto and Windus, 1926; London: Penguin Classics edition, 2000), pp. 171–2.

15

Peace, multiculturalism and development

Professor Kader Asmal

Introduction

Professor Kader Asmal spoke on the 4 February 2008 about the preoccupation of a lifetime of academic study, activism, work on constitutional ideals and public service – which was a passion for and commitment to human rights, equality, justice and development. He spoke from his own experience of life in a system that had lacked basic justice and equality: apartheid South Africa; he spoke as one who had been obliged to leave in order to find opportunity and where he worked diligently to effect change from afar; and he spoke as a prodigal son returned, determined to help his broken homeland heal, shape peace and build prosperity.

His scholarly lecture signified his academic background as Professor of Law at Trinity College Dublin, where he developed as an authority in human and labour rights and international law, and as a board member of the Centre for Human Rights at the University of Pretoria. His work as founder of the Irish Anti-Apartheid Movement and as member of the African National Congress's (ANC) Constitutional Committee that contributed so much to South Africa's post-Apartheid Constitution also had great bearing upon his ability to speak to the issues of peace, multiculturalism and development. Reflective, too, of his post-apartheid career as a politician, his talk contained a clear South African emphasis; in describing what lessons for his own country had been gleaned from the Northern Irish peace-building experience, how these had been applied and developed in the South African context and what resonance they had in the greater global scheme.

The Good Friday Agreement, which saw its ten year anniversary that spring, was much commended by Professor Asmal, who then focused his address on issues of identity, cosmopolitan multiculturalism, democracy, the reconceptualisation of the nation-state, development and the ways in which potentially divisive and destructive forces might be transformed into powers for the public good.

No doubt influenced, in part, by rising food and fuel prices in the global south at that time and his contact with citizens on the front line of human survival as Minister for Water Affairs and Chairman of the World Commission for Dams, he targeted globalisation as a 'source of despair' for many. It was also, however, a 'repository for hope' as its attendant interconnectedness and technological developments carried with them the power to revolutionise civil society and conceptions of the public good in ways that transcend national boundaries and identities and deepen a sense of international solidarity. With the fortieth anniversary of the civil rights marches in the city of Derry also occurring in 2008, such discourse could not fail to have been influenced by the inspiration and solidarity that the civil rights movements in the United States and Northern Ireland had derived from one another in the upheavals of the 1960s.

The question Asmal then asked: when state sovereignty is 'porous' and states or sub-state groupings are no longer permitted to mistreat their citizens or each other without recourse to international standards of justice, is how these obligations might be enforced 'without allowing such means to become a pretext for selective and/or opportunistic intervention by larger, more powerful states'; directly citing US actions in the earlier part of that decade. This discourse was resonant of his own criticisms of Robert Mugabe's Zimbabwe, the July arrest of Bosnian Serb leader Radovan Karadzic and recent African efforts to bring resolution to the internecine strife ongoing in Kenya at that time.

Asmal decried those simplistic conceptualisations of racial and/or cultural identity and the causes of conflict in the modern world, such as Samuel Huntingdon's *The Clash of Civilizations*, which have, he lamented, influenced the West's counterproductive approach to internal 'differences' in their societies and their external policies in tackling Islamism (again, subjects much under discussion at the time of his talk). He declared: '[w]e cannot afford to allow our world to be reduced to such cruel simplifications … Our multiple identities must be encouraged to flourish, not forced into the mould of some racialised or other stereotypical identity'.

As Minister for Education (which he characterised as a 'public good'), he was responsible for overhauling the South African education system from top to bottom including rewriting the racialist, exclusionary curriculum and increasing representation within the universities; imbuing the system with what he called 'cultural justice', inclusive of all and reflecting the values of the new Constitution that he had been so instrumental in crafting.

This preoccupation was much influenced by his long-time mentor Chief Albert Luthuli, whom he had met as a child, and who once told a sceptical white audience: '[y]ou cannot prove your heritage by isolating yourself or by isolating your people; you can only preserve human values by propagating them and creating a climate where these values will flourish'. This is the path upon which Kader Asmal exhorted his audience to tread in pursuit of peace, justice and development, which he described as the 'intellectual projects' of our age.

In her lecture, then Senator Hillary Clinton quoted John Hume, who asked listeners when accepting his Nobel Prize for Peace, to think what might be achieved when people lived for ideals rather than fought for them. In his autobiography, Kader Asmal remembered a school teacher who evoked apartheid almost fondly, saying that at least it had held people together against a common enemy.[1] The lesson of all his years of study, activism and political representation brought Asmal to the answer then, and one which he shared with his audience that February day, that, in the same vein as his host had asserted, we must find something more powerful to hold us together and that is a common future for humanity; a challenge, he concluded, we can only face together.

Lecture

When I was asked by Professor John Hume, Tip O'Neill Chair in Peace Studies at the Magee Campus of the University of Ulster, to deliver a public lecture on the theme of peacemaking, I should have heeded the sage advice of Lewis Carroll's young man who, in admonishing his father, complained:

> 'You are old, Father William', the young man said,
> 'And your hair has become very white;
> And yet you incessantly stand on your head –
> Do you think, at your age, it is right?'

> 'In my youth', Father William replied to his son,
> 'I feared it might injure the brain;
> But now that I'm perfectly sure I have none,
> Why, I do it again and again'.

Standing on one's head may not be very creative and one's political opponents may consider that this is the exercise one is permanently engaged in but it does provide a somewhat different perspective, not necessarily an upside down one.

If standing on one's head is perverse, it is the perversity of enthusiasm that gladly made me accept the John Hume invitation, for a number of reasons.

First, John Hume has been the peacemaker *par excellence* for the forty years I have known him. Over the past decade, we in South Africa have followed his attempts to bring together the political representatives of what were euphemistically described as the divided community in a sundered society. Your settlement has been 'widely hailed internationally as a remarkable but all too uncommon success story'.[2]

My lecture is, therefore, dedicated to John and all the peacemakers, including the politicians, civil servants and negotiators involved, for their persistence and courage in ensuring that the community is at peace with itself and stability has been achieved through 'an extraordinarily complex yet workable institutional model'. Bravo.

Secondly, Derry City has inspired, through the campaign for civil and political rights – and 2008 marks a special fortieth anniversary – a number of insights for me which are reflected in the South African Constitution, dealing with such vital areas as non-discrimination, corrective action to overcome past discrimination, and the need to enhance economic and social rights by constitutional prescription. In this sense, it is for me a home-coming.

I would like to thank The Ireland Funds and the University of Ulster for making it possible for Louise and for me to be here with my friends tonight.

Finally, the issue of national identity has become a matter of some political importance, particularly after the dreadful events of September 11, and the subsequent breakdown in self-confidence in a number of first-world countries.

When we talk or write about conflicts in today's world, *identity* is one of the words that is most frequently used. Be it à propos of former Yugoslavia, Canada, Ireland, Britain after 11 July 2005, the Netherlands, Belgium ... *identity* seems to provide a simple explanation of those conflicts: people are assumed to belong to a solid, immutable group which responds as one if threatened or ill-treated. *Identity* implies uniqueness and sameness.

Nothing could be further from the truth.

What attracted me to the political settlement based on the Good Friday Agreement was the recognition that many citizens here have multiple loyalties, based on identities that may differ from each other, and even be contradictory.

This is in contrast to some other jurisdictions where the good sense that prevailed before – and which continues to be represented in the Republic – has been replaced by demands for the recognition of the alleged core values of a society to which everyone, especially immigrants, must subscribe, in order to build a single identity.[3]

In South Africa, under apartheid, the core value system of separation in every sphere of life based on racial superiority excluded any sense of identity for the majority of our people.

So, in order to ensure that separateness was replaced by unity, we, the lawyers in the African National Congress, looked at this matter in 1988 and proposed, in the seminal document which formed the basis for subsequent negotiations with the apartheid regime, that:

> It shall be state policy to promote the growth of a single national identity and loyalty binding on all South Africans. At the same time, the state shall recognise the linguistic and cultural diversity of the people and provide facilities for free linguistic and cultural development.[4]

We soon realised though that a single national identity could not be imposed by *diktat* (in a number of European countries, it had been 'created' by subjugation and force of arms) and civil war could result if such a concept had to be 'binding on all South Africans'. What we did in fact was to replace the bogus nationalities created by apartheid with a single citizenship for all South Africans, a revolutionary step which we hoped would provide a basis for a durable peace and an understanding of our common humanity.

We hoped that the 'core' values of our Constitution – freedom, equality, justice and dignity, which do not belong to any one culture, would provide what Fintan O'Toole has called 'a map of integration, setting out the relationship between rights and duties in a way open to everyone'. I think we have succeeded in this aim.

Martha Nussbaum has written of the 1,172 trees in Jerusalem that commemorate the 'righteous goyim' – those who risked their lives in the Second World War to save Jewish lives. For Nussbaum the terror which persists is the 'terror of the question they pose. Would one, in similar circumstances, have the moral courage to risk one's life to save a human being simply because he or she is human? More generally, would one, in similar circumstances, have the moral courage to recognise humanity and respond to its claim, even if the powers that be denied its presence?'[5]

That question presupposes a time in which no peace exists. It asks us to imagine how we would act in a time of violence and grave danger. Would we risk our lives for others – simply because we recognised a shared humanity? I presume that most of us gathered here today would like to imagine that we would, in similar circumstances, act so coura-geously. But those relatively small numbers of trees point to just how exceptional, how much in the minority, such individuals really are.

Those of us concerned realistically to construct a politics of humanity, as opposed to a politics of fractured identities, must hope that it is never tested in such circumstances. We must hope, not that greater numbers would act as the 'righteous goyim' did, but that we are never put to such a test. We must hope for a durable peace.

I want to reflect today on how we in South Africa – a country which, as you well know, for so long denied the humanity of most of its people – has sought to construct the very antithesis of that period: a politics of humanity. We have done so, as I will argue, by infusing our constitutionalism with a cosmopolitan, multicultural ethic. I intend also to argue that this ethic can best prompt reform at an international level as well, so hopefully securing, at both domestic and global level, a durable peace.

In South Africa, we have attempted to secure this ethical and legal dimension not by denying our differences: the Constitution, the founding instrument of our democracy, guarantees rights which best protect our freedom to be individuals, unlike any other, but also guarantees the rights we enjoy only in and through our communities – that protect our enjoyment of the society of those like ourselves. In so doing we continue a tradition that saw the Freedom Charter, in the midst of the madness of apartheid, declare that all South Africans had the right to their own languages and to develop their own cultures and customs.

This determination in some sense to celebrate rather than eviscerate difference may have seemed counter-intuitive. It is not long since we emerged from a past in which our differences were our defining feature, the basis on which the state determined the rights, resources and level of care we were due. The multicultural vision embraced by South Africa's constitution has been criticised by some, and it has been said that rather than unite the disempowered, multiculturalism emphasises social divisions and exaggerates cultural differences among them. It would follow that the politics of identity is counter-productive to nation-building.

But this view is wrongheaded. Multiculturalism is necessary – not only because we recognise that life in the contemporary world makes for multiple allegiances and loyalties that are enriching and that individuals require different contexts, inputs and life choices to develop their fullest abilities. We value multiculturalism because we want to preserve a wide range of human conditions, allowing free people the best chance to make their own lives. In South Africa we seek to value not only allegiances of long-standing but also contemporary trends towards global citizenship. Thus we see the growth of the human rights movement, as well as new forms of women's citizenship and of ecological citizenship.[6]

Multiculturalism is also necessary because a society in which each is able to demonstrate his or her difference and diversity equally is a society much more likely to encourage its members to see beyond signifiers of religion, race, ethnicity as the sole markers of identity.

Here I would emphasise that the multiculturalism we seek to promote in South Africa is not of the type which Amartya Sen argues can best be described as 'plural monoculturalism' – a system in which people are constantly herded into different identity pens. 'Multiculturalism' as 'plural monoculturalism' cannot be used to privilege traditional markers of identity at the expense of other affiliations and associations that are freely entered into. 'Unless it is defined very oddly, multiculturalism cannot override the right of a person to participate in civil society, or to take part in national politics, or to lead a socially non-conformist life. No matter how important multiculturalism is, it cannot lead automatically to giving priority to the dictates of traditional culture over all else'.[7]

In other words, in the evocative language of Judge Albie Sachs of our Constitutional Court, a constitution and its human rights provisions must ensure the right to be the same – equality of rights – and the right to be different.

The type of multiculturalism we seek to promote could be called a cosmopolitan multiculturalism. Cosmopolitans think that there are many values worth living by and that you cannot live by them all. So we hope and expect that different people will embody different values, but in an important *caveat* noted by Kwame Anthony Appiah in his most recent work on cosmopolitanism, *Cosmopolitanism: Ethics in a World of Strangers*, they have to be values worth living by,[8] because there 'simply is no decent way to sustain those communities of difference that will not survive without the free allegiance of their members'.[9]

South Africa's constitutional embrace of multiculturalism can be demonstrated by pointing to the large number of provisions that guarantee the individual's right to belief, language, culture and the rights of communities – whether cultural, religious or linguistic – to practice those activities which evidence their community. But these provisions, even those which apply to collective rights, are not novel. They are to be found in many constitutions the world over and are compelled by countless international instruments.

A more distinguishing feature of South Africa's multicultural constitutionalism is a critical attitude or ethos that at the best of times guides the branches of government in reconciling rights within our society. It is a critical approach that unambiguously seeks to shape a shared future.

Ruti Teitel[10] has called South Africa's Constitution a 'transitional constitution' – one which is both backward and forward looking. It is backward looking in that what counts as justice, going forward, is determined and informed by the depth and scope and nature of the particular injustices of the past. Its meaning is conditioned and created by the particular contours of the prior injustice suffered. But it is not equally poised between the future and the past, equally backward and forward looking. It is backward looking only in that it involves a repudiation of an illiberal past. And a repudiation of the past requires the construction/marshalling of reasons in the present-day in order to justify the rejection of values and practices of the past. Our transitional constitutional project cannot be about safeguarding the traditions and practices of the past.

It is true that we in South Africa, especially, want to reclaim and restore histories that have been negated – histories of marginalised peoples and societies. But in the articulation of our constitutional project – both in the Constitutional Court's jurisprudence and when Parliament considers legislation– we should make our decisions by reference to South Africans' shared future and what we want that to look like, and how that involves departure from our past.

This mode of reasoning – an articulation of the society we are reaching for –strikingly resembles what South African legal scholar, Etienne Mureinik, called a 'culture of justification', a culture he and other South African human rights lawyers hoped would be firmly instantiated by a Bill of Rights. As he explained: '[we] have been looking to the [Bill of Rights] not only for its explicit content, but also to enrich laws by fostering justification-thinking, because it was the poverty of law, in the shape of pervasive authority-thinking that made apartheid possible. A bill of rights ... would restore discipline to a system grown slothful about justification'.[11]

Were it to be otherwise, were it our past (even mythical past), and not the future, that was our lodestar, then I fear we would venture too close to divisive, contemporary political projects, as seen in Britain today with the espousal of 'British values', what Prime Minister Gordon Brown has called 'a clear shared vision of national identity'. This imagining of Britain, based on its rediscovery (a redrawing, if you like) of its past, brings with it the alienation of many immigrants and communities. This is not the Britain which purportedly held dear the values of liberty, toler-ance and social justice. These immigrants, by virtue of their multiple identities and sometimes conflicting allegiances, must necessarily contest such a 'clear, shared vision of national identity'.

In a fairly recent constitutional case – an exemplar of the transforma-tive power of constitutionalism – which involved the right of same-sex couples to marry, the South African Constitutional Court showed itself acutely conscious of the need to formulate a jurisprudence that speaks to a shared future that is formulated in response, as a rejection of what was unconscionable, in our past. Justice Sachs, writing for the Court in the same-sex marriage case noted:

> Our Constitution represents a radical rupture with the past based on intol-
> erance and exclusion, and the movement forward to the acceptance of

the need to develop a society based on equality and respect by all for all. Small gestures in favour of equality, however meaningful, are not enough. In the memorable words of Mahomed J: 'In some countries, the Constitution only formalizes, in a legal instrument, a historical consensus of values and aspirations evolved incrementally from a stable and unbroken past to accommodate the needs of the future. The South African Constitution is different: it retains from the past only what is defensible and represents a decisive break from, and ringing rejection of, that part of the past that is disgracefully racist, authoritarian, insular and repressive and a vigorous identification with and commitment to a democratic, universalistic, caring and aspirationally egalitarian ethos expressly articulated in the Constitution. The contrast between the past which it repudiates and the future to which it seeks to commit the nation is stark and dramatic'.[12]

As Justice Mahomed made clear, in South Africa, our constitutional justification should be unequivocally aspirational, future-bound, preserving from the past only that which is justifiable. And while this style of reasoning, of justification, may seem especially suited to South Africa, I would suggest that it is fitting for much of the world as well.

In our public life and discourse, in our laws and jurisprudence, we need to encourage a culture of justification that seeks to shape a shared future based on a very critical examination of our past. This culture of reasoning/justification is much less likely to alienate peoples whose cultures/societies are not well represented in our past – at least our official past. And it means that people who make their homes in South Africa today, without any representation in our past, are much more likely to find a place, a sense not just of being, but of well-being, in South Africa, as they too participate, as full members, in articulating a vision of a shared future.

I have saluted your political arrangements which have brought peace to a deeply divided society. This form of political settlement is what writers describe as consocial, allowing for weight to be given in the structures of government to ethnic, or in your case, community, representation. In other words, administration is by consensus, not majority rule. In the same spirit, it has been suggested in the Good Friday Agreement and elsewhere that a Bill of Rights for Northern Ireland should be enacted: binding human rights rules would encourage development towards a shared future based on what must not be seen as simply restraints on the government but as instruments of empowerment of citizens.

A Bill of Rights would be part of a healing experience and an instrument to deal with the pathologies of your society which may exclude 'fellow citizens because of their race, gender, religion, sexual orientation or disability, or life-style as in the case of travelling people'.[13]

It is anomalous perhaps that as we attempt to make this multicultural, cosmopolitan constitutionalism the foundation or essence of our South African identity we affirm a sense of national identity or belonging. It is anomalous in that cosmopolitanism is often seen as opposed to national identity: the cosmopolitan is the global citizen rather than the domestic citizen. Mary Kaldor has written that the twentieth century can be described as the period in which the nation-state system reached its apogee and this period will also be remembered for the terrible barbarity of totalitarianism and war. But it is not just the excesses of nationalism that compel, to her mind, a more cosmopolitan commitment. It is a case compelled by necessity too: 'The general case for cosmopolitan democracy is based on the argument that democracy at a national level is weakened by the erosion of the autonomy of the state and the under-mining of the state's capacity to respond to democratic demands'.[14]

Appiah,[15] however, argues for a more rooted cosmopolitanism – whereby people are attached to particular places or homes with cultural specificities, 'but take pleasure from the presence of the different places that are home to other different people' and are also able to choose their own homes. Appiah's articulation is consistent with Kant's vision of a cosmopolitan world: one divided into states in which cosmopolitan right trumps the claim of sovereignty. Specifically, rights accrue to individuals and the nation-state exists in order to best facilitate the realisation of these rights. It is not the reverse: that the nation-state grants rights to individuals and that rights do not exist independent of the nation-state.

Thus a cosmopolitan vision does not entail the evisceration of the nation-state – simply a reconceptualisation. And as I will argue later, it is this reconceptualisation that is also needed at the international level if we are to bring about the reforms needed to secure durable peace.

There is another reason to emphasise nationality, and a sense of belonging, identity predicated on nationhood – albeit not a nationhood based on exclusive, immutable features – and that is because while the process of globalisation affords some positive goods, it has also brought about tremendous political and economic instability and rupture. In the face of such uncertainty, identity politics in the narrowest sense, predi-cated on certain immutable features and ideals, assumes a particular potency. Identities are constructed and emphasised for the purposes of political mobilisation. They offer a new sense of security in a context where the political and economic certainties of previous decades have vanished.

As Kaldor explains: 'They provide a new populist form of commu-nitarian ideology, a way to maintain or capture power, that uses the language and forms of an earlier period. Undoubtedly, these ideologies make use of pre-existing cleavages and the legacies of past wars. It is also the case that the appeal to tradition and the nostalgia for some mythical or semi-mythical history gains strength in the social upheavals associated with the opening up to global pressures'.[16]

Right now Kenya is in turmoil. It is not, as David Anderson, professor of African politics at Oxford, rightly observes, a Rwanda – a comparison which only plays into the hands of unscrupulous politicians who want to use the fear of violent insurrection to achieve their narrow ends. But that Kenya, one of Africa's most stable countries, should now be the site of so much violence and displacement, animated supposedly by ethnic divisions mirroring political affiliations, speaks to the enormous and destructive power of identity mobilisation.

Such political or ethnic affiliations, as we know from other countries, are also used for allocating benefits and resources.

And this phenomenon – the appeal of narrow identity politics – isn't only to be observed in post-colonial states, although the genocide in Rwanda is its obvious apogee, or in post-communist states, and here we think of the break-up of the former Yugoslavia and more recently of the conflict in Kosovo. It is also apparent in societies we take to be among the most established western democracies. We only need witness developments in contemporary Belgium where there exists strong antipathy between the richer, Flemish north and the poorer, French-speaking Walloon region.

I would venture that a sense of identity founded on a nationality that is itself predicated, not on immutable ideals, but on a sense of shared future, will go some way to undermining the allure of narrow, identity politics.

Realistically, however, this emphasis on individual rights and a sense of shared future cannot hope to counter the appeal of divisive identity politics where such politics holds out the prospect of real advancement and where multiculturalism simply becomes a cover for unequal social and economic relations. Again Belgium today is instructive – much of the Walloon/Flanders tension is rooted in uneven development. In securing equitable development within multicultural societies, we have to move beyond a narrow distributionist account of development towards an assessment of the extent to which people's ability to make reasoned choices is positively supported by the social opportunities of education, employment and participation in civil society.[17]

This is what real 'development' is about, harnessing people's energies for the common good or as the preamble to the South African Constitution, puts it, to 'improve the quality of life of all citizens and free the potential of each person'.

I want to make one last point in respect of the construction of a multicultural national identity. That is, national identity, even conceptualised in its most cosmopolitan, multicultural ideal, brings with it certain forms of exclusivity – an exclusion of those who cannot or may not make their homes within the nation-state. This is not a theme I will explore in any detail in today's talk but it is worth noting that Kant, in his formulation of a cosmopolitan ethic, was appreciative of exactly this dilemma. He argued that the enactment of cosmopolitan laws in the strictest sense of the term, that is laws guaranteeing the right of hospitality, would ensure the security of strangers when they set foot in a foreign land. This would address the rights-gap wrought by statelessness. In this formulation Kant makes plain that rights attach to individuals *qua* individuals and such rights are to be realised irrespective of where the person finds him/herself.

I have spoken about the place of multiculturalism within the nation-state and its importance in securing a durable peace. I wish now to address how these same considerations of multiculturalism and cosmopolitanism should inform a more equitable international order.

Globalisation, for better or worse, is an unstoppable process. At its best it promotes democratisation, exerting pressure on previously insulated regimes to introduce political reform as a precondition for economic reform, to reduce corruption, increase respect for human rights and introduce/enhance democratic institutions. At its worst it locks states, particularly weaker states, into entrenched patterns of inequality and uneven development. It promotes the erosion, and often complete negation, of state autonomy and makes the state unable to respond to democratic demands. It offers incentives for supra-national, more exclusive affiliations which lay claim to what were previously the monopolies of the state – i.e. force and taxation.[18] And it is this 'lack of authority of the state, the weakness of representation, the loss of confidence that the state is able or willing to respond to public concerns, the inability and/or unwillingness to regulate the privatisation and informalisation of violence that gives rise to violent conflicts'.[19]

In order to minimise the danger that globalisation's upheavals and uncertainties present, there needs to be reform at the international level. I have already spoken of the individual as a bearer of rights and the nation-state as the means by which such rights are realised. What is needed at an international level is a rights-based system of global governance – where the individual rights-bearer and not the state is placed at the centre. There must be an evolution of the classical international law formulation which took as its subject the nation-state towards what Kant envisioned as the 'status of world citizen' which would afford legal protection to citizens against their own criminal regimes.[20]

Today, for many people, globalisation is a source of despair, not because the global movement of money, technology and people has made the world a 'global village', but because these forces have been widening the gap between rich and poor in an increasingly polarised world. Sen refers to the 'overwhelming power of Western culture and lifestyle in undermining traditional modes of living and social mores. For anyone concerned about the value of tradition and of indigenous cultural modes this is indeed a serious threat'.[21] How could this source of despair become a repository of hope?

If the notion of human rights has a future, it must be in harnessing global forces to a politics of hope. Advancing a powerful critique, while never giving up hope, Nobel Laureate Amartya Sen has argued that we must 'ask questions not only about the economics and politics of globalisation, but also about the values and ethics that shape our conception of the global world'.[22]

When I chaired the World Commission on Dams, we worked out an approach to decisionmaking in development projects that I called 'globalization from below'.[23] Within a human rights framework, this approach considered the rights and risks of global investors but it insisted on highlighting the human rights of people who were most directly affected by the project, as well as the considerable risks they faced. As we brought peasants, workers, women's groups and representatives of indigenous people into the negotiations, we saw the tremendous potential of grass-roots globalisation for advancing human rights in transnational negotiations. In many other areas, I believe the future of human rights will also depend upon this new 'globalization from below'.[24]

Globalisation from below is producing new forms of social activism across national borders. Political analyst Jorge Castaneda has identified these new initiatives as 'longitudinal nationalism', which is advanced by social actors from various nations who work together to challenge policies in one or more states.[25] Unlike the old nationalisms, which tended to represent narrow national interests, this 'longitudinal nationalism' seeks to advance what I have been calling the public good that is ultimately in everyone's interest.

The debate on a Bill of Rights for Northern Ireland – which I support very strongly – has shown a huge degree of community involvement which politicians will ignore at their peril. This in itself is a form of 'public good'.

We might want to say that a public good is just another term for human rights. But it is a term that directly engages the global economy as an alternative to the commodification of values. As such, our commitment to the public good goes to the heart of Amartya Sen's call to clarify 'the values and ethics that shape our conception of the global world'.

Revitalising our conception of the public good – as a basis for national sovereignty, democratic governance and economic development – holds the promise of transforming our despair into hope in a globalising world.

We will find the future of human rights in the midst of the hardest cases. As a transformative agent, human rights will be deployed at their best every time we engage the sources of our despair as avenues for revitalising hope. All of this, of course, requires great courage and imagination. We can only seek to seize this moment for the public good.

We will find enormous value as we work here in Northern Ireland and elsewhere to strengthen international solidarity. Our links with each other should not be seen in terms of our geographical distance. Rather, we should see our relations in terms of the historical closeness arising not out of any racial ethnic lineage but out of our common legacy of displacement, oppression and struggle for freedom.

The human dignity found in genuine multicultural societies, I submit, contradicts any assumption that humanity can be divided into separate 'civilisations'. As a space of mixing and merging, diaspora disproves any apartheid-like attempt to carve up the world into separate and distinct peoples, cultures or civilisations. Samuel Huntington, in his notorious volume, *The Clash of Civilizations*, developed such a 'simple map' of the world. Huntington's map fixes civilisations in place. He allows for no movement; he recognises no exchanges. We would probably have forgotten all about his map by now if it had not been found useful by strategic planners in Washington, DC. I note the ways in which Huntington's map of the world violates our understanding of a non-racial world, a recipe for tension, if not conflict. It is a world of us against them.

First, in Huntington's account, all civilisations are racialised, regarded as natural organisms, with roots and branches, which are unified by allegiances among 'kin countries'.[26]

Second, civilisations are reified, treated like things, like machines, or even worse, like the machinery of war. 'In a world where culture counts', Huntington writes, 'the platoons are tribes and ethnic groups, the regiments are nations, and the armies are civilizations'.[27]

Third, citizenship, with its political rights and responsibilities, is depicted as a unique feature of the West. While societies of the West engage in politics, the rest are supposedly seduced by appeals of cultural identity. 'Politicians in non-Western societies do not win elections by demonstrating how Western they are', Huntington asserts. 'Electoral competition instead stimulates them to fashion what they believe will be the most popular appeals, and those are usually ethnic, nationalist, and religious in character'.[28] Recent elections in Denmark and Netherlands belie this superior attitude and the raising of the spectre of immigration in the US, Britain and other European countries shows that ethnic chauvinism is not the prerogative of the Third World.

Finally, considering national sovereignty, Huntington claims that a state's 'cultural identity', preferably of the Protestant kind, entirely determines its role in world politics.[29] For those who assume the cultural superiority of the West, he provides a rationalisation for intervening in the sovereignty of other nations.

A recent high-powered report prepared for the Commonwealth Heads of Government Conference[30] provides a sharp riposte to those who blithely talk of the new wars of religion. It highlights the urgent need to address the 'many root causes of conflict' and draws attention to the post-9/11 debate that 'culture is neither the defining nor the only fault line over which people conflict'.

While cultural influences can contribute to violence 'they are not the only causal factors, nor are they immutable or irresistible'. The report explores the various ways through which violence is generalised and sometimes 'wilfully nurtured'. There are, doubtless to the disappointment of some who may wish for easy answers, questions raised about the role of poverty and inequality in promoting hatred and violence. These, in the opinion of the commission, require sophisticated analysis. However, the report does not ignore the connections. It draws attention to what it calls 'manifest inequality' and its relationship to the psychological dimensions of humiliation.

It makes devastating reading, and should be compulsory for prime ministers, presidents and their advisers who often display a total lack of understanding of the reaction of their citizens whose culture and religion are demonised and marginalised. It is understandable then but not acceptable that the resulting alienation of some of these citizens leads them, on occasion, to take up violence.

We cannot afford to allow our world to be reduced to cruel simplifications, nor can we permit it to be imprisoned within the confines of Samuel Huntington's map. Our multiple identities must be encouraged to flourish, not forced into the mould of some racialised or other stereotypical identity. Africans, for example, cannot be contained within the racist categories that were designed to dehumanise them. None of us has a fixed and frozen cultural identity, because we live in a complex and changing process of cultural creativity. The people of the diaspora cannot be put in some kind of rigid box, because the world around them is constantly being created and recreated by people who experience themselves as displaced. Recalling the words of Salman Rushdie, we find this creative activity advanced by 'people who root themselves in ideas rather than places, in memories as much as in material things; people who have been obliged to define themselves – because they are so defined by others – by their otherness; people in whose deepest selves strange fusions occur, unprecedented unions between what they were and where they find themselves'.[31]

It is true though that even while some degree of tension and displacement may have a creative result, alienation in democratic societies often leads to instability and disaffection. A recent report by the Joseph Rowntree Charitable Trust[32] draws an alarming picture of what it describes as the 'disengagement' from politics by people in Britain who are neither apathetic nor lacking interest. It is the absence of democratic processes and the absence of opportunities for engaging with the process which is irresponsible. The empirical evidence collected in this massive study illustrates the desire of people to have a greater say over policies and decisions that affect their lives. The move to the centre through 'consensus politics' led to the Bader Meinhof and Red Brigades phenomena in Germany and Italy respectively in the late 1960s and early 1970s.

Of interest to my lecture is the clear evidence of the study that there is a need for ensuring that parties and the electoral process reflects the diversity and complexity of people's lives. Democracy needs debate and the articulation of difference.

As Sen points out, elite representation is an inadequate approach to development, as democracy 'cannot really be so centred only on those in power'. The reach has to be broader, and the need for popular participation is not just sanctimonious rubbish. Indeed, 'the idea of development cannot be dissociated from it'.[33]

Also, the administration of justice shows a greater tendency to exercise authority over those who resort to violence for personal political reasons. Already there is much that heralds progress on this front.

Today in Africa the former head of one state, Charles Taylor of Liberia, is prosecuted by an international tribunal for his complicity in the gross human rights violations that occurred in a neighbouring state, Sierra Leone. The head of the African Union, John Kufor, has recently travelled to Kenya in a bid to mediate and quell tensions arising from the recent elections. The new Southern Africa Development Community (SADC) Tribunal, headquartered in Namibia, in its very first judgment, has ordered that a Zimbabwean farmer be granted interim relief.

All these signify a recognition that the concept of state sovereignty is and must be porous. It may only be claimed by a state to the extent it secures the protection of rights-holders within the state. That said, to the extent that the nation-state is democratically representative of its population and reflective of its democratic aspirations, it must be accorded equality with all other states as the vehicle by which such people and claims are advanced a global level.

There is still much to be done: how best to secure fairer, more democratic representation within international authorities and institutions? In particular, how to secure fairer representation within global financial institutions so that globalisation does not just become a watchword for the inequitable development and enrichment of some states at the expense of others? How can we secure a means of enforcing states' obligations to its inhabitants without allowing such means to become a pretext for selective and/or opportunistic interventions by larger, more powerful states?

How, in other words, to avoid what Jurgen Habermas has called the 'hegemonic unilateralism' pursued by the US in respect of Iraq, by which the US government believes itself entitled to disregard both international law and the opinions of the international community in the pursuit of its strategic interests and in the imposition of liberal-democratic values.[34]

These must be the intellectual projects of our age – peace, justice and development, within and beyond states.

They constitute an exciting challenge. In this journey, we can have for our guidance the torch of Antigone whose free spirit shines down the ages and lights the way forward. As she said: 'I was born for love, not for hatred'. In our troubled world this may appear a romantic vision, yet the world desperately needs this vision, so we can experience the boundless march of humanity for peace. We need it so that the saying of Sophocles will come true – that the universe has many miracles, but the finest of all is humanity.

Postscript

Although retired from Parliament, Kader Asmal continued to speak out against corruption and injustice whenever he came across it, both at home in South Africa and abroad. He died on the 22 June 2011, survived by his wife Louise, his sons and grandchildren, friends and admirers and an indelible legacy in the fight for human rights and justice around the world.

Notes

1 Kader Asmal and Adrian Hadland, with Moira Levy, *Politics in My Blood* (Johannesburg: Jacana Media, 2011), p. 287.
2 John Coakley of the Institute for British-Irish Studies, *Irish Times*, 11 July 2007.

3 For a detailed study of this development, see my 'The South African Constitution and the transition from apartheid: legislating the reconciliation of
   rights in a multicultural society', *European Journal of Law Reform*, 9
   (2007), 155–65

4 'Constitutional Guidelines for a Democratic South Africa, 1988', *South
   African Journal of Human Rights* (1989), 129.

5 Martha Nussbaum , 'Patriotism and cosmopolitanism', in Joshua Cohen
   (ed.), *For Love of Country? Debating the Limits of Patriotism: Martha C.
   Nussbaum and Respondents* (Cambridge, MA: Beacon Press, 1996), p. 132.

6 For a more comprehensive account of these loyalties and allegiances, see
   my Bram Fischer Memorial Lecture, 'Globalisation, human rights and the
   African diaspora', Oxford, 2004.

7 Amartya Sen, 'The uses and abuses of multiculturalism', *The New Republic*
   (27 February 2006).

8 Kwame Anthony Appiah, *Cosmopolitanism: Ethics in a World of Strangers*
   (New York: Norton, 2006), p. 144.

9 Appiah, *Cosmopolitanism*, p. 105.

10 R. Teitel, 'Transitional jurisprudence: the role of law in political transformation', *Yale Law Journal*, 106:7 (May 1997).

11 Etienne Mureinik, 'Emerging from emergency: human rights in South
   Africa', *Michigan Law Review*, 92:6 (1994), 1977–88.

12 At para. 59. Minister of Home Affairs and Another *v.* Fourie and Another
   (Doctors for Life International and others, Amicus Curiae); Lesbian and
   Gay Equality project and Others *v.* Minister of Home Affairs and Others,
   CCT 60/04; CCT 10/05.

13 This aspect for Northern Ireland is covered in my article, 'Devising a Bill of
   Rights for a diverse society', *EHRLR* (2007), 597.

14 Mary Kaldor, 'Cosmopolitanism and organised violence', paper prepared
   for conference on 'Conceiving cosmopolitanism', Warwick, 27–29 April
   2000, www.theglobalsite.ac.uk/press/010kaldor.htm (last accessed 25 February 2013), p. 1.

15 Kwame Anthony Appiah, 'Cosmopolitan patriots', in Cohen (ed.), *For Love
   of Country?*, p. 22.

16 Kaldor 'Cosmopolitanism and organised violence', p. 3.

17 Sen, 'The uses and abuses of multiculturalism', p. 3.

18 Kaldor, 'Cosmopolitanism and organised violence', p. 3.

19 Kaldor, 'Cosmopolitanism and organised violence', p. 4.

20 William Smith, 'Anticipating a cosmopolitan future: the case of humanitarian military intervention', *International Politics*, 44 (2007), 79.

21 Amartya Sen, *Development as Freedom* (New York: Alfred A Knopf,1999),
   p. 240.

22 Amartya Sen, 'It's right to rebel', *Yale Global* (19 November 2002), http://
   yaleglobal.yale.edu/content/it's-right-rebel (last accessed 15 March 2013).

23 Kader Asmal, 'Chair's preface: globalisation from below', in World Commission on Dams, *Dams and Development: A New Framework for Decision-
   Making* (London and Sterling, VA: Earthscan, 2000).

24 Kader Asmal, 'Environment and sustainability: looking to the future', in Susan Stern and Elisabeth Seligman (eds), *The Partnership Principle: New Forms of Governance in the 21st Century* (London: Archetype Publishers, 2004), pp. 184–94.

25 Jorge Castaneda, *Utopia Unarmed: The Latin Left after the Cold War* (New York: Vintage, 1994), p. 308.

26 Samuel Huntington, *The Clash of Civilizations and the Remaking of World Order* (New York: Simon and Schuster, 1996), p. 28.

27 Huntington, *The Clash of Civilizations*, p. 44.

28 Huntington, *The Clash of Civilizations*, p. 57.

29 Huntington, *The Clash of Civilizations*, pp. 125–54.

30 'Civil paths to peace: Report of the Commonwealth Commission on Respect and Understanding' (2007). Extracts here are taken from the executive summary, www.thecommonwealth.org/files/227381/FileName/CivilPath-stoPeace978-1-84859-001-4web-secure.pdf (last accessed 25 February 2013).

31 Salman Rushdie, *Imaginary Homelands: Essays and Criticism, 1981–1991* (London : Granta, 1991), pp. 124–5.

32 The Joseph Rowntree Charitable Trust and the Joseph Rowntree Reform Trust Limited, *Power to the People* (2006), www.parliament.uk/documents/commons/lib/research/briefings/snpc-03948.pdf (last accessed 25 February 2013).

33 Sen, *Development as Freedom*, p. 247.

34 Smith, 'Anticipating a cosmopolitan future', p. 80.

Conclusion

Professor Paul Arthur

In 2005 the United States Senate cited John Hume as 'one of the greatest advocates of peace and non-violence in our time' and as a 'courageous leader of exceptional achievement ... in the cause of peace in Northern Ireland'.[1] In that one statement we get the essence of what this volume is about. It is concerned with the local *and* the global and with the quality of leadership that is crucial in times of crisis – it is a leadership that combines strong analytical ability, immense moral courage and the (realistic) optimism of the visionary. It is a leadership that can attract support from across the spectrum – hence the incredible diversity of opinion and experience presented within these covers (all of whom volunteered their services in the names of John Hume and Thomas P. O'Neill) – combined with an incredible tenacity to stand by one's ideals no matter how dark the hour.

The great conservative political philosopher, Edmund Burke, encapsulated the dilemma when he wrote that '[W]hen bad men combine, the good must associate; else they will fall, one by one, an unpitied sacrifice in a contemptible struggle'.[2] (Less than two centuries later the theologian, Dietrich Bonhoeffer, expressed a similar sentiment in the most dire of circumstances). Hence his call to action and to inclusion; but action has to be built on proper speculation. It is here in his essay *On the Present Discontents*, published in 1770, that Burke expresses the nobility of the profession of politics:

> It is the business of the speculative philosopher to mark the proper ends of government. It is the business of the politician, who is the philosopher in action, to find out the proper means towards those ends and to employ them with effect.[3]

Ends and means, and their relationship, one to another – that is the proper business of the political – and those who are best equipped to deal with it are philosophers in action. Contrast that with a more squalid definition of the role of political parties. It is expressed by the hero of Joseph Goebbels's novel *Michael* when he remarked that '[P]olitical parties live off unsolved problems. That's why they are not interested in their solution'.[4] The contributors to this volume have devoted their careers to the seeking after solutions and in their individual chapters they are able to reflect on the agencies of change that have brought peace to Northern Ireland. More than that, they are concerned with the inequity of the world, with the present insecurities and with the remedies to correct them. This is where the local meets the global.

It is the case, too, that although many have retired from elected office (and two have died in the interim) most continue to make a substantial contribution to public life. President Clinton established his Foundation which has done sterling work in Africa, in particular. Kofi Annan has been involved in an intervention in Syria; and Bertie Ahern has been intimately concerned with trying to settle the Basque conflict. We need to acknowledge that these 'exs', these Eminent Persons Groups (EPGs) have a unique role. The United States Advisory Commission on Public Diplomacy recognised their worth: 'In many ways they can do things better than government. They foster a flexible style that encourages innovation ... They offer the world a winning combination of ... professional skills, a wealth of experience, fresh perspectives, and enormous good will'.[5]

Each chapter speaks for itself. It is not our purpose to provide a précis of what has been written. Rather we want to follow a number of complementary strands – global democratisation and the quality of the democratic model; the role of exogenous forces (particularly those of the United States and the European Union) in shaping the peace process; US–EU relations and their competing visions of world peace; and speculation about a better world. But before that it is important that we put the lecture series in its proper context.

Context

The historian E. H. Carr once noted that besides the title and author of a book it is important to make a note of the date of publication. Perhaps more than we want to admit we are shaped by the emotions and fads of the moment. These thirteen lectures were presented between July 2003 and February 2008 – that is between the aftermath and impact of 9/11 and before the challenges facing the global economic system. At the local level most of the presentations occurred before the historic agreement between the Democratic Unionist Party and Sinn Fein in 2007 – hence there is much that is tentative and even a little plaintive in some of the comments. But all of them carry a sense of commitment and passion.

To deal with the local first: it is important to note the different stages in the life cycle of a conflict. One of the gurus on the literature of peace studies, Johan Galtung, describes these as *diagnosis, prognosis and therapy*. It was primarily the SDLP, under the leadership of John Hume, who did most of the heavy lifting in the diagnostic phase. It was his constant mantra, his single transferable speech, which stressed the joint message of non-violence and the unity of people rather than territory. It was the SDLP and the Ulster Unionist Party with the support of both governments (and, incidentally, those parties more recently involved in constitutional politics – the newly formed Northern Ireland Women's Coalition (NIWC), Sinn Fein, the Progressive Unionist Party (PUP) and the Ulster Democratic Party (UDP) who delivered the Agreement in 1998. But as the title of the third stage suggests *therapy* goes beyond institutional engineering. It takes us into the dangerous territory of contemplating the horrors of our past and inducing fundamental attitudinal change.

A student of peace processes and peace agreements, Robert Rothstein, has argued that peace agreements can be weak and tentative because they have left all the difficult issues to be addressed at the end and in that respect we have to be realistic about how quickly they can alter 'the basic nature of a long and profoundly bitter conflict'. But he has important words to say about political leadership and behaviour. That which got them to the point of agreement (when they attempted to maximise their demands) may not be appropriate for the more collegial expectations of embedding that agreement: 'needs and priorities change, interests must be redefined or revisioned, and a joint learning process must be institutionalised and accelerated'.[6]

Hence the frustration that arises in some of the comments emanating from those who had worked night and day to deliver peace to Northern Ireland: they recognise that trust is a delicate plant and that leaders have to bring their constituencies with them. But like all political midwives they grow concerned that too much nurturing can lead to a form of infantilism – we can see why Galtung falls back on the psychological. Indeed it is only Dermot Ahern and Maurice Hayes who can begin to properly indulge in the sunny uplands. Following the literature on peace studies it is Dr Hayes who takes the debate to a new level when he invokes so strongly the forgotten art of the creative process and the extent to which building peace is both an art and a skill. He could have had in mind the works of the Mennonite John Paul Lederach in his journey from his book *Building Peace* (1996) to that of his *Moral Imagination* (2005) with its emphasis on the wealth spring of the creative process. Lederach's earlier work was concerned with conflict resolution which carried with it the dangers of co-optation whereby lots of good work leads to little real change, whereas conflict transformation is about building healthy relationships locally and globally.

And that brings us to our second consideration about the context. It was the Clinton administration that delivered the parties to the peace agreement in 1998. His historic decision to grant a visa to SF President, Gerry Adams, in 1994 represented a paradigm shift in US foreign policy. His inspired appointment of Senator George Mitchell – first, be it noted, as an economic envoy because economic development is a significant driver in peacebuilding (another theme in many of these presentations) – as Chair of the all-party negotiations; and his persistent cajoling of all the parties in the dying hours and days before the signing was crucial to its success. The same administration nursed it through its teething troubles and President Clinton's visit in the aftermath of the Omagh bomb in August 1998 helped to stabilise what was potentially a game-breaking incident. The destructive role that spoilers can play in a post-agreement period merits close attention; and one of the apparent successes of the Northern Ireland conflict has been the extent to which the spoilers have been marginalised.

When President George W. Bush succeeded Bill Clinton there was a real concern that US involvement would peter out. But the United States understood that Ireland was a singular success in its foreign policy and the administration stayed the course. That was as well because the events of 11 September 2001 turned the world upside down. The political philosopher, Edith Wyschogrod, has described the twentieth century as the century of 'man-made mass death'.[7] She was alluding to such as the Holocaust and the gulag, the killing fields of Cambodia and China's Cultural Revolution and the fact that it was the most violent century in the history of humankind. A moment of light seemed to have occurred in 1989 with the collapse of the Berlin Wall and all that ensued and a New World Order brought new optimism. But that could be compared to a shooting star that burns its way across the firmament and fizzles out. Long before the events in New York, Washington and elsewhere optimism had diminished and a corrosive pessimism has descended. The historian, Tony Judt, captures it well when he sees the 'present century as one of growing insecurity brought about partly by excessive economic freedom ... and growing insecurity also brought about by climate change and unpredictable states'. In this context 'our chief task is not to imagine better worlds but rather to think how to prevent worse ones'.[8] That mood can be found among the presentations in this volume, although none is quite so bleak as this.

By one of those strange coincidences President Bush's 'point-man', Richard Haass, happened to be in Ireland on 9/11. He was there for

a specific purpose. He had come to read the riot act to Irish republicanism after three of their number had been arrested in Bogota airport
after, allegedly, giving advice to FARC on bomb-making techniques.
The choice was stark: either Irish republicanism was part of the peace
process or was part of the international network on terrorism. It could
be said that one of the paradoxes of 9/11 was that it accelerated the
peace process in that the 'peaceniks' inside the Republican movement
had a very powerful argument for moving decisively towards decommissioning. Once again the global impinged on the local. American reaction
to 9/11 – Gore Vidal's quip that 'we no longer have a nation but a
homeland' captures the essence of the dilemma facing the contemporary
world – forms an underlying theme in these contributions; and in turn
we encounter hubris followed by self-doubt. The very theme of Mitchell
Reiss's chapter on the sources of anti-Americanism dissects the debate
and America's standing in the world.

Hubris is not far away from some of the European presentations.
After all European harmonisation was moving apace and the EU was
becoming a major player on the world scene. Europe's contribution to
the Irish peace process was considerable and ongoing. It was a think-
tank based in Belgium, *Pro Mundi Vita*, in the early 1970s that described
the Northern Ireland problem as being akin to the religious wars of
the seventeenth century. It was a blot on the landscape – admittedly
this was before the Balkans had caught light. Europe prided itself as a
model of conflict resolution and as an advocate of human rights. It is
Romano Prodi who cites Kant's 'Perpetual Peace' (as well, it should be
said, Thomas Hobbes) and describes the EU as 'a Union of minorities'.
Through the earlier policy of coal and steel harmonisation the nascent
European Community had removed the sinews of war. They had much
of which to be proud. But in these chapters not enough attention was
paid to *fortuna* – what Machiavelli calls the goddess of unpredictability
– and it is the then President of the European Parliament, Pat Cox,
who had the prescience to warn against hubris. That will be one of the
themes of this chapter.

The democratic challenge

Commenting on the first free elections in South Africa in 1994 Andre
Brink described it as 'a moment so brief and bright that it appeared
all too easy afterwards to discount it as an illusion ... Those of us who
stood in the long queues of that April day to perform the simplest
actions imaginable – drawing a line on a square – will never forget
the exhilaration in what the writer Njabolu Ndebele has called the

discovery of the ordinary. Nothing could have been more momentous than discovering that all of us, rich or poor, black or white or anything in between, business executive or street sweeper, student or prostitute, were ultimately involved in, and defined by this part of Africa'.[9] We may be too inclined to take for granted the discovery of the ordinary. Not so the Bush administration in the aftermath of 9/11: Mitchell Reiss tells us that America's stated objectives were those of 'self-defence and global democratization'. The pursuit of the latter has, in the opinion of many (including those within this book), been disastrous. We need to reflect on the challenge to, and of, democracy because it bears on world security *and* the settlement of the Irish question.

In his *In Defence of Politics* (1962) Bernard Crick describes democracy as 'perhaps the most promiscuous word in the world of public affairs. She is everybody's mistress and yet somehow retains her magic even when a lover sees that her favours are being, in his light, illicitly shared by many another'.[10] One commentator has put the concept of democracy at the heart of the Irish conflict. Richard Bourke asserts that 'the conflict in Northern Ireland was the product of a fundamental misunderstanding about the organising principles of modern politics ... [deriving] from the stubborn assumption that the procedure of democratic government offers a sufficient guarantee for the achievement of political equality'. In his *Peace in Ireland: The War of Ideas* (2003) he maintains that it 'continues to confuse political judgement in the Balkans, in the Middle East and in Central Asia as well'.[11]

The significance of the Bourke thesis is that it tackles the majoritarian mindset at the heart of many conflicts:

> Majorities ought properly to be accepted as decisive in determining both the selection and tenure of democratic governments but not as a means of prescribing the terms of democratic inclusion in the state ... it is of vital importance to grasp the essential difference in political analysis between democratic governments and democratic states.[12]

At the heart of the Irish Republican analysis of the Northern Ireland problem was a core belief that democracy had been denied in Northern Ireland whether one takes as one's starting point the 1918 general election or the nature of the partition question or the issue of gerry-mandering. They argued forcefully that the resort to violence occurred simply because there was no alternative; they were following a model of political violence embraced by Johan Galtung, in that violence = direct violence + structural violence + cultural violence. In the new dispensa-tion, because there was an alternative, that which was acceptable in the past could no longer be condoned. Unionists argued in 1974 that the power-sharing government was illegitimate because it was *imposed*. Equally they protested against the Anglo-Irish Agreement (1985) but were reminded when Westminster overwhelmingly endorsed the agreement that Unionists represented not much more than 2 per cent of the United Kingdom population. And when both governments signed the Belfast Agreement in 1998 they took good care to ensure that it was ratified in both parts of the island through referendums.

One of the reasons why the therapeutic (or implementation) stage of the 1998 Agreement dragged on for so long was an insistence that an equity and human rights agenda had to be delivered. While fundamental questions were being asked about decommissioning/demilitarisation and about policing and justice, the cement that held the agreement together was the doctrine of consent. Political violence had been renounced as a tactic and democratic values were being upheld. The success of the Agreement was such that some (we think of George Mitchell and the former Northern Ireland Secretary of State, Peter Hain, for example) believed that it was a model that had lessons for the Middle East and elsewhere.[13] They recognised that Agreement was impossible unless all parties with a veto power were included in the negotiations. They knew too that, unlike 1974, a solution could not be imposed. They had to be conscious of cultural sensitivities, and they needed to be aware that peace without economic development was a peace on shaky foundations. They knew that 'soft' power had to be invoked.

In 1996 the United States Advisory Commission on Public Diplomacy called for the practice of a new kind of diplomacy where 'policies and negotiated agreements will succeed only if they have the support of publics at home and abroad'. The commission borrowed from Joseph Nye's concept of 'soft' power – the ability to set the agenda in ways that shape the preferences of others, 'which strengthens American diplomacy through attraction rather than coercion'.[14] In striving for democratic globalisation the Bush administration seem to have forgotten many of these lessons – a fact which emanates from most of the European contributions to this book. But not just Europeans: it was Senator John Kerry who warned that above all 'we must remember that democratization is not a crusade'. The anti-apartheid warrior, Kader Asmal – and we need to acknowledge that South Africa's role in the Irish peace process has not been fully recognised – offers a very strong critique of Samuel Huntington's *Clash of Civilisations*. He makes the case for a politics of humanity as opposed to a politics of fractured identities. He seeks a rights-based system of global governance, a globalisation from below based on '"longitudinal nationalism", which is advanced by social actors from various nations who work together to challenge policies in one or more states. Unlike the old nationalisms, which tended to represent narrow national interests, this "longitudinal nationalism" seeks to advance what I have been calling the public good that is ultimately in everyone's interest'.

The very title of Asmal's lecture – 'Peace, multiculturalism and development' (and one could substitute 'justice' for 'multiculturalism') – encompasses what he considers are the intellectual tools of our age. And these could stand as an antidote to the drive for global democratisation and away from what Jurgen Habermas calls the 'hegomonic unilateralism' pursued by the United States in Iraq.

Europe and the United States: two competing visions

Professor Romano Prodi was not the only one to cite both Hobbes and Kant. For many Europeans the actions of the US in the post-9/11 period was a profound shift from bipolarity to a misconceived and misjudged hegemony. Some, particularly in the neoconservative movement, went on the offensive. In his provocative *Of Paradise and Power: America and Europe in the New World Order* (2003) Robert Kagan turned the Prodi thesis on its head by arguing that Europe's new Kantian order could flourish only under the umbrella of American power exercised according to the rules of the old Hobbesian order. It was not that Prodi was being starry-eyed. His lecture was delivered less than a month after the bomb in Madrid which raised the spectre of al Qaeda yet again. Others were equally sanguine. In his lecture Dr Garret FitzGerald noted that Europe was having a rapidly diminishing weight in the world. He noted the paradox of the Yugoslav debacle whereby the European states lacked both the will and the capacity to safeguard isolated communities which forced Europe into action: 'The humiliation of these experiences, and of having to rely on the United States both to resolve the Bosnian problem at the Dayton Conference and later to halt Serb repression of Albanians in Kosovo, led to the emergence of the proposal to establish a European Rapid Reaction Force'.

Contrast this with FitzGerald's statement that 'large parts of the world now associate Europe with a philosophy of humanity, solidarity and integration. The EU is seen as a model of the way to approach international affairs'. The reasons are not hard to define and are stated particularly forcefully by Kagan:

> Europe is turning away from power, or to put it a little differently, it is moving beyond power into a self-contained world of laws and rules and transnational negotiation and cooperation. It is entering a post-historical paradise of peace and relative prosperity ...

Meanwhile, the United States remains mired in history, exercising power in an anarchic Hobbesian world where international laws and rules are unreliable, and where true security and the defense and promotion of a liberal order still depend on the possession and use of military might.[15]

Europe needed to escape from Wyschogrod's 'century of man-made mass death' because Europe was the site of so much death and destruction. After all, as Kagan points out, it was President Roosevelt's desire to make Europe strategically irrelevant: 'the common conviction of Americans was that "the European system was basically rotten, that war was endemic on that continent" ... Europe appeared to be nothing more than the overheated incubator of world wars that cost America dearly'.[16]

Now in the twenty-first century – 'one of growing insecurity' as Judt puts it – both the US and EU need to draw breath. There is evidence in these chapters that the European sense of complacency is being replaced by a hard-nosed technocratic sense of having the correct security apparatus in place to make the world a safer place and to ensure that a humanitarian ethos is upheld. Secretary-General Kofi Annan's nine lessons of peace-building is a sobering reflection on we have learned from success *and* failure in a challenging environment The 2008 US presidential election suggested that America was moving away from braggadocio and the crusading mindset to a more considered sense of its place in the world. The economic challenges from the BRIC (Brazil, Russia, India, China) countries, the failure of nation-building, the increasing turbulence in the Middle East and North Africa and the saddened state of the world economic system – all of these indicate that we need to think afresh.

The degree of reflection within these pages and the quality of leadership that is on display suggest that we need not necessarily share Tony Judt's pessimism. But it is going to take a huge leap of faith and is going to put an enormous burden on political leadership. We can learn from success, we can practice problem-solving, and we can come out on the other side. Above all it calls for vision. We need to challenge the pervasive cynicism expressed by the interrogator, Ivanov, in Koestler's *Darkness at Noon*: 'Since the existence of nations and classes, they live in a permanent state of mutual self-defence, which forces them eternally to defer to another time the putting into practice of humanism'.[17] Perhaps we could adopt as our guide Dietrich Bonhoeffer: 'The essence of optimism is that it takes no account of the present, but it is a source of inspiration, of vitality and hope, where others have resigned; it enables a man to hold his head high, to claim the future for himself'.[18]

The world needs to put humanism into practice and to share Bonhoeffer's vision.

Notes

1 Senate Resolution 54 – Paying Tribute to John Hume, Congressional Record, 151: 15 (14 February 2005), S1356–S1357, www.gpo.gov/fdsys/pkg/CREC-2005-02-14/pdf/CREC-2005-02-14-pt1-PgS1356-4.pdf (last accessed 18 March 2013).

2 *On the Present Discontents* (1770), cited in B.W. Hill (ed.), *Edmund Burke on Government, Politics and Society* (Brighton: Harvester Press, 1975), p. 110.

3 *On the Present Discontents*, cited in Hill (ed.), *Edmund Burke*, p. 113.

4 Cited in Bernard Crick, *In Defence of Politics* (London: Penguin, 1972), pp. 166–7.

5 No author, *A New Diplomacy for the Information Age* (Washington, DC: US Advisory Commission on Public Diplomacy, 1996), p. 7.

6 Robert L. Rothstein, *After the Peace: The Political Economy of Reconciliation*, Inaugural Rebecca Meyerhoff Memorial Lecture (Jerusalem: Harry S. Truman Institute, Hebrew University, 1996), p. 7.

7 Edith Wyschogrod, *Spirit in Ashes: Hegel, Heidegger and Man-Made Mass Death* (New Haven, CT: Yale University Press,1983), *passim*.

8 Tony Judt, 'On intellectuals and democracy', *New York Review of Books*, 59:5 (2012), 7.

9 Andre Brink, *Observer Magazine*, 13 February 2000, pp. 24–5, cited in Paul Arthur, 'Conflict, memory and reconciliation', in Marianne Elliott (ed.), *The Long Road to Peace in Northern Ireland. Peace Lectures from the Institute of Irish Studies at Liverpool University* (Liverpool: Liverpool University Press, 2002), p. 150.

10 Crick, *In Defence of Politics*, p. 56.

11 Richard Bourke, *Peace in Ireland: The War of Ideas* (London: Pimlico, 2003), pp. x and xi.

12 Bourke, *Peace in Ireland*, p. xii.

13 Northern Ireland Office, 'Peacemaking in Northern Ireland: a model for conflict resolution?', speech by Peter Hain MP, Chatham House, 12 June 2007.

14 *A New Diplomacy for the Information Age*, p. 4.

15 Robert Kagan, *Of Paradise and Power: America and Europe in the New World Order* (New York: Alfred A. Knopf, 2003), p. 3

16 Kagan, *Of Paradise and Power*, p. 70, quoting William L. Langer and S. Everett Gleason, *The Challenge to Isolation, 1937–1940* (New York: Harper & Brothers Publishers, 1952), pp. 13–14.

17 Arthur Koestler, *Darkness at Noon* (London: Penguin, 1940) p. 128.

18 Dietrich Bonhoeffer, *Letters and Papers from Prison*, ed. Eberhard Bethge, trans. Reginald H. Fuller (London: SCM Press, 1967), p. 25.

Index